D1563983

VICTIMS

Kari and Kicha. Kicha runs, hikes, and travels everywhere with Kari. Brad Brisbin and Bob Pearson assisted in Kicha's training. *Janet Swenson*

VICTIMS

The Kari Swenson Story

JANET MILEK SWENSON

First Edition

1 2 3 4 5 6 7 8 9

Printed in the United States of America

Library of Congress Cataloging-in-Publication Data

Swenson, Janet Milek, 1936-
Victims : the Kari Swenson story / Janet Milek Swenson.
p. cm.
ISBN 0-87108-775-8
1. Kidnapping–Montana–Madison Range Region–Case studies.
2. Swenson, Kari–Kidnapping, 1984. 3. Athletes–Montana–
Biography. 4. Nichols, Dan–Trials, litigation, etc. 5. Nichols,
Don–Trials, litigation, etc. 6. Trials (Kidnapping)–Montana–
Virginia City. I. Title. II. Title: Kari Swenson story.
HV6601.M9S94 1989
364.1′523′09786663–dc19 89-3712
CIP

TO

Alan Goldstein

Jim Schwalbe

Bob Schaap

and

My Beloved Family

Publisher's Note

The dialogue in the hearings and trials came directly from the hearing and trial transcripts. Ellipses to indicate that other statements came between the sentences used are avoided to make it more aesthetically pleasing for the reader. The transcripts are very long, and repetitious questions and answers have been eliminated without changing the meaning or intent of the transcript.

Contents

BOOK 1
THE KIDNAPPING, SEARCH, RESCUE, AND HOSPITALIZATION

BOOK 2

REHABILITATION, THE CAPTURE, AND THE GOLD MEDAL

BOOK 3

THE ATTORNEYS, THE TRIALS, THE AWARD

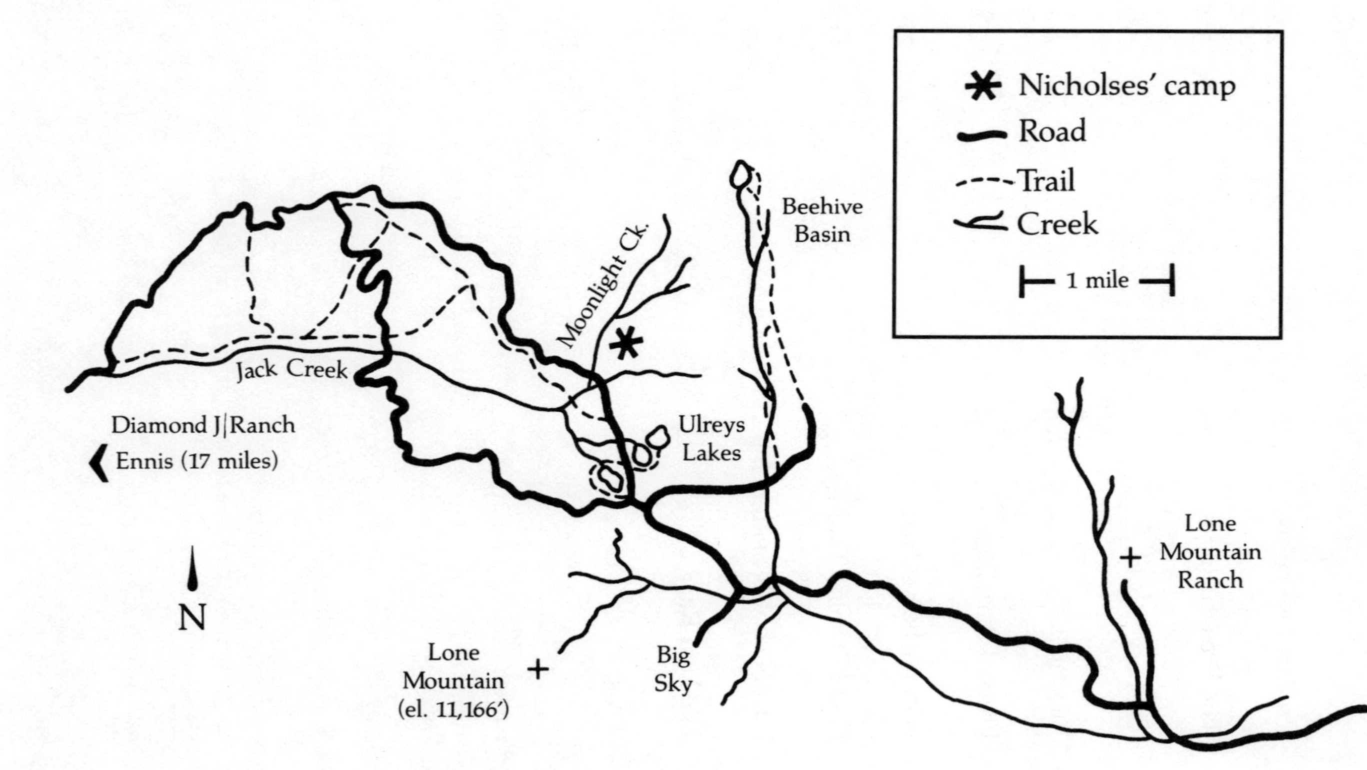
Nicholses' camp
Road
Trail
Creek
1 mile
Beehive Basin
Moonlight Ck.
Jack Creek
Ulreys Lakes
Diamond J|Ranch
Ennis (17 miles)
N
Lone Mountain Ranch
Lone Mountain (el. 11,166′)
Big Sky

Personalities

SWENSON FAMILY

Bob
Janet
Johanna
Kari
Paul

LONE MOUNTAIN RANCH STAFF

Bob, Vivian, & Laura Schaap
Brian Wadsworth
Jay Schreck
Barbara Batey
Diane Goldstein
Terry Gromley
Greg Holler
Deborah Frauson
Steve Shimek
Karen Frauson
Janet Story
Jeff Alm
Neil & Deborah Navratil

IMMEDIATE FAMILY

Hazel Bowman – Grandmother
Milo Bowman – Grandfather
Bob Milek – Janet's older brother
Jim Milek – Janet's younger brother
Dorothy Milek – Bob's wife
Marsha Milek – Jim's wife
Janet & Douglas Milek – Jim & Marsha's children

FAMILY FRIENDS

George Tuthill
Jack Drumheller
Becky Lohmiller
Stu Jennings
Holly Flies
Denny Lee
John Yurich
Bob Naert
Jonathan Jennings
Sally & Dave Hollier

JUDGE

Frank M. Davis

BIG SKY RESIDENTS

Alan and Diane Goldstein
Jim Schwalbe
John Palmer
Bob Donovan
Joel Beardsley

GALLATIN COUNTY OFFICERS

John Onstad – Sheriff
Brad Brisbin
Bob Pearson
Bob Campbell
Bill Pronovost
Don Houghton
Wally Schmacher
Dave Dunn
Ron Cutting
Don Gullickson
Bob Secor
Bill Slaughter
Dave Cashell

U.S. FOREST SERVICE OFFICERS

Bob Morton
Dave Wing
Dan Bauer

FBI AGENTS

Gary Lincoln
Bernie Hubley

BIATHLON TEAM MEMBERS

Marie Alkire – rifle coach
Pam Nordheim
Pam Weiss
Julie Newnam
Peter Hoag
Lyle Nelson

MADISON COUNTY OFFICERS

Johnny France – Sheriff
Jay Cosgrove
Merlin Ehlers
Bill Hancock
Jerry Mason
Doug McLousky
Dick Noorlander
Lee Edmiston

ATTORNEYS

Larry Moran
Marc Racicot
Judy Browning
John Connor
Loren Tucker
Steve Ungar
Don White

Acknowledgments

I am fortunate to be blessed with a husband and children who have patience and a sense of humor. The writing of this book would have been impossible without their love, understanding, and participation. We shared tears and anger while I prepared the manuscript, but I prefer to remember the laughter arising from my typing errors and double-entendres that plagued the first draft of this book.

It is a pleasure to thank the many people who have supported me and my family since the day of Kari's kidnapping . . .

. . . My Mother and Milo, my brothers and their families;

. . . Bob and Vivian Schaap and the crew at the Lone Mountain Guest Ranch, Jim Schwalbe, Alan Goldstein, Brad Brisbin, Bob Pearson, and other residents of the Big Sky community who responded to our request for help when Kari disappeared July 15, 1984;

. . . George Tuthill and Jack Drumheller who shared our panic during the initial frantic search for Kari;

. . . Denny Lee whose generosity and concern made bad situations bearable for all of us;

. . . The friends living in Seattle who opened their hearts and homes to Johanna and provided her with the support and kindness she needed when she was separated from our family;

. . . The friends, colleagues, and members of the community who relieved us of daily burdens by providing meals, and who gave us emotional support with their letters, phone calls, books, poems, flowers, plants, and other gifts;

. . . The hundreds of strangers who sent cards and letters of encouragement to Kari. Most of you did not provide return addresses and this is my only chance to thank you;

. . . The physicians and other medical personnel at the Bozeman Deaconess Hospital and the Harborview Trauma Hospital for the quality care they provided for Kari;

. . . Becky Lohmiller, Jonathan Jennings, Stuart Jennings, Bob Naert, Holly Flies, Lisa Newton, Peter Hoag, Pam Weiss, Julie Newnam, Pam Nordheim, Jay Schreck, Janet Story, Marie Alkire, Todd Boonstra, and Marsha Hoem for providing the love, humor, and enthusiasm that encouraged Kari to return to a normal life and the world of competition. There are other friends, too numerous to mention, who also helped Kari's rehabilitation. You know who you are, and we thank you for your generosity, your time, and your thoughtfulness;

. . . The athletes, coaches, and administrators of the U.S. Biathlon Association who gave Kari the incentive to continue when it would have been easier for her to quit;

. . . The many friends who accompanied us to Virginia City during the trials;

. . . Marc Racicot, Judy Browning, and John Connor, the attorneys who prosecuted the cases. Without their thorough investigations, efficiency, and tenacity, justice for the victims would not have been achieved;

. . . The Madison County Deputies, who provided security at the courthouse during the two trials, for their professionalism and the kindness they accorded both the Nichols and Swenson families;

. . . Sue Erickson, friend and colleague, who encouraged me to start the book;

. . . Michael Malone, Marianne Keddington, and Larry Moran who suffered through the first draft, all nine-hundred pages, and still remained enthusiastic about the project. Marianne provided the first professional editing suggestions, and Mike and Larry encouraged me with their belief that in that stack of paper there was a book;

. . . Dee Marvine, writer-editor, and my friend Merry Lou Henson who encouraged me to continue with the manuscript when I thought I was mired hopelessly in the translation of the taped interviews;

. . . Gerry Wheeler for his suggestions concerning dialogue versus narrative formats;

. . . Brad Brisbin, Bob Pearson, Bob Campbell, Bob Morton, John Onstad, Dave Dunn, Bill Pronovost, Wally Schmacher, Ron Cutting, Don Houghton, Merlin Ehlers, Dick Noorlander, Jerry Mason, David Wing, Murray Duffy, Jennie Nemec, Andi Ross, Bob Naert, and Bob and Vivian Schaap, whose recollections and taped interviews provided me with the information to write about the tragedy from different viewpoints;

. . . Not to be forgotten is my editor, Jerry Keenan, who led me through the maze of the publishing world with humor and patience, and my copy editor, Merilee Eggleston, for her attention to detail.

"Kari is an inspiration to all Montanans. Her courage to overcome a personal ordeal and to succeed in the world of international athletic competition is an example for everyone. Her triumph embodies the will that makes Montanans special."

— *U.S. Senator Max Baucus*

" 'The Kari Swenson Story' is a thoughtful tribute to a great athlete and, more importantly, to a courageous human being. Her disciplined self-control combined with a fierce inner fire are truly remarkable to behold."

—*U.S. Senator Richard G. Lugar*

Introduction

Our family moved to Bozeman, Montana, from Philadelphia in the summer of 1970. My husband, Bob, was leaving Temple University to become the new chairman of the physics department at Montana State University. I was to be a staff nurse at the university's student health service.

Our three children, Johanna, Kari, and Paul, were ages ten, eight, and six respectively at the time. The move was greeted with excitement because Montana and Wyoming seemed like home. Bob had grown up in Bozeman, and my childhood home was in Thermopolis, Wyoming, so the children's summer vacations had been spent in the West enjoying the outdoors with us and their grandparents.

Bob and I enjoyed being parents and spent several hours each evening playing with or reading to the children. Usually a combination of both. Bob's gentleness and sense of humor made him, in the children's words, "the world's best daddy." He teased them out of their bad moods, hugged away their hurts, and encouraged them in anything they wanted to do in athletics, studies, or music. He is a rare parent whose first response is "yes" or "maybe" instead of "no."

We purchased a cozy log cabin in Gallatin Canyon and lived there each summer until the children began taking summer jobs. The cabin is simple, but warm and inviting. Early morning coffee on the front porch was a ritual as we watched the sun rise over the mountains and slither silently over the fence, rocks, and lawn, and up our outstretched legs.

We spent our evenings in front of the fireplace with the children tucked beside us in the recliner or on the sofa. It was a time to share dreams, books, and songs—a quiet, gentle pause in life to realize how much we loved each other.

In the summer we moved Nutmeg, Kari's Appaloosa mare, to the cabin with us and settled in for three months of hiking, floating, fishing, and riding. The children had the freedom to explore the surrounding mountains, study the wildlife and plants, and without realizing it acquire the independence and knowledge to survive outside the bounds of city life. With Bob they built an elaborate tree fort in an ancient Douglas fir behind the cabin and a rock fort on the mountainside behind the tree. When the biting flies were too ferocious for the children to play outside, I taught them to carve caricatures of animals from Ivory soap and played hours of games with them.

They practiced their musical instruments every day, and I drove them into town for music lessons each Friday. Johanna was a gifted pianist who had expanded her interest to the guitar and French horn. She practiced her horn in my bedroom, Kari played her cello in the loft, and Paul bowed his violin on the back porch.

Paul and Kari began competing with each other by the time they were nine and eleven years old. They would sprint the last half mile to the top of a ridge just to see who could be there first. They'd tease Johanna for being the third to arrive, and she'd ignore them with the disdain only a teenager possesses. They were comfortable in the mountains and were avid backpackers. By the time they became serious athletes, running in the rugged country of the Gallatin and Bridger mountain ranges was as natural to them as running on a track was to a hurdler.

Winter weekends were spent skiing at Bridger Bowl or Lone Mountain. Paul used every bump on the mountain as a jump, and Kari streaked down the steep slopes, braids flying, behind Paul. Johanna skied with a group of boys and became a strong, competent, extremely fast skier.

When Kari was fourteen and Paul twelve, a friend took them cross-country skiing. Paul loved it and talked Kari into participating in a race the next weekend. Within two weeks my two youngest children had enrolled in the Nordic race program, and while Johanna and I skied the alpine slopes, Bob, Kari, and Paul became Nordic skiers.

I was stubborn about giving up my downhill skiing, but finally consented to go on a cross-country trip with Bob. Skiing down a hill, I hit a tree and dislocated my shoulder. That accident was the beginning of my involvement with search and rescue, and the following autumn I enlisted the help of Clarence Serfoss, an Alpine professional patrolman, who assisted me and my friend Richard Itoh in organizing and training the Bozeman Nordic Ski Patrol. Our patrol became a satellite of the Gallatin County Sheriff's department, assisting in winter skiing and climbing rescues.

Meanwhile, our children were maturing. Johanna was a blonde, blue-eyed extrovert who loved school, music, people, skiing, and tennis. She was on the high school tennis team and was one of three young women to represent Montana at the first Tournament of Champions held in Washington, D.C., in 1976. For several summers Bob or I happily drove Johanna and her doubles partner Jeanne Rogers to tennis tournaments all over Montana.

Kari was a tall, slim, independent, teenager with long auburn hair and almond-shaped blue eyes. She spent her free time training her horses and seemed to enjoy the solitude and peace the long training schedules afforded her. I spent hours with Kari and her horses, grooming and doctoring both horse and rider, and encouraging her. I loved every smelly horse show we attended.

Paul at twelve years of age was gangly, gentle, and developing a fantastic sense of humor. He loved teasing his sisters, and his huge blue eyes sparkled with glee when he provoked them into chasing him through the pasture or having a water fight with him. Photography fascinated him. We'd see him crawling through deep grass to photograph the wild fox in the field, the owls in the cottonwoods by the barn, a family of ducks on the pond, or some minute insect on a flower. He and the girls set up a darkroom in my laundry area and produced dozens of black and white snapshots. I learned a lot about cameras, shutter speeds, and depth of field during those years. My difficulties with the focus mechanisms on cameras is a joke among my children.

Paul and Kari spent hours running in the hills, wading in the creeks, and cross-country skiing. By the time they were in high school they shared a special closeness. They seemed to know what the other was thinking or feeling and a bond of respect and love made them good friends.

Bob and I were pulled along by the children's momentum. We started running, training for foot races and ski races, playing in local tennis tournaments, and doing speed workouts in the mountains with them.

Stuart Jennings entered our lives through the ski racing program. He and Kari were the same age and shared a lively interest in verbal dueling. Paul and Stu became good buddies because they liked to fly fish and each could consume large quantities of chocolate chip cookies. The three friends began running, roller-skiing, hiking, and skiing together.

For a number of years, Kari, Paul, and Stu were members of the nordic ski team which represented the Northern Division of the United States Ski Association at the U.S. Junior National Championships. At the 1979 championships, the U.S. National Biathlon team sponsored a fun relay race pitting teams from one region against the other. Stu, Kari, and Paul participated. That was the beginning of their interest in biathlon and the three friends were on their way to many years of competing in the sport.

The word biathlon is of Greek origin meaning "two tests." It combines the sport of shooting, requiring the ultimate in concentration and calmness, with cross-country skiing which demands vigorous high-tempo physical activity; diametrically opposite activities. Competitors carry a specially designed ten pound .22 caliber target rifle on their back and shoot at targets fifty meters away. There are two shooting positions, prone and standing (offhand), and the athlete either skis a penalty loop or one minute is added to his/her time for each missed shot. Excellent physical condition and mental control play major roles in this sport, and, for that reason, most biathletes do their summer dry land training on difficult hilly terrain.

In 1982 Paul went to the World Championships in Russia as a member of the U.S. Junior Biathlon team, and Stu went to the championships in Bulgaria the following year. Kari qualified for the women's U.S. team for four years and skied in the United States races until the first World Championships for women was held in Chamonix, France, in February 1984.

Prologue

February 29, 1984
Chamonix, France—World Biathlon Championships

Nervous and introspective, Kari ate breakfast with the other three competitors on the Women's U.S. Biathlon Team. "We're obviously the only team here that hasn't skied in international competition," Julie said, glancing at the Russian women chattering on one side of the dining room, the Swedes on the other. "We must look like a troop of greenhorns!"

Kari, turning to their rifle coach, Marie Alkire, asked, "How can they be so relaxed?"

"They've raced against each other for several years, and have a pretty good idea where they stand with each other," Marie answered. "We know their records, too; they're impressive, but you have an edge because they don't know what to expect from you. When you've finished breakfast I'd like you to go back to your rooms, relax, do some self-talk and imagery."

Kari and Marie left the dining room and walked through the hotel to their rooms, stopping at Marie's door. "I'll wish you luck now, Kari; just remember to relax when you get to the range."

"Yes, ma'am!" Kari snapped to attention, her eyes twinkled with mischief.

Marie watched the young woman walk down the hall. Kari moved with the long, graceful, confident stride of a well-trained athlete, arms and long auburn braid swinging rhythmically with the movement of her hips. If she knew how attractive she looked in her tight racing suit, thought Marie, she would have been embarrassed.

Inside her room Kari rechecked her equipment and placed it beside the door. She began to mentally talk to herself, visualizing exactly what she would do in the race—skiing, then shooting, all the while controlling her pulse and respirations. She would approach the shooting range with pulse bounding, breathing fast, but she was conditioned, physically and mentally, to reduce her heart rate and respirations to the low level she would need to steady her rifle and hit each target.

In five months, this technique would save her life.

Kari bolted out of the starting gate, adrenaline flooding her limbs. The wind whipped tears to her eyes, stinging her face. Her heart pounded, her lungs heaved. Skiing into the shooting range, she lay on her stomach, sighted down the barrel, and squeezed the trigger.

The old man whipped the rifle to his shoulder. She strained against the chain and yelled a warning. Too late! He pulled the trigger. No! No!

All five targets fell. Kari scrambled to her feet and skied out onto the course, moving fast. Again she approached the range and slowed her heart rate as she took the standing shooting position.

Her heart hammered against her ribs. She wrenched one wrist free, clawed at his eyes. His fist smashed into her face, knocking her to the ground.

Stay calm, stay calm. One deep breath, exhale, another breath, exhale, a third . . . exhale—fire. The five targets fell.

The rifle shot roared in her ears and she watched in horror as the searcher's body arched backward, down, down, down to lie motionless among the forget-me-nots and squaw grass.

Kari sped off the range, shouldering her rifle while she skied. Marie chanted after her, "Go Kari! Kari! Kari!"

"Kar-r-i-i. Kar-r-i-i." The sound drifted to her through the stillness of the summer night. Her captors heard it, too, and jumped to their feet. They grabbed their rifles and ran to the edge of the clearing. "Kar-r-i-i. Where ar-r-e-e yo-o-u?"

"Kari Swenson led the U.S. effort that day, with a fifth place finish behind four Soviets in a time of 45:49.6, with an outstanding shooting result of 14 hits from 15 shots," wrote Marie Alkire for a sports magazine. "Swenson bested skiers from the Scandinavian nations—something U.S. men and women Nordic skiers have been unable to do, except on rare occasions. Her finish is the best by any United States woman in a World Championships, or Olympic Games."

Four days later, skiing in second position in the three-person five kilometer relay race, Kari turned in the best performance of her biathlon career. She moved the team from fifth to third place and had the fastest ski time recorded in the second leg of the event, beating Norway, Finland, Sweden, and the USSR. Shooting in a twenty-six-mile-per-hour wind, she hit eight out of ten targets, setting up a bronze medal, the first international medal in world biathlon competition for the United States.

"It was so cold my teeth ached," Kari said over the phone, "but I couldn't stop smiling. Just think, it was the women who won the first international medal for the United States!" She laughed as she concluded the call. "The European coaches keep asking Marie, 'Who iss dis Svenson?'"

"Who is this Swenson? How long has she been gone? Sorry. We don't do night searches. You'll have to wait until morning."

Kar-r-i-i. Kar-r-i-i."

June 9, 1984, Bozeman, Montana

Kari opened her window, flooding her bedroom with fresh night air. Moving the bright ribbons and wrapping paper from her bed, she crawled between the sheets and thought about the past seventeen hours.

This morning she had graduated from Montana State University with a degree in microbiology. After the ceremony her parents had thrown a party celebrating her brother's twenty-first birthday and her graduation. Friends had lit the candles on Paul's cake and had sung to him while he stood beside her, embarrassed, waiting to blow them out. She still couldn't believe that her "little" brother, all six foot three inches of him, was twenty-one years old. Blond like their sister Johanna, Paul had large blue eyes that were accented by thick straight eyebrows and long lashes. His Scots nose came from Great-Grandpa Johnstone and his sense of humor from his father.

They would have one last summer together at Lone Mountain Ranch in Big Sky to train and share the fun of living in the mountains, just as they had as children. Kari smiled to herself remembering the frog races they had had using the little green creatures borrowed from a neighbor's pond, and the day their horses had been spooked by a bear when they were riding up Cinnamon Creek. One more year of competition, and then she would apply to veterinary school, something she had wanted to do since she was five years old.

She shut off the light and slept, unaware that her dream would soon be shattered.

BOOK ONE

THE KIDNAPPING, SEARCH, RESCUE, AND HOSPITALIZATION

1

A SUMMER RUN

June 9, Somewhere in the Madison Mountain Range

Two men tossed carrot and rutabaga seeds on the loosened soil, patted the dirt over them, and sprinkled the area with water. The younger man was impatient with the planting—he missed not having a woman around. His relationship with Sue had come to an abrupt halt last year, so he had traveled to Jackson Hole, Wyoming, to join his father. He had washed dishes, but after a few weeks he decided he hated having to work from eight to five—that wasn't the life for him! For several years his dad had been after him to move up to the mountains with him, and it sounded pretty good after all those dishes. So one night, almost a year ago, he told his dad he was willing to give up society and live in the mountains. It had been fun living away from people and their rules, but it was lonely up here.

"Dad, you remember the plans you and me talked about . . . about getting us a woman?"

The man studied his eighteen year old son and said, "Are you saying it's time?" The boy nodded.

His son had finally come to live in the mountains with him. But getting a woman might not be as easy as he led him to believe. He himself had asked some hippie-like, rootless girls in Jackson to come live in the mountains, but they didn't like the idea. A friend of his had had better luck. A girl had gone off into the mountains with him and had fit right in. Maybe they'd find a girl like that.

July 10

The young man hoisted his pack to his shoulders and picked up his rifle. He checked the pistol hanging at his right hip and the knife in its sheath on the left side of his belt. He jerked his head, tossing his long, greasy blond hair from his eyes, and glanced at his father. The older man was ready to move out—pack on his back, knife in his belt, and his rifle, in its cloth case, clutched in his right hand. Like his son's, the old man's clothes were greasy, patched, and pungent, smelling of sweat and soil. His hat was battered and so impregnated with grease it was waterproof. His father grinned, jammed the hat on his head, and said, "Let's go. It's a long way over the mountain."

July 15, Lone Mountain Guest Ranch, Big Sky, Montana

Kari was in the kitchen by 5:30 a.m. about to take breakfast to the Schaap's backyard where she would help serve the Sunday morning cookout. She loaded the truck and started up the hill. The ranch was nestled between two ridges. The cabins were tucked neatly among the fir and spruce trees with a large grassy meadow between the office building and the log dining hall. A creek gurgled and bubbled its way through the ranch, and the rocks of Yellow Mountain glinted with the first rays of the sun.

Vivian and Bob Schaap, part owners and managers of the ranch, helped her start the fire for the cookout.

"Man, Kari, you should have seen the grizzly I saw yesterday up Jack Creek!" Bob said. "She stayed in sight for about an hour, digging up roots and eating grubs. I sat on the hillside watching her until the elk herd moved in. Then I had to sit and watch the cow elk and their calves for another hour. I liked to have never gotten home!"

"I'd give my right arm to see a grizzly that close," said Kari.

"Not me!" Vivian shuddered. Guests were beginning to arrive. and the subject was dropped.

Paul had been up early, getting a head start on his cabin cleaning job at the ranch. He laughed and joked with fellow employees Jay and Greg as they walked to the Schaaps' for breakfast, and sat down at the picnic table under the old Douglas fir trees. Kari served them and good-naturedly took their ribbing. Jay's eyes twinkled behind his glasses as he smoothed a corner of his mustache. "I heard that Subaru come in pretty late last night, Kari. Doing a little dancing, huh? I'm taking a horse ride to Beehive Basin today. You want to come along?"

"Sounds like fun, Jay, but I can't go today. Thanks anyway."

Paul grinned at Kari. "You look like a zombie, sister dear; just what time *did* you roll in?" She made a face at him. "Want to go fishing with me this afternoon?" he asked.

"Probably not. I need to do some training."

"How can you train? You look like you need a nap! Oh, well, if you're going to play hard, you have to pay for it." Kari threw a potholder at him, and he ducked behind a tree, grinning. A few seconds later Paul slid out from behind the old fir and started down the hill, calling over his shoulder, "Be careful if you run alone, and make sure you tell someone where you're going. Sound like Mom, don't I?" They laughed together.

1:30 p.m.

Kari sat on the edge of her bed cutting the sleeves and neckband from a blue T-shirt. She dropped the scissors and scraps of material on the bed and tugged her red shorts over her hips. Filling a plastic bottle with water, she considered which trail to run.

"Guess I'll try a quick run at Ulreys Lake," she muttered to herself, then closed the apartment door behind her and ran down the hill to her car. Brian and Jeff, two ranch hands, stopped her.

"Want to go into town and help us pick up hay at your folk's place?"

"Thanks, but I need to train. Tell them hello for me. I'm working the split shift today; see you when I serve dinner."

Easing out of the parking space, she pulled away from the ranch and waved to friends standing by the corral fence. The car bumped down the rough ranch road, turning westward toward Lone Mountain and Ulreys Lake.

1:30 p.m. Paul

Paul finished his job schedule early, grabbed his fishing vest and rod, and hurried out to his car. Leaving the ranch, he glanced in the rearview mirror and saw Kari jog across the ranch yard to her car, where she stopped to talk to someone.

Fifteen minutes later, Paul parked beside the Gallatin River and started fishing. Eventually, he tired of catching and releasing the rainbow trout, and climbed a huge boulder to soak up the sun and marvel at the blue sky. He reminded himself how lucky he was to live here. He wished Kari had come with him. They didn't have enough time together because their work hours were usually so different. Kari was special to Paul, and when he returned to the university next year he'd miss her. Paul flopped over on his stomach, nestled his cheek in the soft lichen and moss, and closed his eyes. The hot sun beat down on his back, and far away he heard the screech of a hawk.

2 p.m. Ulreys Lake

The older man hid the packs and rifles in the trees, and he and his son went down to the lake's edge. The young man took out fishing line and prepared to catch dinner. The father sat down and leaned against a tree, frowning as he remembered the events of the day before. A good-looking woman wearing a swimming suit had been floating in an inner tube, fishing. He had yelled at her, "Do you know the day of the week and the date?"

"It's Saturday, July 14."

He had turned and relayed that to his son, who was writing their names and the date on a tree. He had used his knife to peel off some bark and had written on the scarred area with a black indelible marker:

DAN AND DON NICHOLS LIVE IN THESE MTS JULY 14 1984.

He had called to the woman: "Why don't you come over here where there's lots of fish?"

"I'm doing fine," came the reply.

He had walked over to look at his son's work, and turning back to the lake, he had noticed that the inner tube was floating closer to shore. The woman had seemed curious and chatted with him. "You must have been in the mountains for quite awhile, not to know the date," she called.

"Yeah, we've been out here a long time," said the older man, walking toward the shore.

The breeze had blown the inner tube closer.

Then a male voice had drifted on the wind. "Joel, where are you?" The woman had looked startled when she realized she had drifted out of sight of her husband and friends, and kicked with her flippers to propel herself back to the center of the lake.

The older man was brought back to the present by voices from across the water. His son hurried to him and they remained hidden in the trees until the unwelcome hikers left the area.

2:30 p.m. Kari

Kari parked her car near Ulreys, locked the doors, tied a red bandana around her forehead, stretched, and started off at a slow jog. By the time she reached the lower lake her muscles were warm, and she lengthened her stride to run up the steep hill that led to the upper lake. Emerging from the trees, she saw someone on the right-hand shore. Probably a fisherman, she thought, and took the left path to avoid him. Kari felt uneasy—strangers always made her feel that way when she was alone in the mountains.

The trail was treacherous with stones, tree roots, holes, and muddy areas. Great place to turn an ankle, she thought, jumping over a puddle. The trail angled away from the lake and she sprinted up an incline, pushing hard, lengthened her stride, and propelled herself over the rise.

3 p.m. The Men

The son had returned to his fishing, but he was distracted by a woman in red shorts running on the other side of the lake. He stared, then rushed back to his father. "There's a hell of a pretty girl comin' around the lake! Get ready! I wanna see her!"

6 p.m. Paul

"Paul, have you seen Kari?" Barb asked when she placed another basket of rolls on the table.

"No, I haven't. Maybe she's up at the house taking a nap." Paul had returned from fishing just in time for dinner. He had skipped lunch and his stomach had growled so loudly it interfered with his nap on the boulder. When he entered the dining room, Barb had given him a funny look. He hadn't thought anything about it as he seated himself at a table where he could look out at the ranch. Paul started to sweat. If Kari was supposed to serve dinner she'd have been here unless something had happened to her. Maybe her car was stuck. No, she would have telephoned or run back to the ranch for help, Paul told himself.

Barb returned and told him neither Kari nor her car were at the apartment. Jay frowned. "I saw Kari's car parked at the Ulreys Lake trailhead this afternoon. It was there when we came out of Beehive Basin."

Something deep inside told Paul Kari was in trouble—big trouble. Bolting from the dining hall, he ran to his room, grabbed a jacket and car keys, and headed for his car. Bob Schaap and Terry Gromley intercepted Paul and handed him a two-way radio.

"You and Terry check to see if her car is still where Jay saw it," Bob said. "Call me as soon as you get there. I'll phone your parents."

Kari's car was still at the trailhead. Paul was more frightened now, sure she had been injured. Jay and another man arrived with a motorbike and said they would search high along the logging road while Terry and he went into Beehive Basin.

Paul began to walk quickly, then run, shouting Kari's name over and over as he and Terry crossed the creek and began climbing into the steep natural bowl of the basin. Paul's destination was the snow-covered ridges far above them. There wasn't much daylight left; the lower areas were already in shadow.

2

EVENING SEARCH

7 p.m. Bozeman

The phone rang, and Bob answered. When he didn't say anything, I glanced up. He was staring at me with panic in his eyes.

"My God!" he gasped. "I'll call you right back." He banged down the receiver. "Kari's missing!" Quickly he repeated the details Bob Schaap had given him.

"Schaap wants to know what we want him to do," he concluded.

"She must have twisted an ankle. Phone Bob, ask him to get the crew at the ranch out to look for her, and tell him to call the sheriff's office and give the report. She has to be okay!" Bob hugged me so tightly I could hardly talk. "You call while I get my emergency equipment together." I dashed to the next room and grabbed my backpack from under the counter. A sense of alarm left me numb.

Bob shouted, "I'll phone Jack Drumheller, see if he can get a plane to fly me over the area. You call George Tuthill to go with you, ask him if he'll take his car. You'd drive too fast."

I stuffed first aid equipment, flares, flashlight, jacket, and maps into my rescue pack. It gets dark at 10 p.m., I reminded myself. We have about three hours of light left.

"Jan?" Bob interrupted my frantic thoughts. "Jack will meet me at the airport. I phoned Bob Schaap, Kari's car is still there, Paul and Terry are headed into Beehive Basin to look for her. He's getting the rest of the staff out to search, and said he'd phone the sheriff's office. Call George so I'll know you have someone to go with you. Hurry!" He ran to the study to pack his gear.

I misdialed George's number twice before my hands stopped shaking and I got the number right. He is a colleague of Bob's, has known our children since they were small, and said he'd pick me up at the main highway as soon as he got his pack together. I shouted goodbye to Bob, jumped into the pickup truck, and spun out in the gravel as I rushed to meet George.

7 p.m. Bob

Bob backed out of the garage, roared along in third gear to the stop light, then shoved it into fourth, and floorboarded it to the airport. Jack Drumheller and Bob drove into the airport at the same time and clambered into the plane that was fueled and ready to go.

"You realize Kari will be safely at the ranch before we get there, don't you?" Jack said. "She probably sprained an ankle on her run and is sitting waiting for Paul to find her. She'll be okay, Bob, but this is a great idea—beautiful evening to fly. We have about one-and-a-half hours of good light. You ready? How's your stomach?"

"I'm so upset I could get sick without leaving the ground. Damn it! Jack, I'm scared. What could have happened to her?"

Bob's mind raced, wondering what to do next, where to start looking. Kari wouldn't miss work unless she were in serious trouble, he was sure of that. He was a horrible flier and was getting sicker the closer they flew to the rugged, shadowed peaks. Passing to the south of the rocky spires, they looked down on hundreds of miles of timber and mountains. Even the Big Sky development was an insignificant flyspeck. Bob was reluctant to accept how tough it was going to be to find Kari.

The higher slopes were sparsely treed, making it easier to scan the ground as it sped by, but closer to Ulreys Lake the forest became more dense. They saw people on the logging roads or in meadows, but the trees flashed by at 100 mph, making it impossible to see someone stranded in a tree or lying under one. Bob Schaap had told him that he was afraid Kari might have had a run-in with the grizzly bear he had seen, and that possibility scared her father to death.

Jack piloted the plane over the high ridges of Beehive Basin, then dropped lower around the lake. They swooped over the trailhead to Ulreys Lake. The large number of cars and horse trailers jammed together meant, to Bob, that Kari hadn't been found. Flying close to the treetops and the peaks, Jack began a methodical search of the area. Bob was incoherent with motion sickness and dizziness as the plane turned, banked against the cliffs, dropping, rising, circling. They searched for over an hour and the evening light was fading when Jack told Bob they had to head back to the airfield.

"No! Not yet! We haven't found her."

"Bob, I'm sorry. I know how you feel, but we can't stay out any longer. I'm sorry, I don't know what else to say."

Bob, numb with airsickness and emotional strain, cried shamelessly as they flew away from the search area. The wheels touched the runway and the plane came to a stop. He ran for the bathroom, the motion sickness taking its toll. Regaining his composure, he thanked Jack, dashed for his car, and headed up the canyon to the Lone Mountain Ranch, an hour away.

8 p.m. Jan

A thick stand of lodgepole pines at the Ulreys Lake trailhead had been bulldozed to clear an area where fishermen and hikers could park. A small plane skimmed the treetops. Like a bird of prey, it swooped, circled, and crisscrossed above us. George was talking to Bob Schaap while I watched the plane, waiting for it to dip its wings, signaling that they had seen Kari. Poor Bob, I thought, knowing he must be miserably sick by now.

Bob Schaap told us where the search groups were, where we still needed to look, and who had been notified. He mounted his horse to return to the search.

"Bob! When will the sheriff and posse be here?" I shouted.

His jaw muscles tightened. "They won't be coming, Jan. The jerks don't believe in doing night searches!" He nudged his horse forward, and it pranced nervously when I sprang forward, grabbing at the reins.

"Wait! That's not true, I've done night searches with them! What's happening?"

"Unfortunately," Bob said through clenched teeth, "this is Madison County, and they won't help us. We'll have to do it ourselves. I gave George a map. You two search around the lakes; I'll meet you back here later to reorganize if we haven't found Kari by dark."

Bob disappeared into the trees as George and I ran down the trail to the lower lake. Shouting Kari's name, we skirted the lake, which was covered with lily pads and surrounded by bogs. Clouds of mosquitoes descended on us. George stopped. "Listen!" We heard a distant voice: "Kar-r-i-i."

Emerging from the trees onto a logging road, we found Brian Wadsworth, Barbara Batey, and Greg Holler, employees at the ranch. "There are prints all over, but not the ones we're looking for," Brian said. "Barb thinks Kari was wearing her New Balance shoes with this pattern." He used a twig to draw a diagram in the dust. "Nothing like that here. We'll go on up the road."

The three young people continued to follow the road, but George and I scrambled through the thick underbrush looking for the trail to the upper lake. "I found it! Over here," George shouted. He raced up a steep path ahead of me. I glanced into the deep ravine on my right, shouted Kari's name, waited for a second, and followed George.

We ran out of the trees onto the upper lake shore. "You go around to the right, Jan, I'll go left. Meet you half way. Look for prints!"

Two snarling Doberman pinschers rushed me, blocking the trail. I screamed, immobile with fear. A man stepped out of the trees, shouted a command, and the dogs fell silent. My heart raced, and I stuttered as I questioned him about Kari. He said he hadn't seen her but had seen three or four young men across the lake about four o'clock. He thought they were fishermen.

I stumbled along the shore, dazed, realizing for the first time that Kari could have met trouble at the hands of humans. No! No! Oh God, don't let it be that! I cried to myself. I shouted her name louder and ran faster.

I met George in a muddy spot that had at least four different sets of prints—boots, tennis shoes, running shoes, and waders.

"I found lots of prints on the other shore, too," George panted. "Are you sure she wasn't wearing Nikes? There are Nike prints that go up that trail," he pointed to a path leading away from the lake, "but they don't come back down."

"I'll have someone at the ranch go to her room and check on the shoes again. Maybe she's been found. I wish we had a radio!"

We ran hard up the trail, away from the lake, and found ourselves on a logging road.

8:30 p.m. Paul

"Paul, slow down a little! Save some strength for later!" Terry yelled. They had been running uphill shouting Kari's name, but Paul couldn't slow down. It would be dark soon, he had to find her! Terry caught up with him and they split up, each going at his own pace. Paul scrambled up to the high rocky divide, thinking perhaps Kari had gotten up this far and had been injured or had decided to drop over into the Spanish Peaks trails to the north.

"Kari! Kar-r-i-i! Kari!" he shouted and sobbed. The only reply was the echo bouncing back from the far ridge. He stumbled and fell. Catching his breath, he started to rise, and noticed that the sun was setting. The rocky crags of the mountains blazed red and gold, and deep purple shadows filled the valleys. Suddenly Paul was angry, furious that life went on as usual when he might have lost one of the most beautiful people in his life! It wasn't fair! He sucked the blood from a cut on his hand and started running again.

He searched for footprints in the old snow and mud fields along the ridge. A plane buzzed low overhead, making tight turns, flying a search grid between the basin walls. Of course! His dad would have asked Jack to fly him over the area. Find her! he prayed as he jogged down the rocky slope to meet Terry. Please, Dad, find her!

Terry was listening to a tinny voice on their portable radio. "Have they found her? Who was that? What'd they say?" Paul asked, trying to catch his breath.

"That was Schaap telling us to head out, not to be heros."

"Bullshit!" Paul jogged off for the other side of the basin. "I'll meet you in thirty minutes at that little pond down the trail," he shouted over his shoulder.

"Okay, I'll shut the radio off for a little while." Terry grinned, mopped at the sweat running down his face, and started down the trail.

Searching the northwest side of the basin, Paul thought he heard Kari calling. Stopping to listen, he realized he was hallucinating. It was getting dark and the plane had gone. Paul hurried to meet Terry. He stopped and stared, unable to believe his eyes. There was Terry sitting on the ground with Kari cradled in his arms! Paul ran, tears streaming down his face. He'd tell her how much they loved her, how worried he'd been, and would promise never to let her go training by herself again! He stopped in front of Terry who was sitting with his pack on his lap.

"Where is she? Where has she gone?" he yelled. Terry looked at him as if he were crazy. Paul slumped to the ground and sobbed, realizing he had seen what he wanted to see. "Damn it! Damn it! Terry, where is she?" Terry handed him a bottle of water and shook his head.

The long walk out to the trailhead was silent and miserable. In the moonlight tears trickled down their faces. The searchers around the cars were quiet, dejected. Driving back to the ranch Paul tried to pull himself together, figuring his parents would need him to help them.

Paul found his father in the ranch office. He looked scared. Paul needed to be alone. He told Bob to call him as soon as they had any news about Kari, and went to his room. He showered in a daze and threw himself on the bed. Suddenly he saw Kari! She was tied to a log, tethered like a horse. There were men sitting around a fire. She was crying! Paul jerked out of the nightmare, stiff with terror, and ran to the bathroom where he retched until his stomach and throat ached.

9:50 p.m. Jan

George and I hurried back to the parking area where we joined Bob Schaap and his daughter Laura. "Would you go to Big Sky and phone the Gallatin sheriff's office for me?" I asked Laura. "Tell them to call Deputy Brad Brisbin in West Yellowstone and tell him what's happening here. He has a search dog we've used on rescues, he'll come if he knows I'm asking for him. Tell him I'm frantic! I need his help!"

I walked over to Kari's car. I wanted to touch something that was hers, but it was locked. I peered through the windows at the K-2 baseball cap looped over the gearshift, a Junior Nationals medal hanging from the rearview mirror, a plastic water bottle lying on the seat, a pair of cross-country ski poles, and her new "plastic" shoes. I rested my forehead against the cool glass and cried quietly. I hadn't been able to find her. All these years of helping others, and I couldn't find my own child.

10 p.m.

The sun had set and the temperature was dropping. I shined my flashlight through the car windows and studied the contents again. Her fanny pack wasn't there. Thank God she had it with her and would have some protection from the cold. Two weeks ago I had put together a first aid kit for her, and she stuffed it in her fanny pack along with her long underwear and a plastic whistle. Why hadn't she used that whistle to signal us? I wondered.

"I can't leave now," I told Bob Schaap. "I have to keep looking for her. The obvious trails have been searched, but what if Kari went off in a different direction? There's a trail on this map that heads southwest and then angles off between Cedar Mountain and Lone Mountain. Maybe, just maybe, she decided to do a short, steep run and went there."

"You'll have trouble finding the path because of the logging in that area," he said. "But if you insist on going, walk down this road and watch for the trail on the left. It's tough walking. You realize you can't go alone, don't you?" Bob spoke gently, but firmly.

George, Brian, and Greg volunteered to go with me. Bob said he'd remain at the trailhead to wait for Laura. He would also arrange to have someone sleep beside Kari's car in case she walked out during the night.

The radio crackled in Bob's hand, and he stepped aside to take the message as we turned on our flashlights and started down the logging road. "Jan!" he shouted after us. "Your husband just pulled into the ranch. He sounded pretty upset. They didn't see anything from the air. Maybe you'd better head in and let someone else search."

"No! He wouldn't want me to leave. Did Barb check on those running shoes?"

"Yes. Kari's New Balance aren't in the closet."

We left the trailhead and jogged down the rutted road. The footing was difficult, and the farther we went the worse it became. The radio crackled, "This is Schaap. Laura sent your message, Jan, but Brad hasn't called back. What do you want us to do?"

"Have the ranch call the sheriff's office again. I have to reach him! We need dogs and more people. Can you think of anyone else to help us? Maybe someone from Big Sky?"

"I'll do what I can. Hang in there, we'll find her."

Our progress was blocked by a rushing creek that gouged a deep ravine across the dirt road and fell thundering into the blackness below. We were trying to find a way around the mess when Bob Schaap paged me again.

"The ranch repeated the message to the sheriff's office, but Brad hasn't called. Could be they're not relaying the message because this is Madison County."

I knelt on the ground pretending to open my pack, trying to hide my tears. Greg patted my shoulder. "It'll be okay, it'll be okay," he soothed.

I pulled myself together and started back down the trail. I knew Kari was alive. A special feeling we shared would be gone if she were dead. I had to hold on to that thought. She's alive! She's alive! I repeated with each jarring step on the rutted road.

At the trailhead a ranch hand was preparing to sleep on the ground beside Kari's car. Driving back to the ranch, the men in George's car talked in subdued voices. I hugged my pack, rested my cheek against it, and prayed that if someone had taken Kari he wouldn't hurt her. No matter how I fought, images of rape and torture intruded, so I tried positive thinking. I visualized finding Kari, gathering her in my arms, and whispering that everything would be all right. Please, God, just give her back to us alive! Tears soaked the pack.

It was 12:40 a.m. when we pulled up in front of the ranch office. The full moon cast eerie shadows around the corrals and buildings. Perhaps the brightness would give Kari some comfort, wherever she was.

We climbed the stairs to the office where the search was being planned. My husband looked awful. Bob's suffering showed in his eyes, the gray-tinged skin, and the lines around his mouth. We clung to each other. I choked back tears and asked Bob Schaap if he would loan me a ranch truck. I wanted to drive into Beehive Basin and spend the night honking the horn, calling to Kari and flashing the headlights. I wanted her to know she wasn't alone, that we would find her. "Please," I begged, "I have to be out there."

The phone rang. It was Brad Brisbin, deputy sheriff for Gallatin County. He had not received my message until he had gone off duty and checked in with the sheriff's office. He had phoned Sheriff John Onstad, who had given him permission to help us, and he and Deputy Bob Pearson would be at the ranch about 4:00 a.m.

"Jan, I told Schaap not to let you go out alone in a truck. Promise me you won't."

"I have to go! I can't leave her out there alone!"

We argued, and he won when he said I should start thinking about helping my husband and son, and that he'd need me to help reorganize the searchers when he arrived. I hung up and turned to face three weary, frightened men.

"I won't go out in the truck," I sighed, feeling as if I'd abandoned my daughter, knowing what I wanted to do was right, but too stunned to argue. "Where's Paul? Is he all right?"

"He's in his room," Bob sighed, "exhausted, terrified. He can't believe he couldn't find her!"

I suddenly remembered that my family was driving to Bozeman tomorrow—no *today*—and we were to fly to Switzerland on Tuesday. "Why don't you check on Paul while I call Mom? How will I tell her? What will I tell her?" I asked Bob, who just shook his head and went to find our son.

I called my brother Bob, and he promised to phone our younger brother immediately and break the news to Mom in the morning. He tried to reassure me by reminding me that Kari knew the mountains and could take care of herself.

Returning from Paul's room, Bob said, "He doesn't want to talk. He's in bad shape, but he wants to be alone."

Bob Schaap asked Laura to drive George and us up to the ranch house to rest, saying he'd join us later. George, blond, wiry, a first-class athlete whose fields of expertise were orienteering, biathlon, and mountain running, had been working feverishly over the maps, helping Schaap decide which ones should be enlarged for the morning search teams. Now he looked as spent as I felt.

I told Bob I wanted to stay in Kari's room, to check through her running clothes and shoes. I needed to touch something that belonged to her and try to reach her with my mind.

1 a.m. Lone Mountain Ranch

I stumbled across the living room of Kari's dark apartment, fumbled along the wall to her bedroom door, and flipped on the light. Lying on the bed were a pair of scissors and the sleeves and neckband from a blue T-shirt. I picked up a sleeve and crammed it in my pocket. Her bright red running shorts were not in the drawer.

A sweatshirt lay on the floor where she had carelessly dropped it. I picked it up and stared in horror. All sense of proportion and equilibrium left me. Lying on the floor were the running shoes we thought she was wearing, and her fanny pack. She didn't have her first aid kit, whistle, or long underwear! How would she stay warm?

Head reeling, I sat on her bed looking at the posters and photographs on the walls. Snapshots of her friends smiled at me. Next to the door was a small Italian flag given to her by the Italian men's biathlon team last February in Oslo. They could not pronounce her name so they called her "Fox Fire"—a tribute to her red hair. I could see her laughing face as she described those happy days.

"Where is she? Help me find her," I shouted at the frozen smiles.

Bob took my hand. "You can't stay here," he said gently. "Come upstairs."

George and Bob were put in bedrooms, but I stayed in the living room on the sofa. I heard Bob tossing and turning and knew he wasn't sleeping either. For an hour and a half I looked out the window at the moon and sent silent messages to Kari, willing her to hear my thoughts. The week before she had needed a "long distance" day for her training schedule, so we hiked up Sage Ridge. It was steep, and I had to trot to keep up with her long strides. We found a dead tree that had blown over, and I boosted her into its branches so I could take a picture. Getting out of the tree had been harder than getting in; we laughed and joked as I helped her down.

Wandering out of the dense forest, we found ourselves in a meadow carpeted with bright blue forget-me-nots, Kari's favorite flower. After a hurried lunch in the cool breeze, I took a picture of her and the dog sitting in a patch of flowers.

We hustled off the mountain to the warmth in the valley and dinner at our cabin. Reminding me to press the forget-me-nots, she kissed me and drove away, honking and waving until she was out of sight.

3

SEARCH FOR KARI

3 a.m. Jan

Bob Schaap, Bob, and I walked down the winding road from the house to the dining hall where two men sat at a table. One of them was Bob Naert, an emergency medical technician and a Big Sky fireman who had attended search and rescue training classes with Brad Brisbin and me. The other was John Palmer, a fireman who helped with local search and rescue.

Bob Naert was casual, almost cheerful. "Hi! Come and help us sort out these maps. Do you know which trails were searched?" His attitude puzzled me, and I learned later that he did not know Kari was our daughter.

We knew we hadn't missed any trails, but there was a lot of off-trail ground to cover. Other searchers straggled in and gathered in small groups, speaking softly to each other. A strong arm circled my shoulders and gave me a squeeze. Brad! He and Bob Pearson had arrived from West Yellowstone with their German shepherd search dogs Bear and Skip. Dark-haired, handsome, and gentle, Brad gave me a mental boost. He and Bear would find Kari for us! Deputy Pearson stood back, watching, his easy smile replaced with a frown that drew his eyebrows together and turned down the corners of his mouth. "Anybody here from Madison?" he asked.

"Nope!" Bob Schaap answered. "That jerk said the best he could do was send out two men on horseback from their end of Jack Creek. Said they'd leave the trailhead about eight o'clock."

"Eight is too late!" I protested.

"We'll find her, Jan. Go over this map with me again, okay?" Brad's brown eyes said he understood my panic.

The kitchen crew served the group breakfast, but Bob and I pushed our food around, unable to eat. Paul came into the room. His face was as haggard as his father's, and his eyes were puffy and red. He sat down at the table, pushed away the plate in front of him, and asked when we were going to get started. Schaap stood in front of the fireplace and called for order.

"Listen up, everybody. Choose a partner. Each group of two will have a radio and a map. I'll assign trails and areas as soon as you get your partner and map. Hustle!"

Within minutes the group was ready and Schaap asked me to describe Kari. My throat was tight with emotion when I gave the description and showed them the blue sleeve. "Please, when you find Kari, radio the base and cover her, but don't move her until we know how badly she's injured," I said. "Hypothermia has to be a concern here."

"We'll go out with our dogs first," Brad told us. "A half hour later, all of you may begin searching the areas assigned to you. Check in with the base station every half hour, tell us your location, and if you have found any clues. We have radios with several different frequencies, so relay all messages through the base. We want you to search the forest away from the trails, but keep within sight or shouting distance of each other. There are first aid kits for those of you who need them, and the kitchen crew has prepared a sack lunch for each of you. Pick them up. Get moving and we'll regroup at Ulreys trailhead."

Paul stood as if rooted to the floor. "Come on, honey," I said. "Who do you have as a partner? It'll be all right, Kari's probably sitting in the top of a tree shaking her fist at some bear." Paul didn't smile or respond as he turned to leave with Steve Shimek. God help him, I prayed, sprinting for George's car.

As we pulled away I noticed the moon was no longer shining.

5:30 a.m. Ulreys Lake Trailhead

Bob and I were impatient with the delay. He paced back and forth, his face pale and pinched, with deep furrows of fatigue extending from his eyes to the corners of his mouth. He rested his cheek on my head and sighed. He hadn't eaten since the day before, and his hypoglycemia would soon catch up with him. I checked his pack to make sure he had a lunch.

Bob Donovan, director of the Big Sky Fire Department, agreed to go with me. George Tuthill would go with Bob. While they studied their map, Donovan and I checked the nearby trails for shoe prints. Nothing. The radio crackled, and base received a message from Paul. He and Steve had started on foot to search the North Fork ridge and would eventually drop into the east side of Beehive Basin. He told us Kari had hidden a key to her car in a magnetic box if we wanted to get into the car. We found the key. Bob removed the K-2 cap from the gearshift and jammed it on his head, a hint of a smile tugging at his lips. "It's her favorite hat. I'll wear it for good luck." The smile vanished as quickly as it had appeared.

"Ask Paul if they've seen anything up that way," I said.

"Nothing so far," John Palmer answered. "Steve said Paul's in a bad way. Maybe we shouldn't have let him go out."

"Nothing will keep him out of those hills until she's found," I murmured.

6 a.m.

At last we moved out. Bob Donovan and I hurried to the lower lake, picking our way along the boggy shore looking for clues. The lily pad-choked surface sent tingles up and down my spine and the odor of rotting vegetation and stagnant water made me think of death. By now I was thinking that someone could have murdered Kari and concealed her body.

"No!" I shouted.

"What?" called Donovan.

"Nothing, nothing. I was talking to myself!"

We approached higher ground and angled away from the lake, then joined Bob and George and two women from the ranch who were on horses. Brian and Barbara joined us as Brad's voice sputtered from the radio. They had not found Kari.

Brisbin and Schaap

Brad and Bear searched the Jack Creek trail, the dog sniffing through the heavy underbrush and downed timber. The sun had not yet penetrated the tall, dense lodgepole pines, and it was chilly. Bear turned in a tight circle, alerting Brad, then ran uphill through the trees. Brad bashed and battered his way up the slope, thinking to himself, We've found her!

Bear stopped 300 yards up the slope and began circling, searching. He stood still, nose in the brush, whining softly. Brad parted the gooseberry bushes and reached into the grass. Without speaking, he held up an object. It was a bone, slippery with blood and shreds of flesh. It looked like a human forearm. Bob Schaap steadied himself against a tree and tried not to throw up. He knew what a body looked like after a grizzly encounter, and he didn't want to search anymore.

"Let's get this into town to the vet research lab, or to someone who can tell us if it's animal or human," Brad said softly. They slipped it into a plastic sack and took it with them.

Jan and Bob Donovan

Brian and Barbara looked for a trail in the bottom of the ravine, while Bob Donovan and I searched the higher area. The logging in the Jack Creek drainage made it difficult to find the trail we wanted. We bushwhacked through downed timber, crawled over or under dead trees, and occasionally came back to the logging road.

"We found a trail," shouted Barb. "Seems to run along the bottom. We'll follow it."

Brian's voice floated up to us, "Kar-r-i-i! Kar-r-i-i!" I remembered nightmares I had had when the children were small. They were always lost, and I'd run calling their names over and over. No matter how I forced their names from my throat, my voice would be a soft echo. I would awaken sticky with sweat, tiptoe into each child's room, tuck the covers around them, and return to bed knowing they were safe. If only this were a dream!

I pulled branches away from a slash pile, dropped to my knees, and peered into the dark, tangled, cavern. "Why do you keep looking under the slash piles?" Donovan asked.

"Kari didn't have warm clothing with her. If she broke an ankle she might have crawled under one of these to keep warm." Or someone might have shoved her body under one of them, knowing that the loggers would soon be burning the huge piles of brush and dead trees, I thought. No! I knew Kari was alive, I could feel it.

"Kar-r-i-i! Kar-r-i-i!" I yelled.

I took her plastic whistle from my shirt pocket and blew it several times. I decided on a routine that would take most of my concentration: I'd walk thirty steps, call "Kari," continue for forty steps, and blow the whistle. This helped calm my frantic mind.

"Jan! There's a trail off to the left. It must be the one we're looking for." I radioed base to tell them our direction and was told Brian and Barbara were heading back to the trailhead.

We walked into a dense, shadowy forest where the trails were muddy, each depression filled with mosquito-breeding, slimy water. I wore the big old black and red wool plaid jacket that I used to wear when Kari and I rode double on Nutmeg. In those days the large buttoned pockets had held crackers, cheese, and candy; today they contained a blue sleeve, a whistle, a map, and tearstained tissues. I unrolled the sleeves to cover my hands and turned up the collar against the pesky insects. I was overcome with guilt—Kari had no such protection. I prayed as I paced off steps. Please, please keep her safe. Give her back to us alive.

My partner was limping. "A bad ankle," he explained, and I left him sitting on a log while I searched along a stream. I found nothing.

We crossed the creek. My radio interrupted the hum of the swarming mosquitoes. "There are some dead cows up here. Looks like they've been shot." The searcher identified himself, gave the location, and signed off.

"What do you suppose that's all about?" Donovan scowled.

Before I could answer, the radio transmitted again. "This is Brad. I'm going to check out the report on the dead cows. No sign of Kari yet." We picked up various reports, but could hear only the base's responses to other statements or inquiries. I wished we were all on the same frequency!

Forty steps later, as I prepared to blow the whistle, someone shouted through the radio, "We heard a shot! Did anyone else hear it?" I stood still, shocked into inactivity, uncomprehending. The searcher must have been mistaken. Who would be shooting out here? It wasn't hunting season.

Paul and Steve

"Steve!" Paul yelled.

"What'd you say?" shouted Steve from the trees.

"I have to stop and eat something, or I won't be able to go on!" Paul dropped onto a fallen log, and rifled through his pack for food and water. They had been searching the North Fork ridge since 5:30 a.m. and Paul was exhausted. The fatigue from last night's search was still with him, and he realized he hadn't eaten since yesterday morning.

Paul was sure Kari hadn't tried to cross over from Beehive Basin to the ranch, but Steve said they should keep looking since they had been assigned this area. The men looked down into the Beehive's steep bowl at about 7 a.m. and sat down to have some water. The sound of a gunshot startled them. Steve grabbed the radio, reported the shot, and asked if anyone else had heard it. No one answered. We must have been mistaken, Paul thought.

7:35 a.m. Jan and Bob Donovan

We continued to walk, shout, and blow the whistle for thirty minutes. I was preparing to call in our position when a voice exploded from the black box in my hand, "There's some crazies out here with guns. They're shooting at us!" Silence.

Sweat burst out of every pore and my fingers slipped on the radio button. "Base, base, this is Jan, what's happening?"

"I don't know! Someone's shooting!"

I pushed around Bob and took the lead, running, shouting Kari's name at the top of my voice.

Vivian Schaap and Diane Goldstein—Lone Mountain Ranch

Vivian and Diane, the ranch secretary, were in the office keeping the ranch going while everyone else was searching for

Kari. Diane and Alan Goldstein had moved to Big Sky from Michigan the year before. Al loved the peacefulness and space of the Montana area and left behind his partnership in the family business to move to Big Sky.

Vivian was pouring coffee for them when John Palmer's voice burst from the radio on the desk. "Viv! Viv! This is Palmer. Get on the phone and get us two helicopters. Some people have been shot up here! Don't call back, there's to be radio silence! Hurry, Viv!"

Diane was immobile, staring straight ahead. "I know it's Al, I know it's Al!" she cried.

"John, this is Viv, repeat, repeat the message!" She was unable to accept what she heard.

"Get me those helicopters! Fast! Don't call again!"

Frantically, Vivian dialed the operator, who connected her with the Gallatin sheriff's office. The dispatcher told her to call the Madison County sheriff. When the Madison sheriff's office answered, Viv identified herself and said, "They need two helicopters at Ulreys Lake right away!"

"What?"

"You know what's going on over here! We need help. Now!"

"I don't know what you're talking about, ma'am," came the reply.

"Look, you know about Kari Swenson being lost, right? Well, there's been some shooting up there, and they radioed me to find two helicopters to get the injured out. They need help, darn it!"

The dispatcher said he would try to get in touch with the sheriff, and explained that their radio repeater had been struck by lightning several weeks ago and the radio communications weren't good.

Viv ground her teeth and yelled into the phone, "Look, my orders from the search headquarters are to get in touch with your office and get two helicopters over there, fast!"

"I'll check on it, ma'am," drawled the voice. Viv waited for them to phone back, to tell her that help was on its way, but she didn't hear from Madison County again.

8 a.m. Jan and Bob Donovan

I realized I had put a great distance between us, and waited for Donovan to catch up. He hobbled up and Palmer's voice came over the radio. "Listen carefully and DO NOT, I repeat, DO NOT answer or give your location! All searchers return to base immediately! Searchers in sections 7 and 12, be careful! There's someone out there with guns. Repeat, all searchers return to base immediately! Be careful! Stay off the horizon. There are some real dangerous people out there! Jan, Bob, Joy, Debbie—Ennis is it! Ennis is it! There will be radio silence from now on. Radio silence, all units!"

Donovan and I stared at the radio in my hands as if we hadn't heard correctly. I toggled the transmit button and said, "This is Jan. Repeat instructions! Repeat! What's happening? Please, I have to know!" Silence. "Base, this is Jan, answer me!" I wanted to dash the radio against a rock, to lash out at something.

"Bob, what did he mean by Ennis is it?"

"Sounds like they want us to walk out through the town of Ennis instead of circling back on the Jack Creek trail."

"But that's miles and miles from here! In the wrong direction! Are they crazy? What's happening? My God, Kari! Kari!"

"They must have good reason to send us out that way. Don't lose control now, Jan, not now!"

"Walk as fast as you can, Bob, I have to get to Jack Creek!"

I raced ahead, my mind numbed. We sprinted up hills and slithered down slopes. I had no thoughts now, just "Kari—Kari—Kari" echoing in my head. I burst out of the trees into a sunny meadow where the forget-me-nots were brilliant. In a flash I was back on Sage Ridge laughing, watching Kari's auburn hair ruffling in the breeze. The confidence that we would find her alive was shattered.

8 a.m. Bob and George

"What the hell was that?" Bob yelled at George as the echo of a rifle shot rolled and faded against the rugged ridges of the mountains. George shook his head. Bob hoped it was a rescuer signaling for help, that they had found Kari. The men stood in the shadow of the tall trees, listening, but heard only the chickadees and chattering squirrels.

"Why didn't they fire another signal shot?" Bob demanded.

"I don't know." George frowned. They pushed on, wrapped in a depressing gloom that had been with them since meeting Schaap and Brisbin, who had been carrying a bone that looked delicate enough to be a human arm.

Bob and George went on, struggling through the dense underbrush and timber, searching behind downed logs, looking for tracks in ant and mole hills.

The radio crackled, a panicked voice told them to get out of the area as quickly as possible. Someone was shooting at the searchers.

"Come on, Bob, let's get back to base! We won't know what's happened until we get back," George said gently. They ran, crouched, watching, listening, and came out of the trees onto a logging road. Two men on trail bikes gave them a ride to the base.

"There were two guys! They had Kari chained to a log and shot her when she yelled at us to stay away," Jim Schwalbe was shouting to those around him.

"Is she alive?" Bob cried grabbing him by the arm.

"She was when I left. That son-of-a-bitch shot her, and the old man shot Al in the head!" He covered his face with his hands and moaned.

Bob yelled at the Gallatin County sheriff to get a search party together. The sheriff said he couldn't use the civilian posse, that they'd have to wait until reinforcements arrived from Bozeman. Bob shouted, "Get out there! Do something! Help them for God's sake!"

Paul

"Paul! Paul! Kari's been shot!" yelled Brian when Paul reached the trailhead. He and Steve dropped off the ridge and had run for the base after being told that someone was shooting at the search teams. Stumbling through the tangled brush Paul kept saying to himself, Don't let it be Kari! Please! Not Kari!

People milled around, shouting directions. Paul ran from person to person asking if anyone had seen his parents. Some man pushed him roughly, swearing, telling him he couldn't go to the communications van. He shoved a second time, and Paul wanted to hit him, hard. The crowd parted and Paul saw Bob leaning against a car, his head in his hands. He shoved the man out of the way, ran to his father, took his arm, and led him away from the crowd.

"What's happened? Where's Kari? Who's been shot? Where's Mom?" Bob walked beside Paul in a trance.

"Son, we have to be positive. We have to believe Kari will be okay. Jim said it looked like a shoulder wound, but he pointed to his chest, not his shoulder. We can't tell Mom that!" Bob talked mechanically, woodenly. Suddenly his face crumpled. Paul held him. Great heaving sobs tore from Bob's throat, mingling with Paul's.

"We moved to Montana so something like this wouldn't happen to you kids, and now . . . Kari! Oh dear God, Kari!"

8:30 a.m. Bozeman

Jennie Nemec and Andi Ross rushed around the emergency room throwing together intravenous fluids, a portable suction, airways, a disaster bag, and other equipment Jennie would need to take on the helicopter. The call from the sheriff's office had come in about eight o'clock, and Andi had called Jennie in from her day off asking her to fly into the Big Sky area. Jennie had flown with medical rescue helicopters in Kalispell and had the training for this mission.

A deputy grabbed Jennie's bags and ran for his car. A message taped to the cabinet by the phone caught her eye, "Kari Swenson missing." What's that all about? thought Jennie, sprinting for the patrol car. She had forgotten the message by the time she reached the airport. Murray Duffy's helicopter was ready to go. Jennie stuffed her equipment aboard, jumped in, and they lifted off, heading south for the Spanish Peaks.

Jan and Bob Donovan

We left the trail, taking a short cut to Jack Creek. The ground was treacherous with gopher mounds, long slippery grass, hidden roots, and rocks. We took a fall or two. Donovan moved as quickly as he could, limping, grimacing. Finally, we heard the creek tumbling over rocks and logs as we slithered down the last grassy hill, hurried across the bridge, and stopped to reorganize ourselves.

The heat was oppressive. Sweat dripped off our faces and soaked our shirts. Donovan dug into his pack and came up with juice, fruit, nuts, and raisins. I surprised him by radioing to base, "This is Jan. We have reached the creek and will continue on our original route."

"Ten-four," came the reply, hurriedly followed by, "Negative! Negative! Ennis! Ennis is it!"

"Jan, what are you doing?" Donovan demanded, snatching the radio from me.

"If they think I'm going to walk through Ennis they're crazy! Kari is up there, and by damn, I won't leave! She needs me! I have to go back the way we planned, don't you understand?"

"You have to follow orders! We don't know what's going on. If some nut is holding Kari hostage he might hurt her if we stumble onto them. We could make a mess of everything."

We argued. He won. I'd never forgive myself if I caused harm to come to Kari. "Okay, okay, but it's going to be a fast trip out. The sooner we get to Ennis the sooner I'll be back in the mountains looking for her."

We jog-walked down the logging road, but it was the long way out—too many twists and turns. We decided to go out along the creek bottom and returned to Jack Creek.

The miles seemed endless. We gave up trying to find logs across the creek and waded in and out of the icy water. I ran well ahead of Donovan; I didn't want him to hear me sobbing or calling Kari's name. This was a private grief.

A dog dashed out of the trees, barking a warning. We rounded a bend in the trail and confronted two men on horses riding leisurely toward us. I stared in disbelief. These must be the searchers the Madison County sheriff had promised would be out helping us by eight o'clock! No wonder we hadn't found hoofprints along the creek. They admitted they were searching for a young woman lost in the Big Sky area, but they didn't know anything about a shooting. They refused to let me ride double. "It would be too slow," one man said. I was furious, knowing that they could ride into an explosive situation and trigger a catastrophe. But they weren't interested in listening to us.

"How far is the trailhead?" I asked.

"Not far. Less than a mile, won't take you long." They rode on relaxed and unconcerned. I wanted to drag one of them from the saddle, steal his horse, and dash back to find Kari.

It was blistering hot and the trail was dry and dusty. As we limped along the only sounds were the crickets and flying grasshoppers. My shoulders throbbed from the chafing of my pack, and the soles of my feet were on fire from sliding around in wet boots. I was losing hope, but I kept praying Kari would be returned to us alive.

We hobbled into the clearing at the Jack Creek trailhead on the Madison County side of the mountain. A small camp trailer was parked under an old cottonwood tree.

"Hello," I shouted. "Anyone there?"

A young man came from the far side of the trailer. I tried to talk, but couldn't; tears streamed down my face. Bob explained that we needed a ride to the Diamond J Ranch to use a phone. The young man's pregnant wife and two year old son stared at us. The man hurried us into his van, and we bumped down the country road. I sobbed, Bob was silent. The young man looked out of the corner of his eye at me, too polite to ask questions. At the Diamond J, I called the Madison sheriff's office.

"This is Mrs. Swenson, Kari's mother. What happened at Big Sky? Is she all right?"

"We don't know what's going on. We haven't heard anything from the sheriff," came the reply.

"Well, what about the shootings? Who's doing that? Has anyone been hurt?" I yelled.

"Sorry, we don't know anything."

"Could you get a helicopter to come to the Diamond J and pick me up?"

"I'll check." He put me on hold. "Sorry, we can't do that. You could try hiring a private plane in Ennis. I was told to tell you to come in to Ennis and we'll drive you to Big Sky."

"My God, man, that will take hours! I have to get back there right away, that's my daughter in those mountains!"

"Sorry. Just come into town, stop at the Charging Bear Gift Shop, and a deputy will drive you to Big Sky." I wanted to strangle him.

"Have the two girls on horseback come out yet? Why haven't you set up a roadblock at the trailhead?" I demanded.

"We don't know what's going on, ma'am, but some deputies are on their way to set up a roadblock now."

Donovan had explained to the young man what was happening. Worried about his family's safety, he said he'd pick them up, and then give us a ride into Ennis.

"Thank you! I can't sit still, I can't wait here!" I said. "We'll start walking, you can pick us up on the road."

A helicopter coming from Ennis passed overhead with a Stokes litter suspended from its belly. I panicked. Too often I had watched the approach of a "chopper and Stokes"—usually to pick up a body. Kari, Kari!

The van jerked to a halt beside us and we climbed in. I sat in the back with the young woman and her son. I didn't know I was crying until I heard the little boy whisper, "Is she sick, Mommy? Does she hurt?"

"S-h-h-h. Her little girl is lost, that's why she's crying. Don't ask her questions, honey." She drew her son into her arms. We stopped a patrol car coming from Ennis, and asked the deputies for information about Kari. They said they knew nothing and sped off.

Bob at the Base

Bob finally regained his composure, and walked about berating others because they weren't out searching for Kari and wouldn't let him go alone. He kicked patrol car tires and made himself unpopular until Paul insisted that he move away from the people who irritated him. He grabbed Bob Schaap's arm and shouted,

"This is their job! If they don't want to take the risks that go with that badge then they should quit!"

"I know Bob, I know," he answered. "Damn it! I feel so helpless!"

The Gallatin County sheriff had observed Bob's behavior and issued an order for all civilian searchers to leave the area. Paul and George forced him into the car, and they returned to Lone Mountain Ranch, where Bob sat beside the radio anxious, and angry—waiting, waiting, waiting. Paul disappeared. Vivian decided to evacuate the ranch for the day, and while the guests were getting ready to leave she and George armed the ranch crew with guns and told them to guard the trails leading into the ranch.

A woman cornered Vivian in the office, pressing her about what was going on. Joel Beardsley had come to ride a horse she had rented and wondered why no one would help her with the tack. She was persistent and Viv finally told her what she knew. Joel startled Vivian and Bob by saying she was sure she knew who the men were. She had been floating and fishing on the lake Saturday and two men had tried to "entice" her to the shore. Joel said the men were heavily armed with guns, rifles, and knives. They had carved their names on a tree. If the sheriff wanted more information he could get in touch with her at home.

"Bob?" Vivian said, handing him a cup of coffee. "I asked George to tell Diane." Tears filled her eyes. "He's dead, isn't he?"

"Jim said he was. I don't know."

"We're driving the guests away from the ranch until this is over. Will you and Paul be all right?" Bob nodded and Vivian left.

Bob was worried about Paul and asked someone to go look for him. It was 11:35 a.m. Paul stumbled into the office, pale, hollow eyed. "Where have you been? Are you okay?" Bob said.

"I wanted to be alone, I couldn't stand anyone touching me, I didn't want to talk. Why don't we go to the dining room and get you something to eat, Dad?"

"I couldn't eat, and I don't want to leave the radio."

11:40 a.m. Jan

I used the phone at the Charging Bear while Deputy Hancock got us a cold drink. I fumbled with the dial, my hands slippery with sweat. A man answered the ranch phone and I asked about Kari. His voice broke and he said he would let me talk to my husband. I panicked and almost hung up.

"Honey, are you all right?" Bob's voice was soft, controlled.

"Where's Kari?"

"We haven't found her yet."

"What was all the shooting about? I have to know!"

"Kari has been kidnapped. A searcher found her cha . . . chained to a tree." He cleared his throat. "She's been shot, but Jim thinks it was superficial. Probably a shoulder wound." His voice ended in a rush.

"What do you mean? If someone saw her why didn't he bring her out? What's going on?" I was terrified.

He coughed, stalled. "A searcher was shot and may be dead. Jim had to run for his life."

The room started to spin and I grabbed the glass display case to keep from falling. "Is Paul all right? It wasn't Paul was it?"

"Paul's with me. He's safe."

"We have a ride to Big Sky. We'll meet you at the base," I cried.

"No! We've been returned to the ranch and told to stay away from the search area. Sheriff Onstad will keep in touch with his office, so stop at Four Corners and call there before you head up here. If they haven't found Kari, come here; if they've found her he'll tell you what to do. Okay?"

"Okay." I ran for the patrol car.

Paul

Paul left the office and sat on the lawn beside the A-frame where Diane and a guest sat in silence. He had been sitting there about fifteen minutes when his father bolted out of the office shouting, "They've found her! She's alive! They're taking her to the hospital!"

They dashed for the car. Bob drove fast, taking the canyon curves at a dangerous speed. They were silent, not wanting to talk about what might have happened to Kari. She was alive. That's all that mattered.

4

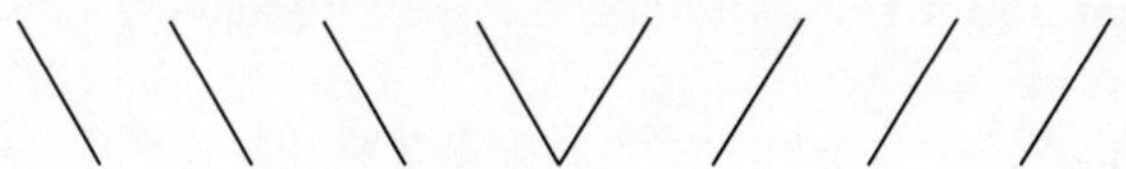

EMERGENCY ROOM

Deputy Hancock's car skidded to a stop at a filling station, and I ran, breathless, to the phone booth and called the Gallatin sheriff's office. The officer told me Kari had been found alive and was en route to the hospital—badly injured.

At the hospital emergency entrance I jumped from the car before it stopped and ran through the double doors. Kari wasn't there. Waiting for her were several physicians, an anesthesiologist, staff from the lab and the respiratory therapy department, and my friend Andi Ross.

"She's alive!" shouted Andi, hugging me, and we dissolved into tears. "Jennie's in the ambulance with her."

From the ambulance radio Jennie's voice blared into the room. "Patient is conscious and oriented. A line of lactated Ringers is open. M.A.S.T. on, uninflated. Blood pressure one-hundred over forty. Respiratory difficulties. One-hundred percent oxygen running."

"Tell Kari her Mom is here waiting for her," Andi answered. "I have doctors Newsome and Sabo standing by. We're ready for you!"

"Great! Tell Jan Kari's still smiling! ETA fifteen minutes," Jennie answered.

"What about the wounded rescuer?" I asked Andi. "Are they flying him in?"

Andi studied her hands. "He didn't make it. He's dead."

"No! Oh, no!" I moaned.

"Who was it?" Bob Donovan asked in a tight voice.

"Al Goldstein was the name I was given."

Bob Donovan gasped, sagged against the stretcher, and we grabbed him to keep him from falling.

"Al was my best friend!" The torment on his face was shattering. He phoned his wife, who was with Diane Goldstein, hugged me, and the Madison deputy drove him to Big Sky.

Bob and Paul

Bob and Paul arrived at the hospital minutes ahead of the ambulance and ran into the hospital where they were surrounded by friends. The wail of the siren reached them and they dashed outside. Ambulance attendants were hurrying to get the stretcher out of the ambulance, and the jostling made Kari open her eyes. She smiled weakly at Bob and whispered, "I'm sorry for putting you through this."

He kissed her and said, "Now that we have you back, everything will be all right."

Paul and Bob followed the stretcher into the emergency room where they were surprised to find me. I tried to hug all of them at once.

"Dad, her hands are like ice!" hissed Paul. At the sound of his voice Kari opened her eyes, smiled at him, and said, "Hi." Her eyes unfocused, crossed, and closed. Paul was shaking. I said they should wait in the corridor with their friends, and as they stepped into the hall, the ambulance driver pressed something into Bob's hand. "Keep this for Kari, Mr. Swenson," he said. Draped across Bob's hand was her good luck gold neck chain. She hadn't had it off for five years. Paul and Bob couldn't control their agony any longer and stood crying in the corridor. Friends closed a circle around them, protecting them from a hovering, persistent reporter.

1:20 p.m. Jan

Sirens, loud voices, and suddenly Kari was there, bundled in a cocoon of gray blankets. Her lips were blue and her freckles were stark against her ashen face. For a millionth of a second the world receded, leaving me alone with my daughter. A hot arrow of pain shot through my chest, my heart felt squeezed.

Jennie Nemec threw her arms around me and whispered, "She wasn't raped!"

Bob and Paul hovered over Kari. After a few minutes I asked them to wait in the corridor, knowing they couldn't watch what would come next. I stood at the head of the stretcher where I could touch her, talk to her. I rested my cheek against her temple. "I love you, Punkin," I sighed into her hair. "You're home at last."

"Hi, Mom," she whispered. Her left cheek and upper lip were swollen and bruised. A drop of blood oozed from the cut on her lip.

Kari's shirt was stained and stiff with blood, and the red shorts were filthy as if she had been sliding in black dirt. Her shoes were missing. Andi cut away the shirt and jog bra, exposing a purple and red wound that puckered against Kari's white skin where the bullet had entered her chest below her right collar bone. A clot had sealed the hole. I swallowed hard.

"Kari, we need to roll you onto your left side so we can see if the bullet went all the way through," the surgeon said.

"It did," she wheezed, "I could feel the blood running down my back." The exit wound was just below her right shoulder blade—close, oh so close, to the kidney and liver! I experienced an emotion I had never felt—hate. It was not pleasant, but I was too scared to worry about it.

The anesthesiologist was trying to draw blood from Kari's left arm, but each time the needle entered a vein, the vessel collapsed on itself. He kept apologizing. "Honey, I'm sorry."

"It's okay," she answered absently.

The room hummed with activity: doctors drawing blood, examining her wounds, nurses setting up sterile instrument trays, the x-ray crew shifting nervously from foot to foot awaiting orders, and the lab people waiting impatiently for the blood specimens. The portable x-ray machine was wheeled into place, films were taken, and the technician hurried away to develop them. A physician listened to Kari's lungs and the surgeon probed her wounds.

Andi cut off Kari's shorts, covered her with a blanket, and inserted a urinary catheter. The anesthesiologist got the blood sample, held Kari's hand, and said, "I'm sorry, honey. It seems like that's all I can think of to say." She smiled at him.

The x-rays were back, clipped to the viewing box across the room. I stared at the shadow of Kari's inner chest outlined against the bright eye of the viewer. The lung was collapsed. The right chest cavity was filling with blood, pushing the chest organs to the left and compressing the other lung, the heart, and the great vessels that returned blood to the heart. My knees buckled and the room tilted. I grabbed the stretcher for support, afraid the surgeon would ask me to leave if I showed too much emotion. I couldn't leave Kari now. I smiled at her and smoothed her hair back, surprised at the amount of debris in her hair.

"Get me a chest tube," ordered the surgeon. He looked at me. "Perhaps you should step out."

"No, no, it's okay! I'm a nurse, it won't bother me." I hoped I wouldn't faint and get in the way.

He shrugged, explained the procedure to Kari, and told her it would hurt. She nodded.

"You're sure calm about all this, sweetie," I said. The activity in the room was suspended for a brief moment as we listened to her answer. "I've had hours, lying in the forest, to get my act together. You all haven't."

I turned away and choked back tears. Andi touched my arm. "Come on, buddy, be half as brave as that kid!"

"Kari, this will hurt," the physician said. He had anesthetized the skin and made an incision through the muscles between the ribs just below her armpit. Pushing forcefully with a surgical instrument to penetrate the remaining tissue, he completed the insertion into the chest cavity. Blood gushed into the container attached to the tube, and Kari moaned. For the first time tears filled her eyes. I dug a stained tissue from my pocket and blotted her tears. The thick tube was sutured to her skin.

"Why is my right abdomen numb? Why do I hurt just below my ribs?" gasped Kari, moving her hand down the right side of her body. The physicians glanced at each other. There was a second of silence. Sounds were magnified—the bleep of the monitor, the sucking of the chest tube, the hiss of the oxygen. The eye of the x-ray box glared at me through Kari's collapsed lung. Fear was becoming a familiar companion.

"We're sending you for more x-rays, Kari," the doctor said. "We aren't sure why you have the numbness and pain, but films of the abdomen and a few more of the chest will help us understand what's happening. Okay?" She sighed and closed her eyes.

Andi and I took Kari to x-ray. The corridor was jammed with friends whose heads jerked in our direction, and I gave Bob what I thought was a reassuring smile. Paul told me later that the expression was more of a grimace.

Moving Kari to the x-ray table was a major project because of the equipment attached to her: I.V., catheter, oxygen, chest tube, and the cardiac monitor. All arrangements made, we moved her with the blankets, then pulled them out from under her. Debris scattered across the floor. She moaned and screwed her eyes shut.

"Hey, Kari, looks like you brought half the forest with you!" joked Andi.

"I picked up some of it when I hit the tree."

Andi and I looked quizzically at each other, shrugged, and tied on heavy lead aprons. We would stay in the room to support Kari for the upright x-rays and keep track of the cardiac monitor. The staff was kind and didn't even hint that I should leave—they knew I wouldn't.

5

INTENSIVE CARE UNIT

2:45 p.m.

Paul and Bob joined us as we took Kari to the Intensive Care Unit (ICU), where she was gowned, transferred to a bed, hooked to the ICU's machines, and given an injection of demerol to relieve the pain. She held Bob's hand and spoke to Paul. "I'm so happy to see you! I hope you didn't worry too much. Did you catch any fis . . ." Her eyes closed, the limp hand slipped from Bob's, and she slept.

The ICU nurse suggested we go home and rest. We were dirty, haggard, and exhausted but afraid to leave Kari. Assured that she would sleep for at least two hours, we went home.

The next hour and a half was a blur of activity. The most difficult thing I had to do was to phone Johanna, who lived in Seattle. I left a message for her to call me, but I panicked when the phone rang and she said, "Mom! What the heck is going on?"

I stammered out an edited version of the kidnapping, trying to sound reassuring and confident. "She's holding her own. Barring complications she'll be out of ICU in about five days. She asked about you, said to tell you she'll be okay."

I knew it would hurt her to see Kari now, so I continued the farce: "It might be best if you don't come for a few days. By then Kari will be more alert, and you'll have a chance to visit. She needs to rest now."

"Mom, is she going to die? Are you telling me the truth? Please . . . I couldn't stand it if . . . if Kari . . ." Gulping sobs spanned the hundreds of miles between us, tearing at my heart. I tried to reassure her and said if she felt it were important for her to come now, she should. She said she'd check with her employer and phone later in the evening. She was still sobbing when she hung up.

I showered, scraping off layers of dirt and sweat. The soles of my feet were covered with blood blisters, and the toenails were black and tender. Water made the mosquito bites itch and reminded me of the numerous insect bites on Kari's body. The image of her wounds and bites made me ill. I threw up, retching, crying, trying to get control of myself.

Friends phoned or came to the house, brought food, and showered us with moral support.

My family arrived after a long, hot drive from Thermopolis, Wyoming. Mother was exhausted and scared. My stepfather, Milo, was bewildered, refusing to believe anyone would harm Kari, and my brothers were as mad as hornets in a fire. They had stopped at the hospital, but were not allowed to see Kari, and they were given little information about her condition.

Mom is tiny, about five feet tall if she stretches her neck, and is normally a talkative whirlwind of a woman, but now she was silent and preoccupied. I saw the anger and sadness in her eyes and tried to make her relax by fibbing a little about Kari's condition.

She looked me in the eye and said, "You never were a good liar, so just keep quiet. I'm going to the hospital to see Kari, and if I'm not pleased I plan to park in that hospital room with her!"

I laughed and hugged her so tightly she squirmed. "What would I do without you, Mom?" I asked, smiling. I hadn't realized how important her strength and sense of humor were to me. I prayed I had inherited her tenacity. I would need it.

5 p.m.

Bob and I stood at Kari's bedside looking at her, listening to the hiss of the oxygen, the bleep of the cardiac monitor, and the gut-wrenching gurgling of the tube as it drained the blood from her chest. Her bruised lip and cheek stood out on her clean face. Her auburn hair was still braided, full of dirt, twigs, and pine needles.

She opened her eyes and whispered, "Hi." Still groggy from the demerol injection, she took Bob's hand, tucked it under her cheek, and slipped into sleep. I pushed a chair under him, and he sat with one hand against her cheek and stroked her hair with the other. He remained there until she awakened an hour later.

6:30 p.m.

Paul stayed with Kari while Bob and I met my family in the waiting room. Mom looked better, and I pressured her, Milo, and Dorothy into going to Switzerland as planned. I knew this would be the last trip Milo, eighty-six years old, would be strong enough to take. We planned an early breakfast together the next morning before their flight.

Pam Weiss, a biathlete from Jackson, Wyoming, was supposed to meet Kari at the ranch that evening to make plans for the fall biathlon camp in West Yellowstone. Bob phoned the ranch with a message asking her to come to Bozeman when she arrived.

Paul dashed into the waiting room and grabbed me by the arm. "Mom, she's in a lot of pain, you better get back in there."

Kari was bathed in sweat and spoke in gasping spurts. "Mom, I hate to ask . . . but . . . I could use something for pain. The demerol . . . didn't help much. My face hurts, too." The nurse got an order for morphine, and Bob took the family home. Kari was turned and propped on her side with pillows, and I sat beside her holding an ice-filled washcloth to her lip and cheek. The old scars on her forehead and chin were blue. I hadn't noticed them for a long time, but now memory took me back to Philadelphia, to a playground with a slide. I remembered the fall, rushing to the hospital in a patrol car, watching the resident take Kari away, and Johanna pacing the floor, sobbing, "Will Kari die?" Suturing completed, the bloody four-year-old had sat in my lap complaining because she hadn't had a chance to play on the swings.

A moan interrupted my reminiscence. "Pam was meeting me at the ranch. This will ruin her few days off." Kari squeezed my hand and slid off to sleep. I looked at her slim, graceful hand lying in mine. It was scratched, the nails were broken and packed with dirt, and a bruise circled her wrist. It was the hand of an active woman; strong, callused, a blister here and there. Love for my daughter engulfed me, and I ached for the Goldsteins.

The surgeon arrived to check Kari, and we discussed the abdominal pain, wounds, and her blood loss. He said they'd check her hemoglobin twice the next day and then decide about transfusions.

Kari was restless and moaned softly in her stupor, occasionally jerking awake with panic in her eyes. I'd assure her she was safe and she'd slip into unconsciousness again.

11:30 p.m.

I sat in a chair, pulled another under my legs, covered them with my sweater, and began writing letters to relatives. Finally, too weary to hold the pen, I propped a pillow against the bedrail, held Kari's hand, and rested.

"No! Please! Daddy, Daddy help me!" Kari's cry split the silence. The nurse came running.

"Stay away, stay away!" Kari's eyes rolled back and she slumped on the pillows. The bleep of the monitor captured the flutter of her racing heart. The nurse put her hand on my shoulder. "You okay, Mrs. Swenson?" I nodded numbly.

I must have dozed and was awakened when Kari squeezed my hand. Opening my eyes I found myself looking directly into hers. She gave me a half smile, said she couldn't sleep because of the pain, and asked what Paul and Bob had done while she was missing. I gave her an abridged version of their frantic search for her.

"I knew Dad was in that plane! The voices I heard might have been yours and Paul's." I wiped her face with a cold cloth. She grimaced when I touched her lip.

"Oh, Mom, I was scared! Just before they found me I was so weak I knew I was going to die." She spoke in short whispered gulps. "All I could think about was Dad, Joey, Paul, and you. I knew how upset you'd be if I died, but I couldn't do anything more to help myself. Who was the searcher who was killed?" She didn't wait for an answer. Sobbing she said, "I tried to crawl to him, but it was too far. If I could have reached him maybe he wouldn't have died." I lowered the bedrail, held her close, and rocked her until she quit crying.

Toward morning she patted my hand and whispered, "I know you don't like puns, Mom, but this sure shoots a hole in my training schedule!" She grinned and went back to sleep.

Tuesday, July 17

The physician removed the bandages and cleaned the wounds.

"Why do I have pain below my rib cage and numbness in my abdomen?" she asked. "That's a long way from my chest."

"I've ordered more x-rays and a CAT scan to be done this morning. The bullet may have ricocheted around as it traveled through your chest and damaged other organs, such as the diaphragm or liver. The scan will give us more information." He replaced the dressings as he talked. "Is the morphine helping the pain?"

"It helps for a while. I'm awfully tired. All I do is sleep."

"The trip to x-ray and for the scan will be hard on you. I'll leave an order for the morphine to be given a half hour before they move you. Hang in there, young lady." He nodded to me and left.

7 a.m.

The family went to breakfast while Kari was being bathed, and what should have been a cheerful goodbye was a sad one. I knew Mom didn't want to go, but she would—for Milo.

The bath had exhausted Kari. Paul sat beside her, silent, attentive, watching her face. She'd open her eyes, smile, and slip into unconsciousness. Paul planned to stay home most of the day and answer the phone, which hadn't stopped ringing since he plugged it in that morning. The national news had carried the story on the morning news shows, and our relatives and friends in the East were calling because some of the stations hadn't reported whether or not she had survived. The Biathlon Association office phoned for news and said they were being deluged by calls from the media wanting photos of Kari and information about her biathlon career.

After the CAT scan, pain kept Kari awake, so we talked. "Pam wants to see you. She doesn't know what to do about renting a condo for the training camp," I said. "What do you think?"

"I'm going to that camp! Stu would never let me use this as an excuse not to train. I have to go!" The effort of speaking left her breathless.

"I can't think of any reason why you shouldn't plan on going," Bob said.

"I had high hopes for the World Championships this year," she said. "Those men sure messed things up for me, didn't they?"

"Maybe not, we'll see. Don't worry about Europe now, let's get to the November camp first."

She smiled, closed her eyes, and drifted in and out of a stupor. Her moans and whimpers made me angry. I wanted to be in the mountains hunting the men who had done this.

"It's awful to see Kari like that, Jan!" Pam said after a brief talk with Kari. "She wants to rent the condo, but do you think she'll be able to ski this year?"

"I don't know, but she has to have something to look forward to. She may not make it, but I guarantee she'll give it a heck of a try!"

The surgeon told us the scan didn't indicate any damage to the liver or diaphragm. He showed Kari a chest x-ray and pointed out the bullet and bone fragments remaining in her chest. He said they might be irritating a nerve and that could be causing the numbness, but they did not plan to operate to remove the metal or bone.

7:30 p.m.

The Pentagon had phoned the Gallatin sheriff's office about Kari, and the FBI had talked to Bob about the possibility of Kari being attacked by an agent of a foreign nation interested in interrupting the Olympic Games in Los Angeles. Bob explained that biathlon was a winter sport and that Women's Biathlon was not yet included in the Olympics.

He told me the names of the men who had kidnapped Kari and what was being done to find them. He had been told to keep certain facts "quiet," and a few hours later he had read the information in the paper. An example was the night search flights equipped with special night vision equipment that were being flown. It was supposed to be a secret, but the story was spread all over the newspapers.

We found Paul holding Kari's hand, looking almost as haggard as he had the night we searched. Gently he disengaged his hand, but she woke up and tried to grin. "See ya, Polly Wog. Sorry I can't stay awake to talk."

He laughed. "You talked all right! I'll blackmail you someday."

Late that evening two units of packed red blood cells were started. She was restless, so we held hands and talked. Around midnight she complained of intense itching, and a phone order from the physician stopped the I.V.s with antibiotics in them. If she were having a reaction to the blood transfusions it was too late. The nurse and I sponged Kari's back, changed her gown, and removed the acrylic pad from under her. Within an hour the itching stopped. We breathed a sigh of relief when we realized the pad was the irritant. She was given a special foam pad that looked like an egg carton to cushion her from the firmness of the mattress.

The rest of the night she was restless and wanted to talk. She would slip into sleep in the middle of a word, wake up later and start where she had left off, or stare glassy eyed until she was oriented. Bit by bit, during the next four hours, she told me her story of fear, pain, and murder. Sometimes she spoke in the third person as if the kidnapping had happened to someone else. Usually, she spoke in the first person, telling me what she had thought to herself and what she had experienced, physically and emotionally.

6

KARI'S STORY

Sunday July 15, Ulreys Lake

I sprinted over the crest of the rise in the trail and dropped over the other side, watching my footing, running fast. I looked up. Ten feet away two men stood glaring at me. I knew instantly that I was in trouble. They were dirty, unsmiling, and the younger man had his hands on a pistol and a knife. The older man stood with his left foot in the trail, staring at me. Rifles leaned against a tree. Rifles? This wasn't hunting season. I took in the scene in a fraction of a second and realized I was running too fast to stop and turn before I reached them. Fear triggered an adrenaline rush, and I dashed forward, trying to push past them. The older man jumped into the trail blocking my way. My mind whirled, grasping for another escape route. I slid to a stop within a foot of him and began to pivot on my right foot to turn back. Jerking my thumb over my shoulder, I asked, "Is this the Jack Creek Trail?" Not waiting for an answer, I continued the pivot, but I felt as if I were in slow motion, in a dream where I wanted to move quickly but couldn't.

"Yeah. It goes to the Hammond Station," one of them answered.

I had almost completed my about-face when he grabbed my left wrist and jerked me around. Before I could get my balance, he grabbed my right wrist, too. My mind raced. There was no way to escape. I'd have to rely on my wits. Act calm, maybe they don't mean any harm, I told myself.

I forced a smile. "Oh, that's the trail I want. Thank you. You can let me go now." I pulled away from him, but he held me fast. Daddy, help me! Help me! I shouted in my head.

I started shaking. Keep calm, keep calm! Don't make him mad. The younger man continued to stand with his hands on his weapons, staring at me, the rifles were within his reach. The wild, glazed look in the older man's eyes scared me.

"Please let me go!"

"No, no, no. We don't run into pretty girls up here very often, we'd like to talk to you," he drawled, his grip tightening. "What's your name?"

I hesitated. "S . . . Sue."

"Are you married?"

"Yes."

"What's your husband's name?"

"Bill. Bill Sowa." I said the first name that popped into my mind.

"Where's your wedding ring?" The tone of his voice was changing. He was angry, leaning closer, breathing in my face.

"I . . . ah . . . I work in a kitchen where I'm around machinery all the time, so I don't wear my ring. It might get caught in something."

I tried to twist my wrists out of the older man's grasp. His grip tightened, and my fingers tingled. The other man moved closer and I was afraid he'd use his knife on me. He stared at me, then his eyes slid away, and he began looking up and down the trail. I thought he was waiting for another person to join us. I finally realized he was making sure there was no one in the area who could help me. *Please, someone, come and help me,* I prayed, but I knew I was alone.

"Do you think she's married? Do you think that's her name?" the older man asked the other as he sneered into my face.

"No, I don't think she's married."

"Well, I am! You better believe that. Let me go! I have to get back to work!"

"All women lie," said the young man without expression.

I started to yell, but the old man shook me, cutting off my cry.

"Now shut up and listen! I want to talk to you, do you have any children?" he demanded.

"No. Please let me go! I don't want to talk to you!"

"Nah. We've been looking for companionship up here. We'll take you along for a few days to see how you like it."

"I'm married, I don't want to go with you! Let me go!" I struggled. He shook me and I lost my breath.

"Well, what'da ya think? Should we keep her?"

"Yeah, let's keep her," said the young one excitedly, grinning.

"We better tie her up. Bring me the rope."

"Help! Help! Someone help me!" I screamed. I pulled hard. He released my left hand and hit me. Hot pain burst on the left side of my face. I reeled backward, stunned, desperately trying to catch my balance and run. The old man jumped me, and we wrestled on the ground. He shouted at me, grabbed me around the throat in a necklock, and grappled for my wrists. I opened my mouth to yell, but his arm tightened around my throat, cutting my scream to a gag. I felt the muscle of his arm as he wrenched my head to the side, and I tried to bite him. He twisted my head farther and I bit my own cheek.

"Get her wrist out from under her!" he yelled. He choked me so hard I quit struggling. The other man pried my right arm from under me and tied a rope around my wrist. They flopped me over on my back. The older man was gasping, his chest heaving. "I've never beat up a woman, but I sure as hell will if you don't stop strugglin' and yellin'!"

He held me while the young man lashed my right wrist to his own left one, leaving only an inch or two of slack. They tried to drag me to my feet. I resisted. Angrily, they jerked me to my feet, and I started struggling again.

"I said I'd black your eyes and I will!" snarled the older man.

"You're young," I pleaded with the younger man. "You don't want to get involved in something like this do you? Let me go! Please let me go! I don't want to go with you."

"I want to keep you," he said.

"No! No! I want to go home! Please! Please!"

"We're gonna keep you for four or five days 'til you get to like us. You can go home later if you don't like it up here."

"I don't believe you! After what you've just done how can I believe you'll let me go instead of killing me?"

"Nah. We'd probably let you go."

"Probably? Will you help me find my way out of the mountains if I don't want to stay?"

"We'll turn ya loose, but you'll have to find your own way out." He smiled, and I knew they were going to rape and probably murder me. This is just a nightmare, I told myself, thinking I'd wake up any minute, but the throbbing in my face and wrists made it clear this was no dream.

"My family will miss me. They'll come looking when I don't get home."

They ignored me. "We'd better get away from the lake before someone shows up. Come on. Hurry it up," urged the younger man.

The men became more nervous as they collected their belongings. The older man shouldered his pack and untied the young man's wrist from mine so he could get his pack strap over his arm. I grasped the chance and pulled away. The older man yanked the rope and tears sprang to my eyes. I was dizzy with fear, and my knees kept buckling like a puppet's. I sat down.

"Get up!" the old man snapped. He was agitated, becoming more hostile with the delays.

"Okay, okay," I said, getting shakily to my feet.

The younger one headed uphill into the forest. I wasn't going to make it easy for him, and hung back making him drag me.

An unusual calm came over me. Awareness of my surroundings was magnified, even the birds' songs, and the heat of the sun was intensified. I realized I couldn't get away. I'd have to be careful until I figured out their personalities, or I'd never make it out of the mountains alive.

The older man plodded along behind me, his rifle aimed at my back. He glanced around nervously.

Pretending to be submissive, eyes on the ground, I studied the direction we were traveling, the lay of the land. When I escaped I didn't want to make the mistake of running in the wrong direction! We traveled uphill along the ridge, paralleling the trail, moving in the direction of the Jack Creek drainage. The lodgepole pines were so thick that in places the sun couldn't get through them, and the dense underbrush was filled with scratchy gooseberry and wild rose bushes. We bashed our way through the forest, slowed by downed, rotting timber. I hung back as much as I dared. The left side of my face throbbed in the hot sun. I touched my lip with my left hand and wiped away blood.

A push from behind made me stumble, and I began listening to their conversation. They walked along, ignoring me, talking easily, as if they kidnapped a woman every day. They discussed their philosophy of society, law, religion, and the mountains. The old man was angry about the development of the Big Sky area, and the fact that ranchers were allowed to run their cattle on "my land." He told the young man that he could learn everything he needed to know about life without going back to school. If he went back to society, the law wouldn't allow him to live free, the old man said. The rich man's laws and taxes would make it impossible for a man to make a decent living, and, he added, the preachers of the world shackled a man's natural urges. The young man agreed and added his two bits' worth. Their bizarre remarks made me worry that they were crazy or on drugs.

"I'm thirsty and hot," I interrupted. "Could we find some water, and sit down and talk about this?" I had to delay them somehow. I decided to tell them I was a diabetic, and if I didn't have my medicine by dinner time I'd get sick. It might have worked, but I couldn't remember the symptoms a diabetic should have.

The older man scowled at me, but agreed. We walked until we came to a swampy area where the older man took off his pack and untied the rope from the young man's wrist, but maintained a firm hold on the rope circling mine. The younger one dropped his pack, offered his wrist, and was retied to me.

"Why don't you leave the rope off for a little while, at least until we get a drink?" I suggested.

"Now, that'd be a dumb thing to do. You'd scram out'a here like a scared rabbit. Nope, you'd better get used to the rope, Sue," said the older man. I started—I had forgotten the name I had given them. My hopes sank further when he picked up his rifle.

We walked to the edge of the bog, and I watched, horrified, as the old man dropped to his stomach and started drinking the gray, stagnant water.

"I don't think you ought to drink that," I warned him.

"Why not?"

"The water in these mountains is filled with a protozoa that causes terrible diarrhea."

"We don't worry none about those things. You better drink some of it, it might be a long time before you get another chance."

Not knowing how far they planned to drag me, I reluctantly drank the muck. It tasted as bad as it looked. I was keenly aware of the men's moods; they were less hostile when I acted as if I wasn't afraid of them. They marched me back to the packs.

"How come you know so much about those things, proto . . . whatevers?" asked the young man.

"It's called giardia, and causes awful diarrhea, and stomach cramps. There's hardly a creek or river in the area that doesn't have the giardia cysts. Haven't you guys been sick?" I kept my voice calm, but my insides were knotted with fear.

"Nope. We been livin' in these mountains for years, and ain't been bothered much with such things," said the young man. He stared at me when he spoke, and I felt naked.

"How long have you two been up here?"

"Well, we been livin' here since last August, but before that we lived up here off and on for maybe twelve years," answered the older man.

"How do you get food?"

"We don't need society for our way of life. We plant a garden every spring, shoot meat whenever we want it, eat roots and berries, and get along just fine," said the younger one.

"What do you do for flour, sugar, and clothes?"

"Those things we buy from a store in Ennis or somewhere. We've made caches all over the mountains and we could live up here for years without going in to society, but we need female companionship," said the young man slyly. I felt as if I'd been kicked in the stomach.

"I know you're going to rape and murder me! I don't want to stay with you! Please let me go!"

"No, no, no! You ain't listening," shouted the older man. "You're gonna learn to like it with us, and wanna stay. We won't rape you because we want you to like us."

"I won't willingly stay with you!"

"Don't be stupid! We live a great life here, free from society. We can start a clan of our own."

Clan? They weren't calling what they wanted rape, but that's what it meant to me. I decided to try a different approach.

"My family and friends will miss me, and will come looking for me. You said you'd free me sometime. Make it now. I don't want to go with you."

"Quit threatening us with your friends!" raged the old man. "You just better be quiet. If anyone finds us that's looking for you, or if anyone walks into our camp, we'll shoot 'em!" He was trembling, glaring at me.

I glanced quickly at the young man, hoping he would argue, but he sat nodding his head in agreement and said, "You'd better shut up."

"I don't know why you're so upset, Sue," said the older man. "You'll have a damned good adventure story to tell your grandkids someday." They laughed. "Yeah, you'll have a great story," said the younger man.

"Let me go!"

In a fit of temper, the older man jumped to his feet, grabbed the younger one's pack, and started the untying-retying process again. He pulled the rope too tight and I flinched, but he didn't loosen it. I couldn't pull at it to loosen it because I had my head band in my left hand. I planned to drop it as a clue for the people who would be searching for me. I didn't want the old man to see it. I appealed to the young man.

"Could you loosen the rope a little? It hurts."

He looked at me with his chilling stare. "Well, maybe."

"No, no, no, Dan! If you loosen it she'll be able to wiggle away from us. Leave it that way."

So! One of them was named Dan.

They pushed and pulled me, heading up the ridge through the dense timber. I hung back, slowing their progress, stepping in the soft dirt of gopher and ant hills, leaving tracks for my family. I was shoved from behind. "Stop that! Dan look where yer walkin'. She's leavin' prints."

With nothing to lose, I continued leaving prints. Glancing at my watch, I realized I wouldn't be missed yet. It was only

4 p.m. It seemed incredible that all of this had happened in such a short time. Picking my way over logs, through spider webs and thorny wild gooseberry bushes, I wished I had gone fishing with Paul.

Out of the corner of my eye I saw the older man wandering off to our right. I released the headband, dropping it at the foot of a shrub. Seconds later the old man confronted me, holding the headband in his hand. "That ain't very smart. If someone finds us and walks in on us we'll shoot 'em!" he snarled so close to my face that his breath made me gag. "Come on, let's get away from here, Dan." I continued to crush bushes and leave tracks. Just as diligently, he covered them.

They pushed, shoved, and pulled me along for another five or ten minutes. The older man said, "I'm dizzy. We better stop again." He chose a shady area and untied the young man, who then sat next to me tightly clutching the rope still looped around my right wrist. The men ignored me and discussed how far to travel today, where to camp tonight, and what their ultimate destination was. I loosened the buckle on my watch, let it slide silently to the ground, and shifted my left thigh a few inches to conceal it.

The men reached a decision. They would camp on this side of the ridge tonight, cross Jack Creek early in the morning, go south between Lone Mountain and Cedar Mountain, and head for the high country where I'd never be found.

"How will I find my way back?"

The older man glared at me. He was pale, and was sweating profusely. Great! Maybe we wouldn't get too far away tonight. I wondered if he was having a heart attack, but he didn't show any signs of chest pain. I decided all the excitement must have given him an anxiety attack. Blast! Just a case of bad nerves. I wondered if the threats against my family were made to intimidate me, or if they were real. My throat tightened with fear. I wanted to cry, sob, beg, and promise I wouldn't tell the authorities about them, anything to be free before my family or friends could be hurt, but I knew it would make them angry, and I couldn't risk that.

"We'll be walking thirty, forty miles tomorrow, Sue. Can you make it?" said the older man.

I didn't answer. Why let them know I could run thirty miles in the mountains as part of my training schedule? If they thought I was a weakling, maybe they'd go slower. I was considering jumping off a steep embankment, pulling my captor with me, and injuring him. But what if *I* ended up with a serious injury? I didn't doubt for a moment they'd shoot me to get me off their hands. They'd never let me go. These mountains would be crawling with law enforcement people, and they'd be on the run until they were caught. I knew in my heart they wouldn't risk their freedom by turning me loose—now, or in four or five days.

Without being obvious, I studied the men, wondering what their relationship was. They shared the same philosophy about society, laws, and women, and agreed about kidnapping a woman and making her a member of their clan. But there was something else, a physical resemblance. I scrutinized the older man, committing to memory his features, mannerisms, speech, and clothing. He was thin, about six feet tall, and had stooped shoulders. His bushy dark hair and beard were peppered with gray, and he had a habit of twisting the ends of his mustache into curls. His face was weathered, leathery, and lined, and I guessed he was in his middle fifties. His eyes were cold and shifty. His clothing was old and dirty, and it was impossible to know what the original colors had been. Perhaps the shirt had been black or dark green. His pants were a faded black with many patches, and he was wearing hiking boots. He never removed his hat, even in this heat. It didn't look like felt, more like old leather rubbed with grease or resin. He had no visible scars, but his chin appeared to recede under his beard.

I glanced at the young man. He was a little taller than I and walked stooped, like the old man. His eyes were an unusual color, either green or a light brown, and there were freckles across his nose and cheeks. His face was long with full, feminine lips, a sharp nose, and a receding chin beneath a sparse beard. Sunburned scalp showed through his thinning, greasy, shoulder-length blond hair. His jacket looked as if it had been accidentally bleached here and there, and his dark pants and jacket were covered with holes and homemade patches. His tennis shoes looked almost new. His hat lay on the ground at my feet. The label indicated it had been purchased in Ennis.

I studied the men while they continued to discuss where they would hide me and decided they must be related. A lull in their conversation gave me the opening I'd been waiting for. "You two seem to have the same values and thoughts. Are you related?"

"That's none a yer business!" snapped the older man.

"Come on, we better get movin'," urged Dan. "We're too close to the lake."

"The rope is too tight and my hand has gone to sleep. Could you leave the rope off?"

"Ha!" snorted the old man.

"Well, could you change wrists?"

"Okay. Dan, you untie the rope. I'll hold both her wrists while you tie up the left hand." He stared into my eyes, and my stomach flip-flopped. "You didn't think we was dumb enough to leave you free for even a second, did ya?"

Dan pulled the rope tight. I grimaced.

"For heavens sake, does it have to be so tight? Loosen it a little," I demanded. He answered by hauling me to my feet. My heart pounded as the older man checked the area and found my watch. His jaw muscles tightened and he stepped close to me.

"You don't mean to leave this watch here for someone to find, do ya?"

"That's not real smart," smirked Dan.

"You shouldn't be doing that kind of thing. If someone finds us we'll have to shoot 'em!"

The old man handed the watch back to me, and I buckled it above the rope. I wished he would return the headband so I could drop it again, but it was tucked securely in his back pocket. I went back to stepping on the gopher mounds, knowing that's what Mom would look for.

The men discussed religion, their lack of respect for the laws of society, and how the influx of people and houses into the Big Sky area angered them. They attempted to draw me into the discussions, but I was too scared and upset to talk to them. I hoped Paul would be worried about me by now, and would alert the Schaaps and our parents. Someone would be out looking for me soon. I wanted to be found, but the thought of Paul, my parents, or one of my friends being killed was more painful than anything that had happened to me so far. The only way I could prevent someone else from being harmed was to escape.

"They had no right invadin' my country like that," the older man was saying. "Buildin' all them roads, and houses, and running all over the place, and cutting down the trees. This has been my country for a long time, they don't have no business here. And those damn cows running all over in the mountains! It ain't right!"

"I don't live at Big Sky," I said. "I simply work in a kitchen, so why are you taking out your hatred on me? Let me go. No one will believe me if I tell them you kidnapped and released me. They wouldn't come looking for you. Please, my family will be worried and will be searching for me by dinner time. I don't want you to hurt them. Please, please, let me go!"

"Shut up! Just shut up, and stop threatening us with your family! How come you haven't mentioned your husband lately, Sue?" drawled the old man.

They were laughing at me, enjoying their power. I got angry, and decided to try a different approach when the time was right. No more pleading. When I had played tennis in high school the coach had said, "Change tactics if you're losing. Why continue playing a losing game when you have the ability to try a different strategy?"

We struggled through the thick timber. "Wait a minute," the old man said, "this don't look like the right place. We wanted to drop into the ravine above the creek, and we must 'a gone too high."

We came to a small spring. The older man stopped. "This'll do. We'll stay here tonight. Take her to that high point, Dan, and we'll chain her to the largest tree up there."

Chain! My hopes of escape narrowed. Dan hauled me to a large tree, where he waited for the older man to bring the chain from his pack. It looked like the type of chain one would buy to restrain a dog—long, strong links. They wrapped it around me and the tree, pinning me to the bark, and fastened it with a heavy padlock. The older man slipped a key into his pocket, untied my wrist from the young man's, and gave him the second key.

"Come on, we better get camp set up. She ain't going anywhere. You keep that key, Dan, but maybe we ought'a put mine up in a tree somewhere." I couldn't see what they did with the key.

5 p.m.

The mosquitoes and deer flies used me for a banquet. I swatted at them absentmindedly, and watched the two men setting up camp. I was frightened, hot, thirsty, and in a real predicament now that I was chained to a tree. There was no way to escape unless I could talk them into letting me go. I was surprised they had stopped so early in the afternoon instead of putting miles between themselves and the people who would be looking for me. It didn't make sense unless they thought no one would look for me, the older man was sicker than he let on, or they were overconfident.

I glanced at my watch and hoped that Paul had realized I hadn't returned, and that he had phoned Dad and Mom. But would they know where to look? Had I remembered to tell anyone where I was going? I didn't leave a note for Barbara! What about Brian and Jeff? What had I said to them? I tried to remember.

The men put three stones together to form a fireplace, and emptied their backpacks. They worked together without speaking. I leaned my full weight against the chain, testing its strength. I thought I could spring one of the links, but the men had fastened me too close to the tree, and I didn't have enough slack to lean into the chain and add stress to it.

Around the base of the tree were a number of different sized rocks. If I could hide one of them, maybe I could smash through the links when the men were sleeping. Now was a good time to try out my new strategy. I decided to be nasty.

"Hey! I'm tired of standing up against this tree. Loosen the chain so I can sit down!" They gave me a startled look.

"Let her wiggle her way down the tree if she wants to sit," the older man said.

"Well, thanks a lot. Do I have your permission to sit?" I asked sarcastically.

Amusement flickered across his face and he told me to ask permission *every* time I wanted to stand or sit.

I reached behind me, sucked in my stomach, pulled outward on the chain, and inched it down the tree trunk. My shirt slid up and I left some skin on the bark of the tree. By the time I was sitting down on the pine needles, sweat was dripping from my chin. I sighed, closed my eyes, and hoped that I would not attract their attention.

Watching the men through almost closed eyelids, I reached for a large rock. They were talking quietly to each other, preparing to start a fire with dried twigs and grass. Suddenly the younger man whirled and walked toward me. I tried to flip the rock under my right hip, but didn't quite make it. He dropped to his knees in front of me and began clearing away the stones and sticks within a four-foot radius of the tree.

"What're you doing?" I asked sweetly.

"Wouldn't want you to get into trouble," he grunted. He spied the rock, not quite hidden by my hand and thigh. "Move," he said. I ignored him. He repeated the word with more emphasis. I looked at his dirty fingernails, and the thought of his hand touching me made me sick. I let him have the rock.

The older man told Dan to choose a sleeping place. He chose a site under some trees about twenty feet away and leveled it by brushing at the pine needles and dirt with his hands and branches. Dan picked up his rifle, said he was going hunting, and disappeared into the trees. The other man mixed biscuit dough beside the fire.

"How do you make biscuits?" I asked, feigning interest, and he jabbered on about cooking in the mountains. My mind whirled with escape plans. Then he asked, "How old are you?"

"What? Oh . . . twenty-two."

"I was hoping for an older woman for my son."

Son! The relationship was so obvious I couldn't believe I hadn't figured it out earlier.

"If I'm not what you want, if I'm too young, why don't you let me go?"

"Nope. You'll stay 'til you decide which one of us you like best."

Which one! They were never going to let me go.

"See, Dan told me he didn't want to stay up here unless we had a woman for him. I've asked some hippie-like girls who live in Jackson to come up here, but they wasn't interested. I bought that chain five or six years ago to keep a woman with us 'til she decided she liked us, and wanted ta stay." He added water from the tiny spring to the flour mixture.

"You mean you've been planning this for years?"

"Yup. We been hangin' around Ulreys Lake the last few days to find a woman. We been waitin' for someone like you."

"How . . . how did you know I would be running around the lake?"

"Luck. Dan saw you on the other side of the lake and told me, 'Get ready. There's a damn pretty girl comin' around the lake. She might be the one we want.' Why, I couldn't believe my eyes when you run over that hill. An' the way ya run right up to me, an' started talkin', why I couldn't believe it! You was just like a five-year-old, all smiles and friendly like."

"Look, my family will have missed me by now and will come looking. Let me go before someone gets hurt." I was trying to reason calmly with him. I didn't want to make him angry.

"If they find you it won't be us that gets hurt." He shrugged, stretched his neck, and threw some sticks into the fire.

"You don't understand! My family will be coming for me. My mother will be worried sick."

"That's your problem. Don't make no difference if it's your folks. You haven't mentioned your husband lately, Sue." He chuckled knowingly.

A gunshot, crashing in the brush, and a deer burst past us on a dead run. My heart thundered in my ears.

"Dan musta missed. Looks like he's trackin' it downhill," said the father from the edge of camp.

"Maybe you'd better check on him. He might have run into a search party," I said.

"Do you think I'm stupid?" His eyes squeezed into slits and he frowned as he turned back to the fire and dropped blobs of dough onto a hot skillet.

I choked back tears, fearing they would make him more angry. As long as I carried on a normal conversation and asked them to explain their way of life to me, they seemed calm. If I could keep them in a peaceful frame of mind maybe they'd unchain me for awhile and I could run. With my finger I wrote my name in the dust by the tree. Maybe, just maybe, someone would find it.

6 p.m.

The young man squatted beside the fire eating a biscuit. He handed me one, but the dry dough gagged me, and my stomach cramped in protest. I swallowed back the acid stinging my throat and tried again, knowing I'd have to eat to keep up my strength. It was no use. I crumbled it, worrying what would happen to me if I didn't escape. I decided to try a new scheme.

"Do you have some paper and a pencil?" I said.

"Wha'da ya want it for?"

"Just thought I'd draw to occupy the time." I had decided I'd try to leave behind little pieces of paper, and maybe a note for my parents to tell them where the men were taking me.

Dan searched through his pack and finally produced pieces of flour sacks and paper to draw on. I tried sketching skiers and horses, but I was so frightened that my hands wouldn't cooperate and the drawings looked like a kindergartner's scribbles.

"Why don't you show her the pictures in your pack, Dan?" said the old man. "I taught him how ta draw a tree stump, but he's darned good at everything he draws," he said proudly.

The young man moved closer to me, searching his pack for the drawings. The odor of his unwashed body and clothing made me squirm and strain against the chain. He finally found the drawings and handed them to me.

"These are my favorites," he said.

I stared. There was a drawing of a unicorn, and an explicit drawing of a nude woman in a very different pose! The female drawing left nothing to the imagination, and I was acutely aware of the role they planned for me in these mountains. They were after sex, plain and simple. Fear, and the odor of his body, made my head spin.

"Those are pretty good." I shoved the drawings at him.

"I painted a mural on the school wall in White Sulphur Springs. Used the unicorn and a girl, but she had clothes on." He smiled.

You little toad! I shouted in my head.

The older man watched me like a hawk, making it impossible to drop paper scraps. I handed the paper back to the young man, hoping he'd move away. For some reason his father decided Dan should teach me how to do some pencil shading so my drawings would look better. Dan sat beside me, talking and sketching, until he realized I wasn't paying attention. Pouting, he moved to the other side of the fire and began reading a comic book.

"May I read your magazine when you're done with it?" I asked. He tossed it to me. It was a *Mad Magazine*. I stared at the grin of Alfred E. Neuman and felt even more uneasy.

"Thanks." I threw it back to him.

8 p.m.

"I don't suppose you guys thought to bring along clothes for a woman, did you? I'm cold, and the mosquitoes are getting worse." I shivered. Dan dug in his pack and came up with a pair of cotton tube socks and a brown plaid cotton shirt. I wanted to thank him but instead I said, "Is that all? You don't expect to keep me in the mountains dressed like this, do you?"

"We've stashed away some of my ex-wife's clothes that might fit ya, but we left 'em in an underground cache in the Bear Trap on the other side of the mountains," the father explained.

"Wait 'til you see the neat underground caves we live in, Sue. We have hideouts where we won't never be found. There's plenty 'a winter supplies and clothes for you. We can live up here forever without going into civilization." Dan was excited, raving about gardens and caches as if I had agreed to live with them. The father was excited, too, and told me about their skills with weapons, shelters, and avoiding people in the mountains. "Our country," as he put it.

I heard a voice calling from the trees and, trying not to be obvious, I strained to listen. Oh, please, please, let it be someone to help me. It came again. The shout was close, but I couldn't understand what was yelled because the men were still talking.

"Quiet!" The old man stopped Dan in mid-sentence. A shout from a different direction floated to us. The men jumped to their feet, grabbed their loaded rifles, and peered into the forest.

A plane was flying nearer, nearer. The older man grabbed my wrists. Dan removed the lock and tugged the chain tight around my waist. Holding my wrists, the older man dragged me, and Dan held on to the end of the chain. Like a leashed dog, I was dragged and pulled under the shelter of the trees where they planned to sleep.

"We gotta keep her out of sight! Those bright-red shorts can be seen from a long ways off. Hold her, Dan, while I get the rest of our gear."

Dan tightened the chain around my waist and twisted my arm behind me, holding me securely while his father scrambled around collecting their belongings and putting out the fire.

"Please let me go!" I whispered. "All you have to do is turn loose of me. Please!" I pleaded. He pressed my arm upward. Pain throbbed in my shoulder, but I wouldn't let him see me cry.

They hid me under the trees while the plane flew over time and time again. Could the people in the plane be looking for me, or was someone else lost? Could Dad have arranged for a plane so quickly? I looked at the dying fire, willing it to smoke. It didn't.

"You must be a pretty important person if they're already looking for ya with a plane," the old man said caustically.

"I told you my family would look for me."

"Like we said before, anyone finds ya with us, we'll shoot 'em."

"My parents will be worried to death. We're a close family, they'll look until I'm found."

"Don't threaten me with your family!" the old man shouted, gripping his rifle so tightly his knuckles were white.

The plane made a tight turn, banking sharply. Poor Dad. If that was him in the plane he was going to be sick. After circling for over an hour, the plane left. The men returned me to the campfire tree, and chained me tighter than before.

"May I sit down?" I asked.

"Yeah," grunted the older man.

The men left me to the mosquitoes while they sat in sullen silence next to the dead campfire. Removing my shoes, I pulled on the socks and shrugged into the shirt. I was scared to death of the coming night and what might happen to me. Occasionally, one of the men would creep to the edge of the small clearing, gun in hand, listening to the sounds from the woods.

10 p.m.

I held my breath and listened. I thought I heard someone calling my name. It sounded like Paul! It was difficult to be certain where the voices came from—maybe the ridge above and the area below. I heard a motorbike traveling back and forth on the road about a quarter of a mile below us. I decided to try again to be free of the chain.

"I have to use the bathroom. Would you take off the chain?"

"You'll just have to squat right there. We ain't lettin' you go, not for one second." The older man was nervous.

"You can't be serious?"

"Well, if you're shy about it, we'll turn our backs." He nudged the younger man.

I was mortified. People treat dogs with more respect. Anger made me breathless as the men whispered just out of my hearing, occasionally laughing. I was certain they were discussing who'd rape me first.

11 p.m.

Darkness closed around me. I was cold and wished I had my fanny pack and long underwear.

"We might as well turn in and lay low," the father said. "Sounds like too much goin' on out there for us to move around."

"Where am I sleeping?" I choked. They stared at me until the hair on my neck stood up.

"We'll chain you to a tree, give you one sleeping bag, and we'll share the other one."

My pulse slowed. They'd been bluffing, scaring me.

"Look, you could release me and disappear into the mountains. If I walked out now, I doubt if anyone except my parents would believe I had been kidnapped. I'll bet the law wouldn't bother to follow up on my story. You'd be free and so would I. I want to go home!"

They ignored me, rigged up mosquito netting over their sleeping bag, dragged me to another tree, made me sit down, and replaced the chain. It was too tight to provide movement and I wiggled around until I could semi-recline. I couldn't turn over, and it was impossible to tug the bag higher than my waist because of the chain. I didn't complain—they might take the bag back. Placing a tarp on the ground, they opened the second sleeping bag, pulled it over themselves, and arranged the mosquito netting for their protection. They were just out of my reach.

11:30 p.m.

Tears dripped off my chin onto my bruised wrists while I watched the full moon rise above the trees and illuminate the camp. Far off I heard a voice calling. Its echo made me sad.

The men were sleeping, breathing heavily, and I allowed myself to sob. My head ached, and my eyes were gritty. I hadn't eaten since breakfast, and the bog water on an empty stomach had given me terrible cramps. My face throbbed. The swollen lip cracked open and I tasted blood mixed with my tears. Why wouldn't the men let me go? They could creep off into the dark and never be found if what they told me about their life-style was true. They must be confident they could avoid the searchers, otherwise they would have moved me miles away before sunset.

Time passed with agonizing slowness, and the mosquitoes tormented me. I wanted to live, to return to my family, and go on with my life. There were so many things I still had to do. I thought about friendships, and recognized that I had left so much of life unlived.

To keep my mind occupied I thought of all the people who had drifted into and out of my life over the last five years. I had wanted to be closer to them, but I was either training or competing when my friends wanted me to do something. There had never been enough time for everything, so I chose studies and athletics. Maybe I'd been wrong, but Dad said that once you make a choice, live with it, don't look back at what might have been. Now I wanted to look back, to fill my mind with loving people and happier days.

I couldn't have asked for a better brother and sister than Paul and Johanna. We'd been close friends despite the usual sibling scrimmages. We had shared the excitement of hot summers at the cabin, studying insects, birds, animals, and plants. The year we studied edible wild plants Paul put cattail roots in all of Mom's salads. Our backpack trips with Dad and Mom had been fun, and we learned to survive in the mountains if we had to.

One summer we found a water snake and named him Oscar. Johanna didn't mind looking at Oscar, but she wouldn't touch him. Paul teased her, saying he would hide Osc in her sleeping bag some night. She promised she'd wring his neck and the snake's, too, if he did. The day we freed Oscar, Paul had come back to camp carrying a huge, bumpy-skinned toad. Johanna had yelled "Yuck!" and refused to have anything to do with it. That summer our parents gave us nicknames. Johanna was Fraid-a-Bug, Paul was Croaking Toad, and I was Half-a-Horse.

Summers were my favorite time of year, especially when we moved to our cabin and took my horse Nutmeg with us. The days were filled with adventures: hiking, fishing, floating rivers, panning for gold, building a tree fort, playing games, and lying in the grass watching the mile-high white thunderheads build up over the mountains.

I remembered the long rides on Nutmeg. I'd sneak out of bed about 5 a.m., tiptoe down the stairs, groom Nutmeg, and noisily open Mom's bedroom door. I had insisted we'd have to hurry if we wanted to ride before the flies were out. Of course, Mom had been awake the moment she heard my feet on the stairs, but she gave me those precious early morning hours alone with my horse.

Nutmeg loved attention. The moment she had heard my boots on the front porch planks she'd whinny softly—a deep-throated, contented sound that was meant just for me. I'd crawl through the jackleg fence, pockets bulging with horse pellets, and stroke her soft nose and lower lip while she munched the sweet treats. I remembered the odors of those mornings: the smell of deer, pine trees, the river, and occasionally a skunk. Shadow, a pet raven, had paced along the rails of the fence, and I'd fed him pieces of the pellets so he wouldn't scold me.

Mom and I had ridden double, enjoying the nippy air, laughing at the scolding camp robbers, and fascinated by the jewels of dew on a spider's web woven in the sagebrush. With my arms around her waist, cheek against her rough wool shirt, I'd tell her my dreams. No matter how farfetched they were, she never laughed or discouraged me.

One day we watched the 320 Ranch wrangler taking dudes out to ride on the Cinnamon trail. He had smiled, tipped his battered felt hat, and talked to me while the guests filed through the gate. I thought he was the most handsome cowboy I'd ever seen, and my heart soared when he praised Nutmeg as a beauty. I told Mom I'd like to be a wrangler someday, and ten years later I had wrangled for the same ranch.

Johanna would invite her friends to the cabin, and Paul and I had eavesdropped on their conversations, giggling and sputtering, until we were discovered and chased away.

Those summer evenings Johanna played her guitar, singing softly to herself or dragging Paul and me into a few folk songs. Each evening Dad or Mom would read aloud with all of us cuddled together on the sofa in front of a roaring fire. Mom always built an evening fire, even when it was too warm. It was "good for the heart" she said.

1:30 a.m., July 16

The moon shining on my face brought me back to reality. I was shivering and the aches in my wrists, face, and back were intensified by the cold. I had heard shouts after the men fell asleep and knew people were searching for me as late as midnight. Squeezing my eyes shut, I concentrated on images of my family and talked to them. I'm here. Please don't give up. Find me. I want to go home. I called their names over and over until it became a silent chant.

3:30 a.m.

My teeth chattered so violently that I was afraid the noise would wake the two men. No matter how I tried, I couldn't protect my upper body with the sleeping bag. I rubbed my numb hands together and tucked them in my armpits. My legs ached from the cold and my cramped position.

I closed my eyes and conjured up Stu's image. I saw his warm brown eyes, wavy hair, and teasing smile. When I tried hard enough I could hear his voice and laughter. I thought about the years Stu, Paul, and I had spent growing up together; the hikes, fishing trips, and ski competitions we had shared. I could see him standing in Mom's kitchen looking at the plate of chocolate chip cookies, saying he'd better not have any, then eating a dozen or more.

He was fun to train with, always making it a game. We teased each other unmercifully. I stared at the moon, wondering if he were awake. He was in the mountains somewhere with the geology field camp group. Ah, friend Stu, what would you do in a mess like this? I asked the empty night.

The old man grunted and turned over. Through half-closed lids I watched the men settle themselves. It was 4:30 a.m., time to think about escaping. I had to get away! While I schemed, the sky turned gray with the first light of day.

Dawn

I was stiff from the cold. Ravens and camp robbers began their search for food around the camp, and their squawking woke the younger man. Darn! I wanted them to sleep as late as possible, hoping someone would find us. I knew my family would be out looking by now, but I hadn't heard any shouts. The young man stood up, stretched, and picked up his gun. "I'm goin' to find breakfast," he told his father.

I pretended to sleep, listening to the man crashing through the brush. The old man continued to lie in his bed, and I faked sleep until the younger one returned. A squirrel chattered overhead. Dan aimed and shot. The tiny animal fell dead at my feet. These guys must be crazy! Searchers were probably looking for me, yet they risked rifle shots that could bring people running into camp. I shook my head at their arrogance.

"What's your problem, Sue?" I realized the older man had been watching me. I didn't answer.

He turned to his son. "We better move camp this morning." I was surprised to see him stop not more than fifty yards away, move three rocks into position for a fireplace, and return to the sleeping area. They moved their packs, rifles, and bedding, and then turned toward me.

"I wonder how your woman's doing, Dan. Let's go get your woman up." It frightened me to hear them refer to me as "your woman." I had no intention of being anyone's woman!

"Let's get her up and move her over to the camp."

Refusing to talk to them increased their anger, so they hauled me to my feet and walked me to the new camp. It was a good thing they held me up, because my legs were so numb I would have fallen. They shoved me down into a sitting position and chained me to a fallen log.

"I'm freezing! Could I have the sleeping bag again? What have you done with my shoes?" They tossed me the sleeping bag. I pulled it over my legs and hips, and tucked my hands in my armpits. My shoes were under a tree.

The mosquito bites itched, my head ached, and I was thirsty, but I wasn't going to ask them for water or food. I was busy thinking about escaping. I decided to ask the younger man to loosen the chain around my waist and I'd grab his pistol from the holster on his belt. Okay, smarty, once you get the gun what are you going to do with it? Are you tough enough to shoot them? I asked myself. The thought of killing upset me, and I tasted bile in the back of my throat. I knew I couldn't kill them, but they wouldn't hesitate to bash my brains out or shoot me if I threatened them with a gun and didn't use it. I scrapped that plan.

"I think we should move out and eat later. Someone might find us if we stay here," the young man said to his father.

"That don't make sense. The fire's goin', let's eat first."

The two men argued while I listened, hoping they'd stay and have breakfast here.

"What are you going to cook for breakfast?" I said.

"Squirrel and biscuits." Dan held up the bloody carcass of the squirrel. I wondered if they cooked squirrel better than they did biscuits.

"Well, okay, fix breakfast here, but we gotta do somethin' about her red shorts. They're too bright, and someone might see her if we have to cross an open area," said the old man.

Dan said something to his father and the older man turned toward me with that glazed look in his eyes. It was the same look he had when he hit me yesterday.

"Take off your shorts and give 'em to me," he demanded.

"No!" I yelled at him. The image of the drawing of the nude woman flashed through my mind.

"You heard me! Give me them shorts. Now!" He stepped toward me, hand extended, waiting. The muscles in his jaw tightened as he ground his teeth.

"Better do it, Sue," Dan urged.

Inside the sleeping bag I wiggled out of the shorts, and my face flushed with anger and embarrassment. He took them to last night's dead campfire.

The son squatted by the fireplace, three feet from me, preparing to cook the squirrel. For the first time fear began to win the battle. I swallowed to hold back the tears. This was my last chance to talk him into letting me go. If they avoided the search party this morning, I'd be dead.

"Please, let me go! I don't want to go with you. I have a husband and family I love. They'll be worried about me."

Dan ignored me.

"You can turn me loose, you have a key. This is kidnapping. You don't want to get involved in this anymore than you are. Let me go! The law will never find you. If you keep me I'll run away as soon as I can. I'll never stay willingly."

He turned slowly and fixed me with hostile eyes. There was no smile, no frown, no worry, no regret in his expression.

"No. I want to keep you for myself. You're purty."

"Oh, please, please, let me go! I want to go home! Please don't do this to me." I sobbed and gasped, suddenly out of control.

He sat calmly beside the fire, shaking his head no. He fed twigs to the flames, paying no more attention to me than he would a trapped animal. I tried to stop crying but more sobs welled up.

The old man returned to the fireplace, and I held my breath to stop crying. He stood beside his son and stared at me. I felt as if I were suffocating. He tossed me the shorts that he had rubbed with charcoal from the dead fire. They were now a dull, blackish red. The old man's eyes reminded me of cold glass marbles, and the son had no more response to me than he did to the dead squirrel dangling from his hand.

Choking back tears, I struggled to pull on my shorts inside the sleeping bag. I had them halfway on when I heard a rustling in the brush to my right and saw a man kneeling in the grass outside the camp. Dan jumped to his feet, pulled his pistol from its holster, and aimed it at the man.

"Get back! Stay away! They have guns! They'll shoot you!" I screamed.

The old man grabbed his rifle, pointed it at the man in the grass and shouted, "This the girl ya lookin' for?" His son was working on his jammed pistol, fumbling another shell into the chamber.

"Yes, that's her!"

"Stay back! Get help! They'll shoot you! They'll shoot you!"

"Shut her up, Dan!"

Out of the corner of my eye I saw the young man's feet and legs turn toward me. In two steps he was standing directly above me.

"Get away, get away! They'll kill you!" I shouted again.

There was an earsplitting explosion and I was slammed back against the log. I smelled gunpowder, and a searing arrow of pain shot through my chest.

"I didn't mean to shoot her!"

"My God, he shot me!" My vision blurred, then cleared, but everything was black and white. I felt something wet and warm on my shirt, and heard a funny sound, like someone sucking on a juicy peach. I listened. Horrified, I realized the noise was coming from my chest. I'm going to die! Of all the stupid things to happen just as help arrives.

"Help me! I've been shot!" The wound gurgled and bubbled.

The young man towered above me, gun in hand. "Come in and help her. I can't believe I shot her!"

"No, no no! Everyone stay out. Dan, shut up, just shut up!"

He fell silent and made no attempt to help me. The old man whirled to his right, shouting, "Stay out, stay out!" On my left a man stepped into sight.

"Help me!" I wheezed, and realized there were *two* searchers.

"Do you have guns, do you have guns?" The older man leveled his rifle at the man walking into camp. The searcher raised his hands in the air saying, "No guns, no guns. I'm coming in." The old man walked slowly toward the rescuer, his rifle trained on him.

"Help me! He shot me!"

"I didn't mean to shoot her!"

"Where is she?" The searcher was looking frantically around the camp, unable to see me.

"Over there, over there," Dan answered.

"Damn it! Where?"

Dan pointed. The searcher saw me, dropped his pack, rushed over, and knelt beside me. He shouted over his shoulder, "Where's she shot?"

Dan stooped beside the searcher and tried to pull up my shirt but the chain was so tight it wouldn't slide up. The searcher looked shocked when he realized I was chained.

"What the hell is going on here? Get that chain off!" He glanced at the older man who was pointing a rifle at him, and eased open the neck of my T-shirt, looking at the wound. Dan laid his pistol on the ground and fumbled under me for the lock.

"Al! Call for help! Get help!" yelled the man leaning over me. He said his name was Jim.

The older man's rifle was still pointed at Jim, but he yelled at the man called Al, "You got guns? You got guns?"

"Yes, I have a gun! You can't get away!" Al yelled back.

The old man moved behind a tree, leveling the rifle at Al. Seeing the rifle move in the direction of his friend, Jim jumped to his feet and grabbed for the gun, trying to protect Al. The old man swung the rifle back in his direction, and Jim raised his hands. "Everything's cool. Nobody's going to get hurt. Put your gun down," he said to the old man.

"You're surrounded by two hundred men! You can't get away! Give yourselves up!" demanded Al.

Dan jerked hard on the chain. I screamed in pain, and Jim turned to look at us. Behind him the old man raised the rifle, stepped out from behind the tree, and aimed at Al.

"No!" I moaned.

The rifle report roared, and we heard something fall in the grass. Jim whirled away, shouting, "Al! Al!" The old man aimed his rifle at Jim as he ran to his friend, still calling, "Al! Al!"

Jim ran to a spot about twenty feet away, paused, then disappeared from my sight. The old man slipped another cartridge into his rifle and aimed in the direction Jim had run.

"Don't do that!" I wheezed.

The whole thing had happened in about ninety seconds.

"Get your stuff together, Dan. Let's get outta here!"

"Do ya want the chain?"

"Yeah!"

"Is she gonna die?"

"Nah. I see these kinds of wounds all the time. It's no big deal."

They yanked at the lock and chain, hurting me in their hurry to escape.

"I'm . . . so cold. Please . . . please leave . . . me . . . the sleeping bag."

"You won't be needing it!" the old man said and they each grabbed a corner at the foot of the bag and flopped me out on the ground like a dead fish. Pain shot through my upper body and the sucking grew louder.

"I'm going to die. Please . . . don't leave me . . . alone. Help me!"

Dan pulled up my shorts. His father shouted, "They'll never take us alive." They ran away. Silence. The wounded searcher's radio crackled. The men hadn't tried to help him, hadn't even looked at him. They knew we were both going to die, and they wanted to save their own skins.

"No, I won't die!" I said to an empty camp. Talking hurt my chest, so I was silent, listening for the footsteps of the two hundred people returning for me.

I heard the radio again, and thought if I could get to it perhaps I'd be able to get help for us. The effort of turning from my back to my stomach made me dizzy, and pain splintered through me. I felt something warm and sticky on my back and knew the bullet had gone all the way through. Everything was out of focus, and the ground was lurching and spinning under me. I struggled to push myself to my hands and knees. My right arm was numb, useless, and I had a sense of total weakness.

I inched along the ground like a worm, pulling with my left arm, pushing with my toes. I paused to breathe, to stop the spinning sensation, then started forward again. I wanted to reach the campfire, hoping there were a few hot embers to start a fire. The cold went all the way to my bones. It took me a long time to reach the fireplace, which was only three feet away.

I couldn't sit up or get on my hands and knees. Lying on my stomach, I scraped up pine needles, twigs, anything within reach, and tossed them onto the coals. Nothing happened. I raised my head and tried to blow on the fire. My wound gurgled, the trees tilted, and my vision faded. I collapsed.

I lay for a long time with my head resting on my arm, barely conscious, cold, afraid to move, inhaling the dust from the ground. Don't fall asleep or you'll die, I kept telling myself. I hadn't heard the radio since reaching the fireplace, and I wondered if the batteries had died or if those two searchers had been the only ones looking for me. If there were more people out there, wouldn't I hear them talking to each other on the radio? Had the searcher been bluffing the old man? I moaned at the thought.

Something brushed across my cheek. I tried to focus, to clear the gray mist from my vision, and saw an army of huge black ants crawling over my arm, heading for my blood-soaked shirt.

"No!" Frantically, I brushed at them with my left hand. They scurried around in a rage and came back. They renewed my desire to find the radio and the injured searcher.

I could make out the silhouette of something bulky a few feet away. Inching my way to the object, I discovered the backpack dropped by the rescuer when he had come into camp. Maybe there was a radio, water, or clothing in it. I fumbled with the buckles, but I couldn't unfasten them because my fingers were too cold and weak. Okay, sissy, I told myself, just lie here and die of hypothermia and shock. I had to keep scolding myself, urging myself to do things, to live.

I worked on the buckles, resting frequently, and had the sensation that my body was as light as a feather, that I was floating above the ground. It made me nauseated. The last buckle undone, I reached blindly into the pack and pulled out its contents: a bottle of water, a candy bar, and a sleeping bag, but no radio. I lay panting, hungry for air, and the wounds bubbled moistly.

Curling up on my right side, I slipped my feet into the sleeping bag, tugging and wiggling until it covered me. The trees and ground whirled and tipped. I closed my eyes and talked to myself. It would be easy to drift into sleep, but I knew I'd die if I slept.

When I felt less dizzy I opened the water bottle. It was warm lemonade, but I drank it and took a bite of the candy bar. The sweetness was sickening. I dropped the candy and gagged down more lemonade.

The sun shone on the ground at the base of a tree closer to the injured searcher. I had to get to the patch of sunshine, to warmth. Wiggling along the ground was more difficult now because I had to drag the sleeping bag with me. I imagined I was a fuzzy caterpillar creeping along the forest floor. Paul would have enjoyed my performance. In my mind I saw him laughing, encouraging me every inch of the way. Finally, I turned onto my back, exhausted, welcoming the sunshine on my face. This was it, I couldn't go any farther. I wondered if the injured rescuer was conscious.

"Hello! Can you hear me?" My voice sounded peculiar. I tried in a louder voice, but quit when the sucking sound started again. I knew what was wrong, but I couldn't do much about it. I tried to relax, to think things through, and to stop feeling sorry for myself.

I looked up at the sun filtering through the branches, and concentrated on my injuries. There was a difference between the sucking sound on the outside and the gurgling noise inside my chest. I tried to understand, and decided the gurgling was due to blood inside the chest wall, and the sucking noise was the sound of air and blood rushing back and forth through the bullet holes. I didn't want to die, not alone.

"Mommy! Mommy! Help me!" I whispered. Thinking of death wasn't going to help me. I had to come up with a plan that would keep me alive.

I lay still and experimented with different types of breathing, trying to find the pattern that caused the least gurgling and sucking. I closed my eyes and concentrated on slowing my pulse and inhaling correctly.

The flies discovered me. I pulled the sleeping bag up as far as I could, but the insects wouldn't go away. I knew they were biting me, but I was so numb it didn't hurt except on my face and around my eyes. I used the flap of the sleeping bag and tried to shoo them away. It gave me something to concentrate on, to keep myself awake. Something rustled in the bushes.

"Help!" I croaked. A squirrel dashed up the tree by my head, scolding me. "Poor fellow. They shot your friend, too." I started to cry. The gurgling increased.

I continued shooing the flies and shouting each time I heard a noise until my strength was so low that I didn't dare call out. I needed every ounce of energy I had to stay awake, alive. Where were the searchers? Surely the man who got away had had time to get a few people organized to look for me. Maybe he had run into the kidnappers again and they had shot him.

There was a new buzzing sound. I looked around for a large insect, and through a haze, I saw a helicopter. At last, at last! I tried to sit up or crawl. I couldn't. I realized that because of the thick tree cover they'd have to fly directly overhead to see me. There it was! I flashed the bright lining of the sleeping bag at them, hoping it would attract their attention.

"No! No! Don't go! Come back, come back!" I sobbed, as the sound of the chopper grew fainter. I lay panting, afraid they wouldn't find me. I concentrated on breathing again and stayed calm the next time it returned. For what seemed like an eternity the helicopter crisscrossed not far from me. I lay watching, listening, praying, and imagined them rescuing me.

Several hours later the helicopter passed directly over me. I could see the people hanging out the door, looking down. Why couldn't they see me? Please, please find us soon, I pleaded silently. They continued to fly close to me, but I decided they'd never see us. As if reading my thoughts the helicopter disappeared, and I was left with the flies, the mosquitoes, and the scolding squirrel.

The activity of flapping the sleeping bag and yelling at the searchers opened the wounds, and they oozed. I didn't have the strength to keep the insects away, so I closed my eyes and the flies crawled on my face, drinking the salty tears.

I didn't want to die, I wanted to do so many things. I took a long, slow, deep breath, listening for the gurgling. I couldn't give up. I'd held on this long, what was a few more hours? Someone would find us, they knew we were out here, and they had the right area. Be patient, be patient. My mind was foggy, and it was more difficult to encourage myself.

The sunshine moved away from me, behind a log. I wiggled as close to it as I could and waited. I couldn't keep my eyes open. My body was numb. I struggled to stay awake. I had a pleasant feeling, the sensation of floating like an autumn leaf drifting slowly from the top of a tall tree. After a time that peaceful feeling gave way to a frightening one. I felt myself sinking toward a black hole, falling in slow motion, tumbling head over heels, over and over.

I brought up the faces of my family and whispered to them "I'm sorry. I couldn't help it. I tried to come home. Don't cry. Polly Wog, don't be sad. Joey, oh Joey. I'm sorry, I'm sorry. I love you."

I heard a noise and forced myself to concentrate, to listen. Branches snapped in the underbrush. I summoned the strength to yell, but the voice I heard didn't sound like mine. I tried again.

"Help me!"

The blackness curled around me, sucking away my breath. I struggled to stay conscious, gasping, wheezing.

I heard radio static. "Help me!"

"There! There she is! Onstad, over here. She's here!"

"It's okay, Kari, we've found you. Can you hear me?" asked a man.

"Yes."

Another voice asked questions and someone tugged at my shirt. I was turned onto my left side. Someone whispered, "Cripes! It came out the back."

I wanted to shout, yell, and thank them for finding me, but all I could do was smile. It was hard to open my eyes because the lids felt like lead. Between questions I drifted toward the black pit, tugged by an invisible tide. The men's voices kept me awake when I needed it the most. Radios broke squelch, men transmitted messages and shouted directions. Their voices sounded far away, as if echoing through a long tunnel.

"We've found Kari! She's alive! We also have a DOA. Is the medical team coming in, or do they want Kari flown out?" a man shouted.

I felt so sad. I knew what DOA meant.

"They've decided to take you out in the chopper," someone said, "it'll only be a minute."

I listened to the hovering helicopter as gentle hands slid beneath me, lifting me. It hurt and I moaned as they placed me in a stretcher and tightened the straps.

"Pull those straps tight," snapped a deep voice.

"Pearson, if I pull it any tighter I'll cut her in half!" someone answered.

"Kari, don't be afraid, but I'm going to cover your face with the blanket. The wind and dust from the helicopter can be pretty uncomfortable. I'll leave you plenty of breathing space."

I felt them lift and steady the stretcher as the helicopter began its ascent. When their hands left the stretcher it swung gently like a canoe on a lake.

There was an earsplitting crunch and a horrifying jolt! A thousand shards of pain shattered through my body. I screamed as the stretcher lurched wildly, tipping from end to end. I started to slide. I couldn't see what was happening because my face was covered. Frantically, I clutched at the rails of the stretcher, but I couldn't get a grip because of the blankets. The stretcher continued its erratic end-to-end tipping, and I slid back and forth. After all this, I was going to die anyway. What a fitting end to this whole stupid soap opera!

The swaying decreased. The stretcher leveled out, and I felt myself being lowered to the ground. I decided with my luck they would probably drop me. Then I heard shouts and felt the stretcher being caught and steadied. I was almost home. I had made it.

The blanket was pulled back.

"Kari, my name's Jennie, I'm a nurse. How're you doing?"

"Fine," I wheezed.

I tried to answer the questions the nurse asked me. I was lifted from one stretcher to another, and moved to an ambulance where a man Jennie called "Naert" took my blood pressure while she checked my wounds. Someone asked if they should cut off my clothes. Jennie said, "No, the bra will make a good pressure bandage."

Good thing, because I was wearing my new jog bra, and my best shorts. I smiled at my silly thoughts, and someone said, "Those blue lips sure make her teeth look white!"

The man taking my blood pressure shook his head and muttered, "That can't be right!" He took it again and said, "I don't believe it, Jennie, but it was the same both times—seventy over thirty."

Jennie frowned and said something about the pressure not matching a pulse of eighty-eight and respirations of thirty-six. "Kari, what's your normal pulse?" she asked me.

"Forty to fifty."

"Ha! Now it all fits together," she said. Someone outside the ambulance whispered, "She's really shocky!"

Jennie ordered them to turn up the oxygen flow in the mask they had over my nose and mouth. "Get the M.A.S.T. suit on her, but don't inflate it," she ordered. I felt pain in my arm and watched her trying to start an I.V.

"Do my parents know where I am?"

"You bet! Finding you will sure make them happy!" Jennie grinned at me.

The man patted my arm, jumped from the ambulance, and asked who my parents were. I think the doors closed before he got an answer.

"Let's go guys, keep it slow over this rough road," shouted the nurse. Every bump we hit sent waves of pain pounding through my body.

The oxygen helped clear my mind and vision. Jennie finally got an I.V. started, and an ambulance attendant sat next to me squeezing the bag, pushing the fluids into my vein. They turned on the heater. I was warmer, but the gurgling in my chest increased. Jennie listened to my lungs and called in a message to the hospital. I heard them say Mom was waiting at the emergency room, and I wondered where Dad and Paul were.

The ambulance jerked to a stop, the doors were flung open, and I saw Dad. He looked awful. I felt guilty for his pain.

He kissed my cheek and whispered to me. Behind him I saw Paul. They walked beside me, but the rapid movement of the litter made me dizzy and I closed my eyes until it stopped. Dad kissed me again, and Paul's hot hand squeezed my cold one.

4:30 a.m., July 18

The phone rang at the ICU desk. Kari was still telling me what had happened to her. "I was glad the doctors let you stay in the emergency room, Mom. I was really scared when they started sticking all those tubes in me."

She sighed, and asked for more ice for her lip. Her hand slipped from mine, and she slept.

7

THE DEPOSITION

7:30 a.m. Wednesday, July 18

"Sweetie, the detectives are coming this morning to take your statement." Bob's voice was tight with emotion. "The physician said he thought you were strong enough to talk to them, but if you don't think you are he'll stall them for a few days."

Kari's eyes begged me to run interference for her. I knew she didn't want to talk about the kidnapping again, especially with strangers.

"You'll do just fine," I said. "You don't have to tell them everything, just the facts. They've made a tentative identification of the two men and need your statement to verify their information."

Tears pooled in the corners of her eyes, and she brushed at them with the corner of a sheet. "Okay, but I want both of you here with me. If the doctor thinks I'm strong enough to do this do you suppose he'd let me start eating real food? I'd love a cup of tea!"

The surgeon agreed to her food requests and told her she would be given morphine, taken to x-ray, and would have time to rest before the law officers came. Something new was added to her routine: agonizing respiratory exercises designed to expand the collapsed lung. Following the deep-breathing session, a loose plastic mask was placed in front of her face, and she inhaled a cloud of mist. The moisture would loosen blood or mucous so she could clear it from her lungs.

Kari's mail was piling up, and I opened it when she went to x-ray. There were letters from strangers wishing her well, and it occurred to me that we should screen all the mail because of the publicity the case was drawing.

Bob and I discussed the SWAT team that was coming from Billings to help with the search. It was to be a secret operation because Sheriff Onstad thought the kidnappers had a radio, and he didn't want them to follow the search through the news media. I laughed and asked how long he thought it would be kept quiet. We placed bets. I won.

Kari returned to her room so exhausted she fell asleep without drinking her tea. Bob sat beside the bed studying her face, committing every detail to memory. This interview will be painful for him, too, I thought.

11 a.m.

Detectives Don Houghton and Ron Cutting from the Gallatin County sheriff's office arrived. The gurgling of the chest tube made them nervous, and they avoided looking at the large container of evacuated blood at the foot of the bed. Holding a page of slick white paper, one officer explained that they were going to show Kari some photographs. He turned the page so she could see it.

"That's . . . that's the younger man," she said, pointing. "The one named Dan." The photograph was one of many on a page from a school album. Kari's abductor was smiling.

"That's what we needed to know! When you've finished your statement we'd like you to help make up a composite of the other man. Do you think you can do that?" Kari nodded. Bob pulled a chair up to her bedside, gripped her hand, and smiled at her. I stood behind the bed where I could watch her and touch her hair, but she couldn't see me.

Kari gave an abbreviated version of the kidnapping and murder. Her voice broke, she wheezed, and the chest tube rattled. After a brief pause, she collected herself and continued. Bob's face was a mask of agony. He blanched when she told how the kidnappers had dumped her from the sleeping bag.

I stared at the I.V. fluid dripping into the tubing and experienced a wave of hatred for the kidnappers. A phrase from a poem I had written ran through my mind: The dignity of the human spirit shrivels and decays./Hate becomes an all consuming malignancy.

Detective Houghton thanked Kari and said he wished all witnesses could remember details as well as she did. She grimaced and said she'd had plenty of time to study her abductors. They worked on the composite picture until she was too exhausted to continue.

Finally she slept, and Bob dozed in the chair beside her bed. His hand was clasped in hers and tucked beneath her cheek.

8

NIGHTMARES

2 p.m. Wednesday, July 18

Washed, dried, and untangled, Kari's long red hair fanned out around her, glistening with golden highlights. I fashioned it into two thick braids that hung over her shoulders. She looked like a little girl. Paul helped her unwrap gifts and open her mail.

"How do all these people know about this?" she exclaimed, looking at the stack of mail in Paul's lap, and Bob explained about the news coverage. We hadn't allowed her to watch the news yet because we didn't want her to know about Al until she was stronger.

Big Sky Search Area

The search continued at Big Sky, where deputies awaited the arrival of the SWAT team from Yellowstone County. Someone had leaked the news to the press, and reporters were clamoring for details. The Madison County sheriff held a news conference and talked about the country where the Nicholses usually camped.

The July 18 *Bozeman Daily Chronicle* quoted France as saying, "We don't have these people pinpointed. . . . We have six general areas that we think they may be in." He went on to say that the SWAT team would fly into the mountains in two helicopters and then search by foot because "We don't want any advance notice that we are arriving."

Several deputies and the Gallatin County sheriff discussed among themselves the possibility that if the fugitives had a radio, they would be alerted and could avoid the areas to be searched. Sheriff Onstad shrugged, "Well, we'll do the best we can. Keep an eye out down here in case they're flushed out and make a run for it in this direction."

5 p.m. ICU

The *Bozeman Chronicle* was full of interviews with the Nicholses' relatives and friends, calling them "misunderstood men who wouldn't hurt anyone." The older man's ex-wife was quoted as saying that Don and Dan weren't "happy with the system," but that they weren't "the cold-blooded killers news reports are making them out to be." She described her son as "a nice boy." Sheriff France romanticized the kidnappers by referring to them as the Daniel Boone type, stating they were "no longer a threat." Sheriff Onstad, referring to the shooting of Al, compared Don Nichols's actions to that of a grizzly bear: "You threaten the cub and the sow becomes unglued."

Back in Kari's room I looked at her bruises, the tubes running in and out of her body, and my anger mushroomed into a headache. "A nice boy! You bet!" I mumbled to myself. I thought about the anguish the Goldsteins were going through while I dug through my purse for an aspirin.

The respiratory therapist had come and gone, leaving the mist mask on Kari's face. When he returned to collect his equipment he told us a visitor was waiting in the hall. Jay Schreck, a wrangler from the Lone Mountain Ranch, clutched a handful of wild roses and looked uneasy as he settled beside Kari's bed. He discussed her horse Sassacus and told Kari he would take care of the filly until she returned to the ranch.

Jay looked at his watch. "I promised not to stay more than five minutes; it's been eight. Don't worry about Sassy, Kari, just get well. We miss you." Leaving the room with Jay, I saw Kari reach for the TV volume control. I heard the name "Alan Goldstein," and my heart missed a beat. I said a hasty goodbye and ran back to Kari's room. Bob and Paul were trying to calm her. "No! No! Not Al!" she sobbed. Two nurses rushed in to help us, and I explained what had happened while they checked the equipment. Bob sat on the edge of the bed rocking her. The chest tube sucked ominously. What was there to say? Her friends had gone out to find her and one had lost his life because he was a caring, sensitive man who believed in helping others.

Kari was given more morphine and fell into a fitful sleep. Exhausted and haggard, Bob and Paul went home.

1:30 a.m.

Kari was twitching, tossing her head from side to side. I touched her wrist and all hell broke loose. She jerked upright, screaming, "Al, Al! Oh no, help! Help!" She screamed again, struck out with her hands, and the vase of wild roses shattered on the floor. The struggle subsided when she awoke enough to realize where she was. Her eyes begged me to make the bad dreams go away.

I bathed her face and talked softly to her. Crying had given her the hiccups, increasing the pain, and she welcomed the foggy world of drugs. At 3:30 a.m., she whispered. "Those men didn't try to help Al or me." Her voice broke. "I was so cold! I begged them to leave me in the sleeping bag, but they just flopped me out!" I held her. My tears soaked into her fresh-scented hair.

Big Sky Search Area

Sheriff John Onstad drove down Gallatin Canyon, heading for home and a few hours of sleep. Earlier he had met with the other officers at the temporary Madison headquarters at Big Sky to set up plans for Thursday's SWAT assault. He had hoped that making plans so late would preclude someone leaking the operation to the press.

Madison Deputy Merlin Ehlers, helicopter pilot Murray Duffy, and Dave Evans, the director of the SWAT team, had studied maps and decided on the landing zone, which direction the team would go on foot, and their ultimate destination. They gulped strong black coffee and changed their minds a half dozen times before they were happy with the plans. Merlin munched on a roll, stabbed at the map with his finger, and indicated precisely where he would spend the rest of the night.

Merlin and Deputy Doug McLousky would go to a high point in the Madison mountains by the radio towers. They would stay there through the night and the following day until the operation was concluded. Equipped with "Probeyes" (night vision equipment), they would watch for campfires or people moving across the open areas of the wilderness below them.

Meanwhile, sheriffs Onstad and France met and agreed that the news media would not be present at the pre-dawn operation. Reporters would remain at the Big Sky headquarters and wait for news releases. Onstad would drive up the Spanish Creek road to a selected point, and, using his patrol car lights, he would direct the helicopters to where the SWAT teams would board for the flights into the mountains. He was to be there by 4:45 a.m.

4:30 a.m. Thursday, July 19

Sheriff Onstad turned off the highway onto the Spanish Creek road and headed toward his early morning rendezvous with the SWAT team that was being transported by van to the take-off point. Onstad rounded a curve in the road and stared at the string of taillights snaking for a mile into the distance. He jammed the accelerator to the floor and passed the vans and cars packed with news media personnel.

"What are you doing here?" he yelled at a woman reporter standing in the middle of the road.

"Johnny told us there's a big operation going on up here!"

Damn! he thought. Someone should have told me the plans had changed. He jerked to a halt at his appointed station and was besieged by the press. The sheriff turned on his patrol car lights and waited. The sound of helicopters filled the air and the TV camera crews were turning on their lights, expecting comments from Onstad or the SWAT team.

Madison County had low-band radios and couldn't communicate with the Gallatin force, so Sheriff Onstad had loaned a high-band radio to Sheriff France, who now used it to announce, "The first flight is off!"

"Who the hell is he talking to? What flight?" John asked his bewildered deputy, Wally Schumacher.

"France, this is Onstad, where are you?" he yelled into the radio.

"Why, I'm on the Spanish Creek road. Where you at, John?"

"I'm on the road, too, where I was supposed to bring in the helicopters! Instead I'm entertaining the press!" The media realized they had been tricked and were furious.

Sheriff Onstad sped to the new take-off area, where the next to last team was ready to go. The Gallatin sheriff took Sheriff France aside and told him how angry he was. France looked at Murray's chopper sitting across the road from the patrol car.

"I have to talk to Murray. I'll be right back," he said and walked away. Onstad fumed as France climbed in beside Murray. The helicopter flew away.

"France! What are you doing?" Onstad yelled into his radio.

"Well, I changed my mind. No sense both of us sitting here. I'll keep in touch."

The gray light of dawn silhouetted the chopper as it disappeared over the mountains. Sheriff Onstad and Deputy Schumacher poured themselves some coffee and prepared to wait.

7 a.m. ICU

Sitting in the waiting room, I read the release Bob had written for the papers:

"Kari and her family would like to express their appreciation for the generous concern and support received from the community and around the country. Thank you! Kari is making great progress towards recovery.

"We are deeply saddened that Al gave his life. Our love and sympathy go out to his family and friends. Our indebtedness and appreciation are inexpressible to Al, Jim Schwalbe, Bob Schaap, Brad Brisbin, Jack Drumheller, George Tuthill, Bob Donovan, the Lone Mountain Ranch Crew, and the many others whose prompt response on Sunday night and Monday morning made the difference between finding Kari and not. A few hours' delay and she would have been taken from the area. We thank and love you all.

"Some news articles and quotes from relatives and friends of the abductors, as well as the two sheriffs involved, seem to be portraying the kidnappers, as 'mild, gentle men', as 'not dangerous', like 'a sow grizzly protecting her young', and so on. Let us not forget the facts!

"1. Kari was forcibly abducted, being threatened with a knife and sidearm. 2. She pleaded with them to let her go. 3. She was told repeatedly that they would kill anyone who came after them. 4. She was tied to the young man with a short rope and dragged to their camp. 5. She was chained to a tree. 6. When the abductors heard shouts and whistles of rescuers, they again repeated their intent of killing anyone who came into camp.

"This all took place before the presumed accidental shooting. We do not interpret this as behavior of mild, gentle people.

"After the shooting, they unchained Kari so they could take their chain (for another similar use?) and dumped her out of a sleeping bag with the words, 'they'll never take us alive—we'll kill anyone who comes after us.' Mild, gentle people? Do the law enforcers need an excuse to wind down the search? To calm the justifiable fears of the public?

"We feel the facts of what they did speak to the necessity of finding them before someone else is killed."

The *Bozeman Daily Chronicle* printed an edited version of the statement, changing the emphasis. Bob was so angry he refused all future contact with the newspapers. *The High Country Independent News* printed the statement verbatim.

10 a.m.

Kari, exhausted but excited, sat in a chair. The chest tube and urinary catheter had been removed. "By Sunday I'll be able to jog up and down the halls," she grinned mischievously. "I'd like to meet the little boy who sent me this picture." She held up a bright crayon drawing.

She stayed awake longer and finally had a good visit with Paul. She asked Bob to set up a memorial for Al and suggested that her friends send money to the memorial rather than sending flowers or gifts to her. Bob and Paul went home and returned an hour later with Johanna, who had just arrived. She looked frightened, but Kari's smile reassured her. The children laughed and talked, and Johanna had a soothing effect on Paul and Bob. That night she cooked them a scrumptious dinner, the first full meal they had felt like eating since the kidnapping, and made them forget their fear and grief for a few hours.

Big Sky Search Area Thursday Afternoon

Sheriff Onstad and the press were parked on the Spanish Creek road, sweating and waiting for word from the SWAT team. At 2 p.m. Sheriff France informed the base the search had been abandoned and that he would meet Onstad at Cosgrove's house at four o'clock. After waiting until 8:30 p.m. with no messages from the Madison County sheriff, Onstad drove to the take-out point for the SWAT team. Halfway there he met one van of dirty, exhausted men on the Jack Creek road. They said another van was somewhere behind them. John intercepted the second group and Sheriff France at the campground at the Jack Creek trailhead. A SWAT team member told him that two of the squad were missing. One searcher hadn't returned and another went in to look for him—alone.

John was so mad he gave the other sheriff a dressing down in front of everyone. Johnny pushed his hat back, squinted at Onstad, and said he had left a car there to bring them back when they walked out.

Head aching with anger, Onstad drove toward the take-out point, where the car was waiting for the missing men. Halfway there he spotted them driving toward him. He made sure they were all right and drove home to cool down. He wondered how deputies Ehlers and McLousky had survived the day.

Doug McLousky and Merlin Ehlers had been sitting by the radio towers watching for the SWAT team to come into sight. Their eyes burned from lack of sleep, the strain of using the Probeyes during the dark hours, and the bright sunlight. At about 9300 feet, they sweltered in the sun. Flies swarmed around them. At noon, Gary Lincoln of the FBI and Dave Evans joined them on the ridge. The four men sat wondering what had gone wrong with the operation.

The SWAT teams ended up about four miles too far south and were eventually ferried back to the right search area. From there they had bushwhacked into Bear Trap Canyon on the Madison River and met their vans at the power plant. The men were exhausted, blistered, thirsty, and angry. What had gone wrong? There were varying opinions, but it was never resolved.

Friday Morning, July 20

Bob wheeled Kari to the room where the young crayon artist was lying with his shattered leg suspended in a traction unit. She thanked him for the drawing and admired his model horses.

Flowers, plants, gifts, and cards brightened Kari's room. Becky Lohmiller, Kari's long-time friend, had come to the hospital each day with humorous self-illustrated letters, balloons, or something cheerful. Today was the first time Kari truly enjoyed the letters, because she could stay awake to read them herself. Two friends on the United States rifle team must have cleaned out the card shops in California.

Kari wanted to walk to the bathroom, a room's width away. She started creeping across the room, clutching Bob's arm for support, shuffling along a half step at a time. I followed behind, pushing the I.V. stand. We tried not to laugh, but the procession was too comical not to. She stopped, clutched her side and chest, and giggled with us.

Johanna and Paul entertained Kari by visiting with her and reading her mail to her.

7:30 p.m.

Bob met Stu Jennings in the corridor and explained Kari's condition. Stu had come as soon as he could get out of the mountains. He hesitated, took a deep breath, stuck his head in the door, and said, "Some people will do anything to get out of training!"

"A-h-h-h, Stu, you always pick on me!" moaned Kari.

"Whether you know it or not, you've given biathlon more press in five days than its had in thirty years!"

"Good grief! I don't have to do something like this every year, do I?" she said in mock horror.

"You'd better check the fine print in next year's contract." Stu's smile faded and his dark eyes looked serious. "It's good to see you," he said softly, kissed her cheek, and turned away to greet Johanna and Paul.

Kari complained of pain during the night. Unable to sleep, she talked.

"The flies, mosquitoes, and ants were awful! I kept thinking of the flies laying eggs in my wounds and almost went crazy! I know I'm no raving beauty, but for the first time in my life I wished I were ugly, really ugly. They said they wouldn't rape me, but I knew they hadn't kidnapped me to wash their dishes!"

"Rest, honey. Don't hurt yourself by going over it again."

"I have to talk now. I feel so guilty because Al was killed. If I hadn't called for help, Jim and Al wouldn't have tried to help me and Al would be alive. Why did they shoot him? They let Jim come into camp."

"Who knows? It wouldn't have made any difference if you had yelled or not. Al and Jim would never have left you there."

"Why did it take so long to find me?"

"I don't know, Punkin."

"Weren't you there?"

I told her how I got out of the mountains.

6:30 a.m. Saturday, July 21

Wind-whipped raindrops against the windows and rivulets of water etched patterns on the dusty glass. A vase filled with forget-me-nots, prairie smoke, pussy toes, and bedstraw stood on the windowsill.

"Remember the forget-me-nots on Sage Ridge, Mom?" Kari startled me. I thought she was asleep.

"You bet! That was a great hike, wasn't it?" I answered.

"Do you think I'll be able to get up there again this summer?"

"Why not? You'll walk a little slower, that's all. Maybe I can keep up with you next time."

"You do okay, Mom. It's the weight of the camera equipment and the lunch that slows you down." Her eyes twinkled. "Time for my sprint across the room. I'll try pushing the I.V. stand."

She sat on the edge of the bed, frowning. "My chest feels heavy, and the pain in my abdomen is worse this morning. Guess I didn't get enough sleep last night. I didn't mean to upset you, but I needed to talk."

The surgeon was gone, but his partner arrived early, listened to her complaints, ordered x-rays, read them, and ordered another CAT scan.

Kari wanted her address book and some clothing, so Johanna, Johanna's boyfriend, and I drove to the ranch. We parked at the A-frame and Bob and Viv Schaap hurried down the steps, looking tired and sad. We talked, oblivious to the fine drizzle dampening our hair and jackets.

Johanna and I went to Kari's apartment. I was vertiginous with shock when I saw the scissors and scraps of blue material still lying on the bed. The horrors of last Sunday night flooded back. I was frozen, unable to move.

"Mom, help me find what Kari wants, and let's get out of here," Johanna urged. Kari's biathlon rifle and case were lying on the floor. She kicked the lid closed with a bang, and said, "Let's go!"

Back in town we hurried up the stairs of the hospital and were accosted by a reporter. "Isn't it good news about Kari's scan?"

"What?" I gaped at her.

"The scan was negative." We pushed past her and ran up the stairs. I stopped at the nurses' station and asked the nurse why the reporter knew about Kari's scan.

"Jan, you've got to do something about her, she's driving us crazy! She questions everyone and even followed Kari over for the scan. Andi and Jennie saw her following them and led her on a wild goose chase in the parking lot while the nurses sneaked out the other way with Kari. She must have been hiding around the corner and heard the physician's report. It's driving us nuts!"

The day supervisor and I mulled over the problem. She decided to phone the editor and ask him to remove the reporter from the hospital. She returned ten minutes later, red faced and angry. "He refused! Said she was doing her job. Well, I'll have her thrown out if she continues to upset my staff!" She swished down the hall, reminding me of a supervisor I had had many years ago. She had been a sweetie but it was a mistake to make her mad.

Kari was upset. "I know the x-rays and scan were okay, but something's wrong. It's harder to breathe than it was yesterday. Am I complaining too much?"

"Nope. We need to know how you feel."

The nurse came in with a note from John Yurich, a college friend of Kari's who was on his way to Seattle. Kari asked me to explain to him that she couldn't see him today, maybe tomorrow. We didn't know then how ill she would become in the next twenty-four hours.

3:30 p.m.

Johanna and Paul popped in and out throughout the day, and Johanna took over Paul's care. He had been neglected to some extent because I spent so many hours at the hospital, and Joey was making up for it. I opened Kari's mail, and Bob sat on the bed reading the notes and letters to her. There were many from strangers wishing her well, some telling of their own tragedies and recoveries. One card contained a six-inch length of rainbow-colored ribbon, which she tied around the neck of a miniature teddy bear swinging from the handle of a vase.

Shock and revulsion paralyzed me when I read the obscene words scrawled in the next letter. Some sick mind had worked overtime to produce such evil. I jammed the letter into my pocket, hiding it from Kari, and opened another envelope with sweaty, shaking fingers. Every unknown name and address was a threat.

Later, the wind and rain lashed the trees, knocked tender green leaves to the lawn, and filled the room with sweet, clean air. I pressed my forehead against the chilly window and thanked God Kari wasn't out in the mountains with those men.

She slept sporadically and talked about friends and past events. I fell asleep in the chair and jerked awake when Kari screamed. She clung to me, her heart pounding so hard I could feel it against my chest.

"I dreamed the old man had me by the wrists and was hitting me in the face!" She was drenched with sweat. I washed her, changed her gown, and got her up to the bathroom.

While she dozed I thought about her behavior. She was strong willed and didn't like people to know she was vulnerable. She had handled her problems this way since she had been a child. When her young horse had injured a hoof on barbed wire, Kari had refused to have her destroyed and convinced the veterinarian to let her try to save Sassy. He told her the horse needed four penicillin shots a day, and Kari proudly said, "My mom knows how to do that. She's a nurse." He rolled his eyes at me and showed her how to change the bandages.

Our neighbors loaned us their barn, and Kari cleaned and organized it in a whirlwind of activity. It was a bitterly cold winter, and caring for the horse hadn't been easy. She made a game of hauling water by making a harness for our dog and training her to pull the water container on a sled.

Kari had one good laugh at my expense that winter. Sassy knew who caused her pain with the penicillin shots, and the last day she was to get them she revolted. When I stepped into the small room in the barn, the horse wheeled to meet me, ears flat, teeth bared, and charged. I ran up the wall and clung there helplessly. Kari crawled under the poles, against my orders, murmuring to Sassy. She scratched the horse's withers, put the halter on her, and led her away, giving me a chance to sneak to safety.

"Wow, Mom, you sure climbed the wall fast!" Her voice trembled with mirth, and she blurted out, "You looked pretty funny, too, kind of like a big spider on a wall." We rolled on the hay laughing, and she kissed my cheek. "I'm glad you're okay. Sassy just doesn't want any more shots."

The horse had her way and slowly recuperated without more penicillin. Kari learned about patience and responsibility that frigid winter and never complained about her frostnipped fingertips or the hard work.

I knew she would apply the same push and stubborn optimism to her own injury. It was a healthy attitude as long as the physicians approved.

Sunday, July 22

I stood at the window watching the gray sky turn pink, purple, then gold. Suddenly, the sun was shining on the leaves outside Kari's window. The breeze was cool, and I quietly closed the window. Turning, I found Kari watching me. I cocked my head at her and said, "Those pigtails make you look ten years old."

Her smile didn't reach her eyes. "Mom, something's wrong. My side is numb and the pain under my ribs is terrible! I feel like I'm sliding backward."

"Maybe you've had too much company. I'll see that the visits are kept to five minutes today."

Johanna came to say goodbye. There were hugs, kisses, and promises to phone and write often. The girls' embrace was long, silent, tearful. Joey returned to Seattle.

Kari regressed before our eyes. We elevated the head of the bed higher and higher when it became more difficult for her to breathe. She got up to the bathroom, and the effort exhausted her. She was too nauseated to eat, and for the first time in twenty-four hours asked for medication to stop the pain. Bob pushed me out the door. "Go get some coffee! You're making me nervous!"

In the cafeteria I crumbled a piece of toast and sipped cold coffee. I had decided Kari must be bleeding again. It was the only explanation for her symptoms. Or was it empyema, a pocket of infection in the chest? The specter of empyema snatched at my mind. I had had a case study in nursing school, a man with this condition. The physician had fought a battle with the infection: daily draining the purulent fluid from the chest, mega doses of antibiotics, days and nights of agony, a complication, surgery, death. I lost my appetite and hurried back to the hospital room.

Kari was pale and lay sweating, eyes closed. She appeared so lifeless that I had to touch her and feel her warmth to reassure myself. Bob's face was dark with anger. A difficult session with a respiratory therapist had ended with Kari in tears. Bob was more upset than I had seen him since the day she had disappeared.

"What's that sloshing in my chest when I roll over?" Kari asked after we had turned her. "I can hear it and feel it." The nurse listened to Kari's lungs and hurried away to phone the physician. Hours crept by. Kari slipped in and out of sleep, gasping, sweating, confused. I was upset because she wasn't being given oxygen.

Paul sat on the edge of Kari's bed and read to her, not caring whether her eyes were open or closed. "She can hear me," he said. "She'll know I haven't left her alone again." He looked miserable.

Evening

Kari asked me to rub her head, a technique Bob had used when she was a child to soothe away hurts and troubles. I thought she was sleeping until the tears slipped out from under her closed lids. I wiped them away and rested my cheek against hers. "It'll be all right, sweetie. Sleep if you can," I murmured.

"When I sleep I dream men are chasing me or shooting at me. I can't run away. I move in slow motion, and the men get closer and closer. I scream for help, but there's no one to hear me. I don't want to sleep!"

Kari's evening respiratory treatment was only the mist mask. She was too sick to do the rest. The head nurse poked her head in the door and said Sheriff Onstad wanted to talk to me. I asked a friend who had just arrived to stay with Kari while I was gone. John Onstad leaned wearily on the nurses' station counter. A tall, big man with kind eyes, Onstad was usually cheerful and easygoing. Tonight he drooped with exhaustion. We sat in the cafeteria with our coffee, and he said, "Brad tells me you're unhappy with the way the search for Kari was handled."

"We're angry because no one except Brad Brisbin and Bob Pearson would help us. Darn it, John, you and I have done night searches in the dead of winter, and I couldn't get one law officer to respond on a summer night! We had to phone for Brad personally, and even then the dispatcher wouldn't put through our call. Why?" I gulped for air and continued. "It was hell for my husband and son waiting at the base for the official search to get organized. Jim Schwalbe said he wasn't allowed to go back into the forest the way he and Al went in, so he couldn't find the camp. He was angry, too!"

John explained the problem of searching in someone else's jurisdiction, and I reminded him that he had done many of Madison County's rescues, at least for lost hunters. He said he was there Monday morning simply because Brad's phone call had jolted him from a deep sleep and, without his glasses, he had misread the map and thought Kari had been lost in his county.

John's story jumped from incident to incident, and I was beginning to get a clear picture of what had happened after Jim Schwalbe had run out of the forest. He shook his head when he described the stretcher accident.

"When I saw the litter hit that tree I was scared to death, We had finally found her, knew she needed immediate medical attention, and it looked like we'd lose her after all. I almost . . ."

"Code Red, West Wing One! Code Red, West Wing One!" blared the intercom. I jumped up, knocked over my chair, and ran. There was a fire in Kari's ward! I dashed into her room and was lost in a wall of swirling white. I thought it was smoke, then realized it was moisture.

"What's happening? Is that the fire alarm?" Kari's pupils were dilated with fear. I tried to calm her.

"Could you help me into the chair. Maybe I could breathe better sitting up," she said. I eased her out of bed, my mind whirling, trying to remember the placement of the nearest fire exit.

The door banged open. A fireman ran in and yelled, "This is it! Has anyone been smoking?"

"No, the mist is from the respiratory machine," I said. "Could that have set off the alarm?"

"Probably," he said, looking at us for the first time. He must have recognized Kari from the newspaper photographs because he jerked his helmet off, smiled, and said, "It's sure easy to see why they decided to take you, young lady." The moment the words were spoken he realized what he had said and stammered, "I mean . . . I'm sorry, I didn't mean to say that!" His face flushed a deep red and he beat a quick retreat. Kari looked startled, then burst out laughing. She clasped a pillow to her chest and the two of us laughed hysterically, inappropriately, relieved.

A humorous ending to an ugly day, I thought. The night was yet to come.

9

THE RESCUE

Sheriff John Onstad

John waited at the main desk of the hospital and watched the firemen come and go. The woman at the desk confirmed that it had been a false alarm, and he walked wearily to his car, wishing he could have finished the conversation with me.

Driving home his thoughts were occupied with my questions. There were answers, plenty of them. The manner in which the crime scene had been investigated haunted him, and he got mad just thinking about it. If Kari died, the conviction of the Nicholses would depend on the evidence found at the scene, as well as the photographs and measurements that should have been taken. John thought back to the events that started his participation in Kari's rescue.

Sunday, July 15

The phone had rung about midnight, shocking him out of a deep sleep.

"John, this is Brad Brisbin. I'd like permission to help with a search at Big Sky. There's a girl missing in the Ulreys Lake area."

"That's in Madison County isn't it?" John responded. Brad didn't know for sure, but pressed hard for permission to go. He also wanted to take Deputy Pearson and his dog.

"Pearson's dog is green, isn't he? Aren't you supposed to teach an Accident Investigation Class in Yellowstone Park tomorrow?" the sheriff said.

"I don't think the investigation class is that important. I'd like to go to Big Sky." Brad's voice had a sharp edge.

"Well, go ahead and take Pearson with you. I've been trying to read my map without my glasses and I think this could be in our county after all. I'll get the posse up there about 7:30 a.m. to give you a hand. Keep in touch with me."

John phoned his office and asked the dispatcher to alert members of the posse to meet him at the Conoco gas station at Big Sky at 7 a.m. The Madison sheriff's office was informed that deputies Brisbin and Pearson and their dogs would be joining the search at Lone Mountain Ranch at 4 a.m.

West Yellowstone

Bob Pearson moaned when the phone rang, and glanced at the clock. It was 1 a.m. He had returned from a float trip on the Snake River and hadn't been to bed yet. His eyes were gritty from lack of sleep, his sunburned back throbbed, and the aspirin hadn't tempered his headache.

"Yeah?" he growled into the phone.

Brad explained the situation and asked if Pearson wanted to join him.

"Sure. What do you think we're walking into, Brad?"

"Your guess is as good as mine. Jan wouldn't have asked for our help unless she felt it was necessary, but I'm not sure what our position is. After I talked with Bob Schaap I rechecked my map. There's no doubt in my mind that Ulreys Lake is in Madison County's jurisdiction. I assume we're going in as a resource, not as search organizers. Odd, though, neither Bob nor Jan mentioned other law enforcement officers."

7:25 a.m. Sheriff Onstad at the Conoco Station, Big Sky

John stood around impatiently with members of the posse waiting for one more person to arrive. He had been keeping track of Brisbin and Pearson by listening to the communications between the two of them. He assumed Sheriff France and his boys were the initial search party, and that his deputies were just backup men. He had planned to show up and offer the Madison sheriff their services if he wanted them. If he didn't, it would be a good day for a search drill for John's crew. Onstad's radio popped and he intercepted a frantic message from the base at the lake. Someone was shooting at the search teams.

"Come on, Dave!" John yelled, and Sergeant Dave Dunn and he jumped into the pickup. "The rest of you wait for the last posse member, then get up to the lake!" Onstad shouted at the startled faces around him. Dave pushed the accelerator to the floor, and the truck and horse trailer lurched forward.

"Dave, that must have been one of the searchers firing a signal shot! It doesn't make sense that people would be shooting up there."

"Let's hope so!"

The Ulreys trailhead area was crammed with cars and horse trailers. The pickup rocked to a stop, and the law officers jumped from the truck. They heard someone yelling and saw a bearded young man running down the Beehive access road shouting, "Call the sheriff! Call the sheriff! They've shot and raped the girl and killed my friend!" He shouted the message over and over.

"Okay, son, calm down. What's your name?" John said.

"Jim Schwalbe. Let me go. I have to talk to the law!" he said, jerking away. Dave and John weren't in uniform and couldn't convince him they *were* the law. Jim whirled away and ran down to the communications center, shouting, pleading for someone to do something, to go back with him to look for his friend and the girl.

John pushed his way through the crowd to the man operating the communications system and shouted, "Is Sheriff France here? Anyone know where he is or if he's coming?" The answer to all three questions was no.

The sheriff took stock of the situation. He was out of his jurisdiction, had two people wounded, two men with guns who might be on a shooting spree, and there were about thirty civilian searchers out there, as well as Brisbin and Pearson. "How'd I get into this mess? he wondered."

Dave and John gave up trying to isolate Jim from the crowd and did an interview right there.

"One of them shot Kari, and when I went in to help I found her chained to a tree! Al radioed for help, then told the men they were surrounded, couldn't get away, and they shot him! Oh, God, they shot him right in the face!" He buried his face in his hands and moaned.

"Okay, okay, take it easy. Is Kari still alive?"

"She was when I left. Why are you just standing around? Why aren't you out looking for them if you're a sheriff?"

"Take it easy. First we have to know where this happened," John said. "Dave, I want you and Jim to look at this map and try to figure out where Kari is. Get back to me as soon as you have the information I want. Find out the name of his friend." Dave nodded, took the map, and moved Jim away from the crowd.

"Anyone here know who this girl is?" John shouted above the confusion.

"Kari Swenson. She was working at the Lone Mountain Ranch," said the man at the radios.

"Who are you?"

"John Palmer, Big Sky Fire Department," he answered as Dave handed Onstad the map. He indicated where Jim thought the shootings had taken place.

"Are you taking charge?" Palmer asked. Onstad didn't answer him and he asked again. The sheriff didn't want the job, but realized he had no choice.

"Okay, Palmer, get the searchers out of there. From looking at the map I'd say the people in sections seven and twelve may be in the way of whoever is shooting. Tell them to be careful coming out. The two girls on horseback and that man and woman on foot are to walk out to Ennis. They're not to come back into this area once they reach Jack Creek. They could run right into the gunmen."

Just before Palmer transmitted Onstad's messages, there were a few squelch pops on the radio. The sheriff wondered if the kidnappers had taken the wounded man's radio and would be able to monitor the search, possibly picking off members of the group as they made their whereabouts known.

"Palmer! Tell those people out there not to radio in their positions! They are not to use the radios! I want total radio silence. Total!"

"Yes, sir!"

John radioed his office and asked for reinforcements with bulletproof vests, rifles, plenty of ammo, and maps. "Hurry! We've got real problems up here."

He heard Palmer radioing the ranch requesting helicopters, and knew they'd have trouble getting a helicopter without a sheriff's order, so he called his office again.

"Call Murray Duffy," he ordered. "We need his helicopter. Have him pick up a medical team and fly them in."

Behind him he heard Jim telling the story again.

"Who's Jim talking to?" John asked.

"That's the girl's father. Looks like he's coming apart at the seams. Poor guy."

Bob urged Onstad to get into the forest, to find Al and Kari. It was an uncomfortable confrontation. John knew how Bob felt, but he couldn't do anything until his deputies arrived. (Much later John realized he and Bob had grown up in the same neighborhood, and that Bob had been a member of John's father's church.)

Onstad turned to Palmer and growled, "Get a message to Madison and tell Sheriff France to get over here. Now!"

Two miles away, Brad Brisbin and Bob Schaap ran downhill, and eventually came out on the road. A pickup truck with Sheriff Onstad, some of the deputies, and Jim Schwalbe stopped them, discussed where they thought the shots had come from, and the men headed into the dense forest on foot. Schaap and two other searchers hopped in the truck and were driven to the base. Jay Cosgrove, the Madison deputy stationed at Big Sky, and Brad Brisbin joined forces. Under the cover of the trees, they began moving cautiously along the road towards Jack Creek.

Bob Pearson heard the order to evacuate the area and started to return to the command center. Suddenly, his dog streaked away into a small ravine. Bob's heart flopped over once or twice, and he prepared to defend himself. Skip returned, tail between his legs, his muzzle covered with porcupine quills. Bob sighed in exasperation and gave Skip's head a reassuring pat. At the base he watered Skip and made a comfortable bed for him in the back of the patrol car.

"Bob!" shouted Don Houghton, limping up. "Would you fly as a spotter in the helicopter with Murray? Morton and I have been up, but my knee is killing me, I have to uncurl my legs for a while."

"Sure!" Pearson tossed his pack and firearms in the trunk of the car, locked it, and jumped into the chopper with Bob Morton, a law enforcement officer for the U.S. Forest Service, and Murray

Duffy. The helicopter began flying a tight grid at treetop level and several times the pilot gave Sheriff Onstad and his ground crew a true north-south bearing.

Dave Dunn, Jim Schwalbe, deputies Wally Schumacher and Don Gullickson, and John Onstad continued to the end of a logging road. They spread out with Wally as the point man, flanked on the right by Dave and on the left by Onstad. Jim Schwalbe and Don Gullickson brought up the rear. Jim took a few minutes to orient himself; he knew approximately how much of Lone Mountain Peak should be showing above the ridge where he and Al had walked. They would walk a ways, wait for Jim to catch up, discuss the direction he thought they should take, and start off again in the same formation.

Jim was upset because the area didn't seem quite right. He wanted to hike back in following the route he and Al had taken earlier, but John was afraid it would be too time consuming, and Kari didn't have time to waste. Eventually, they arrived at a meadow on top of a ridge and had a good view of the surrounding terrain. John saw Murray's helicopter passing back and forth to the west of them and made radio contact with Bob Morton in the chopper.

"Sorry, John," Bob replied. "We haven't been able to locate a large clearing, Kari, or any equipment."

"Tell Murray to put 'er down. We'd better send Schwalbe up to have a look," John yelled into his radio. While they waited for the chopper to land they were joined by Deputy Bill Pronovost and Detective Bob Campbell from the Gallatin sheriff's office.

"Any sign of Madison County yet?" John shouted at Bob Campbell.

"No! Sorry, John, it looks like it's us again." He gave his lopsided grin. Bob was tough, and a great search and rescue manager, John thought.

"Jim, I'd like you to go up in the helicopter with Pearson. Maybe you can spot the clearing or packs from the air. Will you go?" Onstad asked.

"Sure!" Jim's face was pale and his eyes reflected the panic he barely managed to control.

The helicopter landed. Murray leaned out the door and shouted, "I brought a nurse with me, left her at the base with Bob Naert."

"Thanks!"

11:20 a.m.

Bob Pearson and Jim Schwalbe went up with Murray Duffy. Another helicopter had just arrived on the scene, and Bob radioed the other chopper's position to Onstad. It was Brad Brisbin and Sheriff France in a chopper from Ennis.

The two choppers crisscrossed the area in a tight grid, hoping to find the clearing Jim had fled three and a half hours earlier. The forest was dense, and it was impossible for the men to see objects at the base of trees. They could not locate a large clearing. Murray talked with Jim Schwalbe, then radioed John that they were going over the ridge to the west and would fly a grid in the next drainage.

Much earlier, Jay Cosgrove and Brad Brisbin had stationed themselves at a spot on the logging road where they could see a large slope. If anyone tried to cross the hill, they would be seen by the officers. The two men had been in this position for a long time when a helicopter hovered over them and landed. It was Sheriff France. Brad filled him in on the search. They checked the information they had against the maps and had the pilot start flying grids. Unable to spot anything, Sheriff France had the helicopter drop them off in a clearing, and they started searching on foot.

"That's it! That's it!" Bob Pearson's voice exploded from the radio on Brad's hip. "We've spotted the area! There's the pack!" Brisbin and France scrambled back into their helicopter.

From the air, Bob and Jim could clearly see Al's red pack. Murray flew as close to the trees as he dared, but they were unable to see anyone on the ground. There was no clearing to land in, so Murray headed for a ridge a quarter of a mile north of the area where they hoped to find Kari.

"Onstad! We couldn't land!" shouted Duffy into the radio. "The blades wouldn't clear the ridge, so Pearson had to jump three or four feet while I hovered. I'm on my way back to pick you up."

Murray dropped off Schwalbe, and took Onstad and Pronovost back to join Pearson. One more trip with Dunn and Gullickson, and they were all together on the rock slide. The other helicopter dropped Brisbin and France.

"Everyone armed?" Sheriff Onstad asked.

"I locked my rifle in the car when I jumped into the chopper!" Pearson exclaimed. Bill Pronovost handed him a pistol. There were now seven men, armed and ready for the final push to find Al and Kari. They agreed on an open-point assault formation, and with Bob Pearson in the forward position, they began to move through the timber. The deadfall and heavy underbrush cut visibility. The officers crouched, stepping carefully, listening. Somewhere ahead of them an angry squirrel chattered.

"Listen!" They stopped. Someone called for help.

"That's Kari!" whispered Brisbin. Pearson said the voice didn't sound like a female's. It was husky and raspy, almost masculine. Onstad thought it sounded like a wounded animal, like something caught in a trap.

They moved again, stepping quietly. Onstad passed a fireplace with three stones placed together for a cooking surface. It seemed a strange place for a fireplace, too steep.

Brisbin's radio broke squelch, and they heard a soft voice call to him from the underbrush. "Help me!"

"There! There she is!" shouted Bill Pronovost dashing forward.

Brad dropped to his knees beside Bill and yelled. "Onstad! Over here! She's here!"

John had seen her and was running in their direction. A narrow shaft of sunlight streamed through the dense forest, highlighting Kari's red hair. Brisbin, Pronovost, and Onstad knelt beside her, staring at her ashen face and blue lips. "It's okay, Kari, we've found you. Can you hear me?" John said. She shocked them by smiling. A rattling wheeze shook her body.

Sheriff Onstad radioed the base. "We've found Kari! She's alive, badly wounded. Get the medical team or litter in here fast! Tell that nurse to hustle her decision! We also have a DOA."

John asked Kari questions to keep her conscious while they examined her chest wound.

"Okay, Kari, take it easy," said Bill. He rolled her gently onto her left side, and the dark brown stains below her shoulder blade indicated that the bullet had gone through her body. Brad glanced at John, and shook his head. They were probably thinking the same thing—her kidney and liver were damned close to the exit hole!

Looking up, John realized his deputies were standing close to them in a circle. He asked them to move out and form a protective perimeter.

The base reported that the medical team wanted Kari brought out to them because the area wasn't secured. They were right, of course; it wouldn't do to have them pinned down by snipers. The chopper arrived and began lowering the litter.

"That's not Murray's outfit! Who's in that chopper? Does he know what he's doing?" Onstad yelled.

"That's my boy, John," replied Johnny France. "Used to fly in Vietnam, so guess he knows his trade."

"Murray was out of fuel," Pearson said.

The helicopter hovered above the trees, waiting while the men prepared Kari for the ride. They wiggled their hands and arms under her cold body, and Brisbin said, "Move her on the count of three. Kari, we'll be as gentle as we can. One, two, *three.*" She moaned when they released her, and her pain made all of them wince. Bill covered her face with part of the blanket. They tightened the straps that held her in the litter, and attached it to the cable dangling from the helicopter.

"John, there's not much clearance through those trees. That guy better be as good as Murray!" said Bob Pearson, directing the pilot with arm signals. The officers gently released the litter so it wouldn't swing and interfere with the balance of the chopper. Bob gave a signal and the helicopter started upward.

"Shit! No!" shouted Brad. Squinting into the sun they watched helplessly. The pilot made an error and started forward before the litter cleared the trees, and it swung into a dead lodgepole, shattering the brittle branches. The pilot poured on the power, and the litter tipped end to end, shearing off the branches, slammed into the trunk of the tree, pulled free, and went spinning and tipping like a child's toy into the sky above the clearing.

Crime Scene Investigation

The litter disappeared from view, and a squirrel scolded from a tree. John asked Brad and Bob Pearson to start tracking downhill from the camp, and they reminded him that they had been out with the search team since 4 a.m. They wanted to return to the base to eat, rest, and water Brad's dog, and then head down Jack Creek to see if they could pick up the killers' tracks. Jim Schwalbe entered the area with John's officers, who had stayed with him. Bob Campbell and Bob Morton joined the deputies in the outer perimeter, but Jim stumbled past Al's body and began stuffing his belongings into his pack. John watched, waiting for the officer in charge to stop him. When he didn't, Campbell spoke up. "Jim, you'd better leave your things—they're evidence." Dazed, Jim sat down, waiting to be told what to do.

Al was lying on his back, arms thrown above his head. Near his right hand lay an automatic pistol, and the same distance from his other hand was a portable radio. Suddenly, John was mad, really angry, at the waste of this young man's life, and possibly Kari's.

Onstad looked around. Now was the time to go slowly, to do everything right, to collect and preserve the evidence that would put the men who did this in prison. The Madison County sheriff didn't have his equipment or deputies to do the investigation. John knew Don Houghton was at the base, and in the trunk of his car was everything needed for collecting evidence: a 126 visual maker camera and film, evidence bags and tags, flagging tape, and all the supplies needed to properly measure, sketch, and photograph the evidence. He told Sheriff France he and his officers were prepared to help him, and offered him their services. Johnny turned his back on John and walked away mumbling. Dave Dunn heard him and stared, slack jawed, at the refusal of assistance.

John backed off, stung by France's attitude, but realized it was Johnny's jurisdiction. He'd do it his way. Onstad asked Campbell, Brisbin, and Pearson to take Jim Schwalbe to the base area with them.

"I need a camera!" France shouted.

"I have one in my pack," offered Jim. France took the camera, Jim left with the deputies, and Sheriff France walked around taking photographs until he finished the roll of film. He asked for more film to be brought in. There was no request for the special camera or other equipment.

Bob Morton and Bill Pronovost had suggested to Johnny that they do a search of the perimeter. He said okay, and the two men pointed out to him a number of things, among which was a dead squirrel and some white powder at the base of a tree. They didn't touch or collect any evidence.

Pronovost and Onstad discussed the candy bar that was melting in the sun, and John asked for a container and a cold pack to preserve it. The helicopter ferried in the requested items along with the film. Sheriff France reloaded Jim's camera, photographed Alan's body, and said he could be flown out. The officers were surprised because no sketches or measurements had been done.

After the helicopter removed the body, Sheriff France continued taking photos. Stooping beside the white powdery material, he frowned and asked Bob Morton, "Wha'da ya reckon this is?"

Bob stepped forward, careful not to disturb a tennis shoe print. He rubbed a few grains of the powder between his fingers, placed a pinch on his tongue and pursed his lips, tasting. He looked Johnny right in the eye, and suppressed a grin. "Flour!" he said with a deadpan expression. "Ah-h-h, by the way, that cartridge under the toe of your boot may be an important piece of evidence, Sheriff," he added.

France put the spent .222 cartridge in the pocket of his jacket.

"Don't forget the .22 cartridge," John said.

"Huh? Where?" Onstad pointed to the smaller shell casing, and France put it in his pocket with the first one.

Sheriff Onstad and his officers sat quietly on the perimeter of the crime scene and watched the Madison sheriff collect the evidence. There were a number of sticks, sharpened on one end, the lemonade container, Al's and Jim's backpacks, the cartridges, Al's binoculars, a gun, a radio, and some other things. Under a tree were a pair of Nike running shoes that belonged to Kari. Onstad's men gathered one piece of evidence—the candy bar. Normally, evidence cards would accompany each piece collected, stating what it was, where it was picked up, and by whom, so the property officer could correctly record and store the evidence.

Sheriff France completed his crime scene investigation without doing any measurements. He borrowed a medical bag, placed the evidence, all but the cartridges, in it, tied the sharpened sticks to the outside of the bag, and said he was ready. The officers left the area without ringing the crime scene with yellow tape. Madison's sheriff did ask that some trees be flagged on the way out so he could find his way back. They were a quiet group, each busy with his own thoughts, irritated by the flies and mosquitoes.

Ulreys Lake Trailhead

A hundred questions faced Pearson, Brisbin, Schwalbe, and Campbell when they returned to base. Waiting were Madison County deputies Merlin Ehlers and Jerry Mason. They had arrived hours earlier and were puzzled at the lack of communication from their superior. Both men were familiar with crime scene investigations and tracking, and Merlin had brought his dog Gypsy Lady. She had the best record in the state for tracking criminals.

Merlin, Jerry, Brad, and Bob Campbell joined forces and started their hunt. Brad and Merlin led with the dogs, trying to pick up a scent, while Bob and Jerry served as their backup. They picked up tracks leading into the Jack Creek drainage and scrambled through thick brush and downfall. It was rough walking and almost impossible to move quietly.

Leaving the bottom land, they tracked south toward Lone Mountain and passed behind it with Cedar Mountain to the southwest. The dogs were working well, taking turns so they wouldn't get exhausted. The heat, flies, and mosquitoes made it uncomfortable.

Bob Morton and Murray Duffy used the helicopter to do a two-hour search for the fugitives.

The officers with the dogs searched until late, returning to the base about 8 p.m. They were angry when they realized the helicopters and most of the crew were gone. "Damn it! We'd have been in a hell of a fix if we'd run into those guys and had a shoot-out ten miles behind the mountain. Great backup we had!" one of them grumbled.

Jerry and Merlin headed back to Ennis, and Brad and Bob joined Sheriff Onstad at the Gallatin County headquarters that had been established at the Big Sky Conoco station. They accompanied John to the Madison County headquarters, which had been set up in Jay Cosgrove's Big Sky home. Onstad took over the living room and with his deputies worked out roadblocks and patrols of backcountry roads and Highway 191.

John had a map of the Gallatin Forest spread out before him, and he and Brad discussed the lead the kidnappers had on them. Deputies from both counties were sealing off the trails and roads out of the area, but there was no way to completely surround the hundreds of miles of wilderness. Joel Beardsley had been interviewed, and the lodgepole with the inscription "Dan and Don Nichols Live In These Mts July 14 1984" had been sectioned and brought to the headquarters.

It was well after dark when Onstad fell into bed, still wondering about Kari. On impulse, he phoned the hospital and was told she was in the intensive care unit. Surgery hadn't been necessary.

Tuesday, July 17

Another hot day. Two teams of officers went out, one to check an old cabin in the Beehive area and the other to the crime scene. The deputies searching for the cabin were outraged when they realized a circling news helicopter pinpointed their position. They were sitting ducks.

At the crime scene, the second team was accompanied by a group of photographers, reporters, and television crews. Sheriff France had given them permission to go with him. He struck a deal with a photographer: he'd allow her in to the crime scene in return for copies of the photographs.

Onstad and some of his deputies wondered why the media was allowed in, because measurements still had not been taken and undisturbed prints had to be photographed. Their investigation equipment and personnel were there and available to the Madison County sheriff.

On Tuesday afternoon the two sheriffs met with Big Sky residents and reassured them that the killers would "probably" avoid populated areas. Sheriff France looked fresh in his pressed uniform, his .44 magnum pistol in its shoulder holster slung across his body, his hat pulled well over his forehead. Sheriff Onstad wore less conspicuous clothes—a camouflage shirt and faded Levi's that he and his men preferred when they participated in a search. His pistol was on his belt. He put his hat on the table.

About two hundred people jammed into the room. Sheriff Onstad said he assumed that the Nicholses were still in the area. He had sixteen men searching the roads and some of the timber, but deputies wouldn't be searching the dense, deep forest because of the possibility of being shot. The National Guard wouldn't be called in.

France said the Nicholses should be considered dangerous, that they seemed to be "military and jungle oriented." He concluded by saying that even though the two killers had not been sighted, he believed they were still on the mountain.

There were questions: Was a deputy really shot off his horse? Could the men have escaped before the law officers got on the scene or put up roadblocks? Was it true that the men could be hiding out in Ennis with friends? Why didn't Lone Mountain Ranch get help when they called for it? One older gentleman tried unsuccessfully to get Sheriff France to tell him what resources he had used in the search, the rescue, and how many men he had working on the case.

The television stations interviewed tourists in the Big Sky area. Some said they thought it was "exciting." One teenager said she hadn't looked forward to a Montana vacation, but the kidnapping and murder "sure spiced things up." She'd walk in the woods as soon as the deputies quit turning her back—she wasn't scared! A young man said he was sorry people got hurt, but it was "something exciting to write about."

Later that week Sheriff France took the collected evidence into Bozeman. Detective Ron Cutting greeted him at the Gallatin County sheriff's office. "What can I do for you, Johnny?"

"I gotta whole bag of goodies for you, Ron." He shoved the medical bag containing the crime scene evidence across the desk. "I reckon you'll want to put this stuff in your evidence room for me until we get those guys. You know how to catalog this stuff better than I do."

"Johnny, why aren't there any evidence tags attached to these items?"

"Like I said, you know more about this than I do. Besides, we were in kind of a hurry."

Ron meticulously labeled and recorded each piece of evidence. The tally complete, he and Johnny France signed the inventory slip. Later that day Bill Pronovost walked into the office.

"What did you make of the sharpened sticks, Ron? I figured they were used for cooking. How badly did France squash the .222 cartridge?"

Ron glared at his fellow officer. "What sticks? You know damned well there weren't any cartridges!"

Pronovost asked to see the evidence inventory and ran his finger slowly down the list. His eyebrows pulled together in a deep frown.

"Ron, I don't want to ruin your day, but all of the items brought out of the crime scene aren't here. Onstad and Morton said there were .22 and .222 cartridges, and there were sticks tied to the outside of the bag. If you don't believe me, check with the guys who were there."

Ron checked. He spent days asking officers where certain pieces of evidence were. Each officer gave him the same answer, "Ask the guy who picked it up!"

The crime scene investigation and missing evidence would create major difficulties for the state's prosecutors and would give Don Nichols's attorney grounds for asking for dismissal of charges against his client.

10

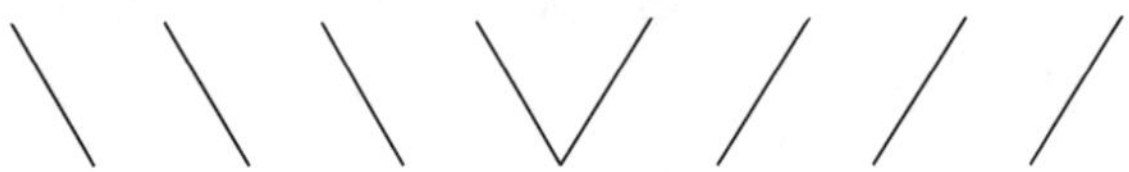

HOME

Monday, July 23

"Am I going to die, Mom?" Kari whispered. Her lips were gray and her skin glistened with perspiration. I clutched her cold hands, trying to warm them.

"No! No, Punkin! Everything will be all right."

"Kari, you're bleeding into the chest cavity again," the surgeon said after a series of x-rays had been taken.

"Does that mean another chest tube?"

"No. I'll insert a needle into the chest and draw out the blood with a syringe. The nurse will get you ready." We helped Kari out of bed and positioned her on a chair with the back of it to one side. A pillow was placed on a table in front of her and she was stretched forward with her head, shoulders and arms resting on it.

"Ready, Kari?" the doctor asked, sitting behind her. She nodded. I sat at her head whispering to her, encouraging her. He numbed the skin and inserted the needle into the muscles between the ribs and pushed deep into the chest cavity. She closed her eyes and moaned through clenched teeth. Blood filled the syringe. I gagged and looked away.

"We're almost done, Kari. There was more here than I expected." He had emptied the large syringe several times and was filling it again.

Bob and Paul arrived an hour later when the color had returned to her face. "Guess what, Pop? No more sloshing!"

Paul took me aside and said he had decided to go back to the ranch because Brian had told him it was difficult to get the ranch work done with both Kari and him gone. I didn't want him near that area until the killers were caught, but I didn't know how to tell him how I felt. I had heard him talking to Bob about obligations to the Schaaps, so I kept quiet. I would regret my silence.

Gallatin Sheriff's Office

Sheriff Onstad called Detective Bob Campbell into his office and told him that he wanted two law enforcement officers out on horseback looking for the Nicholses. As director of the Gallatin County Search and Rescue team, Bob was a logical choice to head up the operation. He chose as his partner Bob Morton, a law enforcement officer with the U.S. Forest Service. The two men had been friends for a long time, and they trusted each other to know what to do in a tight situation.

Bob Campbell was the taller of the two men. Even-tempered and gentle, his deep, drawling voice was usually quiet and calm, masking his quick mind and strength of will. Bob Morton was wiry of build and good humored. His snappy eyes were reminiscent of a little boy bent on playing pranks. Morton's knowledge of the mountain ranges in the area would be invaluable in the months to come.

Tuesday, July 24

"Wow!" Kari exclaimed, looking at the flowers and plants massed on every available surface of the bright, cheerful family room. "Where did these come from?" Bob handed her an envelope filled with cards.

The physician had dismissed Kari from the hospital that morning, saying he wanted to see her in his office on Thursday, her twenty-third birthday. Kari had wheeled down the hospital corridors, making detours to say goodbye to the little boy with the broken leg, and the nurses. We stopped outside and took some flowers to the elderly woman who lived across the street from the hospital. Kari had watched her from the window for the last four days and wanted to share some flowers with her.

"I'm exhausted," Kari sighed. "If the phone would stop ringing I could nap!" The ringing hadn't let up since we walked in the door. Many calls were from newspapers, writers, and TV stations wanting to interview Kari or tell her story. I unplugged the phone.

Bob and Paul had moved a bed into the family room for Kari, but the mound of soft pillows kept slipping and pressed on her back, so Bob dashed downtown and bought the recliner that would be her bed for weeks.

It was a long trip from the chair to the bathroom—twenty-five or thirty feet. "It's hard to believe we jogged up Sage Creek two weeks ago and today I can barely get to the bathroom," she panted. "Darn! This is going to ruin my training schedule! Guess I'll time my trips to the bathroom and try to make each one a few seconds faster. I can see the coach reading my training log: 'Shuffling sprints to the bathroom.' Should impress him, don't you think?"

"He'll be happy you're here to shuffle! Besides, a little humor in the log is just what he needs," Bob teased.

I slept on the sofa that night, thankful to be able to lie down again. Kari was restless and shifted constantly in the recliner.

Toward dawn she slept, and I tiptoed out to the deck to watch the sun come up over the Bridger Mountains. I thought of Al and remembered the beautiful words from a memorial at the castle in Edinburgh, Scotland:

> The Whole Earth Is The Tomb Of Heroic Men
> And Their Story Is Not Graven Only On Stone
> Over Their Clay
> But Abides Everywhere Without Visible Symbol
> Woven Into The Stuff Of Other Men's Lives.
>
> They Shall Grow Not Old As We That Are Left Grow Old.
> Age Shall Not Weary Them Nor The Years Condemn.
> At The Going Down Of The Sun And In The Morning
> We Will Remember Them.

The sun burst over the mountains, flooding the valley with light.

Wednesday, July 25

"Mom, I need a shower. Could you wash my hair and shave my legs? I look like a gorilla!" Kari begged. This was a challenge. She couldn't stand in the shower without getting dizzy, and I wasn't sure I could lift her out of the bathtub. I thought fast. Fifteen minutes later I was scurrying around collecting shampoo, towels, razor, soap, and a lawn chair lined with her foam pad. I arranged them outside, took the screen off the window, passed the garden hose through to the laundry room, and hooked it to the spigot in the sink. Dressed in panties and an old cotton T-shirt, Kari walked ten or fifteen steps and then sat in a chair I'd scoot under her. She'd rest for a few seconds and catch her breath. In this way we leap-frogged across the family room, down the hall, out the front door, and finally to the lawn chair.

I washed her hip-length hair and watched the sun glint and dance in the auburn mass. "Time for the legs," I said. "I haven't shaved someone else's legs since I was a student in the operating room doing pre-surgery preps on patients."

"How badly did you mutilate them?" Kari grinned.

"Ha! They didn't even have razor rash when I finished with them. This will be the best shave job you've ever had."

Our dog, Wister, barked and we jerked around looking down the driveway for an approaching car or a neighbor on foot. Nothing.

"This would be the time for the UPS truck or some dark, handsome stranger to drop in. With my sprinting ability, I'd be caught flat footed."

"You'd definitely give them an eyeful!" I said, wiggling my eyebrows. She flipped soap suds at me and laughed.

"Boy, I'm getting dizzy! Are you almost done? Why does the sun make my chest and side hurt?" she said frowning.

"Maybe the heat irritates the damaged nerves. We'll ask the surgeon tomorrow."

Washed and shaved, she leap-frogged back to the recliner, where she fell asleep. Her coppery hair framed her pale face and cascaded across her shoulders. I gulped coffee, memorizing every freckle on her face, the high, sculptured cheekbones, the thick-lashed, almond-shaped eyes, and the delicate ears pierced with tiny balls of gold. I realized again how lucky we were she was alive.

Big Sky

Douglas Goldstein arrived at the Buck's T-4 restaurant for a meeting with Sheriff Onstad and FBI agents. Everyone was there except the Madison County sheriff. Douglas told the men that his family wanted to hire a professional tracker and asked for their cooperation. They were agreeable. The tracker wanted his visit to be confidential and asked that no publicity be given.

Bozeman

Becky Lohmiller stayed with Kari while I ran to the store. The next day Kari would be twenty-three, and Paul was coming in from the ranch to share dinner with us. He had asked me to pick up a new running outfit for her. "There's a pretty melon-colored set at the Athlete's Foot. Don't get red! I don't want her to ever have red shorts again!" he had said to me.

That evening Kari complained of chest pain and numbness in her abdomen. Her temperature was 100.2°F. She curled up in the chair, and Bob read to her until she slept.

Thursday, July 26

The early morning breeze stirred the wind sock outside the family room window, and a meadowlark sang in the apple tree. It should have been a perfect day to celebrate Kari's birthday, but the drive to the physician's office was hot and uncomfortable. We walked toward the building and she leaned heavily on me, clutching for support, splinting her right side with her arm. "I'm getting dizzy!" We made it to the waiting room before her knees buckled. She sat gasping, avoiding the startled looks of the waiting patients.

After another series of x-rays, the physician told her she was bleeding into the chest cavity again. I wanted to yell, scream, and throw things! It wasn't fair!

"What happens now?" Kari asked, crushing my fingers in her clammy hand.

"I want to see you Monday. If the bleeding continues I'll have to drain it."

I took Kari to the car in a wheelchair. "You must be scared, Punkin," I said, tucking a strand of hair behind her ear. Sweat trickled down her neck.

"No, just hot, tired, and hurting. I want to get home to my chair where it's cool and comfortable. I hated having all those people stare."

Spanish Peaks

Early the morning of Kari's birthday, Bob Campbell, Bob Morton, and Dan Bauer, another Forest Service officer, unloaded their horses at the Spanish Creek ranger station. Dan was about Morton's size and was the youngest of the three. His blond hair and blue eyes were emphasized by his tan, and his grin made him look younger than he was. Campbell's friends teased him for bringing a "green-broke" horse named Red. Bob defended his horse, and his friends grinned, giving each other knowing looks.

The lawmen resembled horsemen out for a pleasure ride. They wore Levi's, western shirts, chaps, and cowboy hats—their badges were in inner pockets. They tacked wanted posters with the Nicholses' description at each trailhead and fork in the trail on their ride up to the Spanish Lakes. On their ride they angled northwest to Lake Solitude and continued toward another group of lakes. Along the way they interviewed backpackers, riders, and hikers, and encouraged them to leave the area to avoid the possibility of another murder or kidnapping.

It was hot and dusty as the men and animals wound their way into the high country. Sharp granite peaks, well above timberline, towered above them as they rode through the stunted mats of Krummholtz, whitebark pine, and huge boulders scarred with parallel grooves that marked the grinding passage of ancient glaciers.

At nine thousand feet they looked down on the crystal blue water of one of the Jerome Rock lakes. The horses, fly-bitten, hot, and thirsty, pulled impatiently at the reins and trotted toward the lake. The three men knelt beside the lake and splashed icy water on their faces, gasping and yelling at the shock. They studied the craggy rocks and scattered pines above the lake for the glint of the sun on a binocular lens and searched the muddy bank for footprints.

Heading back to the trailhead, Dan let his horse, Maynard, have his head. The part-Tennessee Walker pranced along the trail, neck and tail arched, looking like a snooty aristocrat.

"These flies are driving me nuts!" Morton complained. Campbell turned to look back and didn't see the pine branch that switched his horse on the shoulder. Red erupted like a volcano, bucking, jerking on the reins, and throwing his rump from side to side.

"Hang in there!" Dan shouted.

"Damn it!" Campbell exploded. He had been off balance when Red started bucking, and one last heave landed Bob on his tailbone in the middle of the trail.

Morton rushed in and grabbed Red's reins. "You okay?" he gasped. Campbell moaned and slowly got to his feet. A smile started in Morton's eyes, spread to his mouth, and laughter burst from him in a gusty howl. Campbell grinned sheepishly and remounted Red.

"I suppose you two will have this story spread all over the country by dark," he growled.

"Would you deny us the fun of telling the guys at the office about this?" Morton said between guffaws.

"It depends on how much embroidering you do!" Campbell's voice was accusing, but his eyes sparkled with humor.

The Birthday Party

I brought out the cake with twenty-three blazing candles. Kari looked wistfully at me and I realized what a dumb thing I had done. It took her three puffs and some help from Paul to extinguish the tiny flickering heads of fire.

Kari asked Paul to help her unwrap the gifts, one of his favorite pastimes. He cut the strings or ribbons for her and handed her the boxes. The package I had picked up at the hospital this morning rattled. She opened it and found a round metal container full of cookies from another biathlete. There were many lovely gifts from friends and family.

Paul's present was rewarded with a big grin. She held up the silky running shorts and tank top. "Are you giving me a hint, brother dear?"

"Well, you can't lounge around like Cleopatra forever. Besides, I'll need someone to run with me in a few weeks."

Johanna's present had been saved for last. "A teddy bear! And he's smiling!" She tucked the fuzzy toy into the recliner beside her.

Bob and I walked Paul to his car, and when I slipped my arm around his waist I realized he was losing weight. He said it was difficult to be at the ranch, but Jay, the crew, and the Schaaps were supportive and helpful.

Friday, July 27

Kari wandered from chair to sofa to bench and back again—her new strengthening program, she said. Later, I settled her on the deck in a padded chair, and she looked content as the wind sock curled its colorful tentacles around her shoulders, the cat curled up in her lap, and the dog lay across her feet. A phoebe bird called down by the barn as I dashed to answer the phone. It was Sarah Hollier asking if Kari could come to her wedding on Saturday. There were many friends who wanted to see Kari, Sarah said, to know she was going to be all right. I gave Kari the message.

"I'd love to go, but I think the ride in the car would be too much. Let's see how I feel in the morning. Right now, I'd like to try walking as far as the aspen trees."

By the time she reached the bottom step of the deck she was panting and wobbly. "Rats! My muscles are screaming for exercise but the rest of me won't cooperate!"

That evening her temperature was 101°F.

Saturday, July 28

Sarah and Cairn were married in the chapel at Big Sky, and the reception was well underway when a friend hurried toward me, eyes wide with surprise. "She's coming, Jan. Look!" Through the large picture windows we saw Kari and Bob silhouetted against Lone Mountain. A whisper rippled through the guests. Kari was leaning on Bob, but she pulled herself up and smiled when Sarah and the Hollier family greeted them at the door. Surrounded by friends, they slowly made their way to our table, where they stayed for thirty minutes then quietly left. Bob had his arm around her and her arm circled his waist, clutching his shirt for support.

When I got home Kari was pale and nauseated and her temperature was 100.6°F.

Monday, July 30

The appointment with the physician didn't go well—Kari was still bleeding. His attempts at draining away the blood were painful and unsuccessful. He decided to see her the following Monday and if she were still bleeding or had not improved, he would set up an appointment with a chest surgeon in another city.

Big Sky

Driving toward Big Sky, Deputy Brad Brisbin received a radio transmission from Wally Schumacher, resident deputy at Big Sky.

"I got a call about two men in camouflage clothes walking around the Buck's T-4 motel and restaurant asking for information about the Nicholses. I ran a check on their vehicle—it's a rented car from Salt Lake City. If necessary I'll check on the rentee's name, but I'd like to know what's going on at Buck's first. Where you at, Brad?"

"A few miles south of Buck's. I'll meet you in the parking lot."

Brad and Wally questioned the motel clerk, who gave the deputies the room number where the men were staying. Walking softly down the corridor, Wally asked, "Do you suppose these guys are mercenaries, survivalists, or just nuts out to make a name for themselves?"

"We'll soon find out," Brad said, knocking on the door. A man in camouflage clothing opened it. Behind him was another man similarly dressed and a third man talking on the phone. The man who opened the door eyed the uniforms, stepped back, and said, "Come in. What can I do for you?"

Entering cautiously, ready for trouble, Brad said, "Seems like we need to talk with you fellows about why you're here." The man on the phone slammed down the receiver and spat questions at Brad and Wally.

"I think you're a little mixed up here, mister!" Brad interrupted. "I'm the one asking questions!" After a rapid interrogation he discerned that the man on the phone was the tracker hired by the Goldsteins; the others were his assistants. They had insisted on secrecy, and here they were setting the already nervous community into a spin.

Brad introduced himself and Wally and said, "Sheriff Onstad's on his way here. He asked me to accompany you on your tracking mission today." Arrangements were made to leave as soon as John arrived, and Brad and Wally walked back to their patrol cars.

"Good luck, Brad!" Wally chuckled at the frustrated expression on Brad's face, and pulled away as Sheriff Onstad arrived.

Brad Brisbin, John Onstad, Jay Cosgrove, Johnny France, the tracker, and his assistants gathered at the kidnapping scene above Ulreys Lake. Examining the crime scene, the tracker noted that most of the Nicholses' footprints had been destroyed. He studied a set of boot and tennis shoe prints beside the boggy area at the camp and began to take a series of measurements. "Did the investigating officer get photographs of the prints the day the crime was committed?" he asked. No one answered.

The tracker led the group to a draw close to the Jack Creek logging road. From there he began climbing, stopping on a ridge not more than a mile or so from where Kari had been found.

"See, here's where they sat resting," the tracker said. "These indentations were made by their buttocks and those four small areas are their heel marks. They sat here, leaning back, watching the helicopters and all of you running about trying to find that girl and Mr. Goldstein."

"Those bastards! They knew we couldn't find Kari and they just sat here!" Brad said, grinding his teeth.

They agreed to take the tracker into the Madison high country to an area known as Cowboy Heaven. The Nicholses had frequented that area and had usually planted their gardens in that section of the mountains. The searchers planned to leave at dawn the next day.

Tuesday, July 31

Kari's strength and good humor disappeared. She slipped in and out of sleep, moaning, jerking awake, frightened, sweating. Fifteen days ago we had found her in the mountains, and it was beginning to look as if we were back to square one.

While Kari struggled with pain, the tracker was taken into the high plateau country of the Spanish Peaks known as Cowboy Heaven. A rancher had called the FBI to report that his cowboys discovered missing supplies at his mountain cowcamp. Knowing that the Nicholses frequented the area, Dave Wing, law enforcement officer for the National Forest Service, insisted on an investigation. Brad Brisbin, Gary Lincoln and Bernie Hubley of the FBI, Jay Cosgrove, and Sheriff France made up the rest of the search party.

The tracker walked slowly up the dusty road, head down, looking for prints. The rest of the posse were strung out, providing a protective wedge. He found two prints similar to those at the crime scene and moved out, making a beeline for the cowcamp.

A spacious walled canvas tent stood beside a fenced horse pasture. The tracker pointed and said the prints crossed the meadow and went into the cowcamp. Gary glassed with his binoculars and the others moved quietly to surround the camp. Sheriff France stood open-mouthed when the tracker dashed across the pasture to the tent, threw open the flap, and dropped to his knees to study the dirt floor. A tennis shoe track in the tent belonged to "the boy," he announced.

Excitedly, the tracker followed the prints to a spring used as a water supply for the camp, through the grass-sage meadows strewn with wildflowers, and up the steep slopes to the west, where he discovered a trail. He walked around the area, studied the prints, and said this was the Nicholses' "back door" in and out of the area. Dave Wing nodded in agreement, aware that the killers had used the steep, rocky terrain around Barn and Fall creeks for years.

"They're close," breathed the tracker. "See, the grass is still bent. They aren't far ahead of us. If we hurry we'll have them before dark!"

The sheriff looked uneasy. He frowned and looked at his watch. It was 4 p.m. and would be dark by 10 o'clock; six hours might not be enough. He contacted Bob Campbell over in the Spanish Peaks, but Bob and his men couldn't ride the seventeen miles over to Cowboy Heaven because of the steep, rocky terrain.

"Boys, I'm afraid we're gonna have to call it a day," said the sheriff. The tracker objected.

"I'm calling it a day!" France repeated, heading down the slope.

Discouraged, the searchers began the hot walk back to their cars. The tracker and his assistants were silent, remaining apart from the posse. Dave and Brad walked together.

"You know, Brad," Dave began, "Don Nichols and I go way back. He's been living in these mountains off and on for years, and has caused a few problems for me. His poaching, running off recreational hikers or hunters if they got too close to his camp, and keeping Dan out of school created a lot of footwork for me. I think he was responsible for burning down the Cowboy Heaven cabin and the Spanish Creek ranger station, but I couldn't get close enough to him to ask!"

"We could have used your knowledge of the Nicholses those first few days we were looking for them," Brad said. "Where were you?"

"I was fighting a fire on the Rocky Boy Indian Reservation, bad one. The minute I saw the headlines in the papers, I thought to myself, Well, it looks like the Nicholses really got themselves into a mess this time! There was never any doubt in my mind who had kidnapped Kari. That was their style—if you want it, take it."

Wednesday, August 1

I sat on the deck watching the sunrise. Screeching hawks spiraled on the updrafts. Kari refused her breakfast when I returned to the family room. "I'd like some tea if you'll have a cup with me," she smiled. "Do you know anything about the surgeon the doctor wants to send me to? I'd like to know if he works with athletes—I think that's important." The phone rang. It was a man from Vermont who knew Kari through the Biathlon Association. He expressed his feelings about the incident and asked if there was anything he could do. I asked if he would do some research and find out who the top-notch chest surgeons in our region were. He said he'd talk to some friends at Walter Reed Hospital and get back to me in an hour or so.

He phoned later with the name of a surgeon in Denver who was awaiting my call. I phoned and spent the next ten minutes answering questions and reading him Kari's temperature chart for the last eight days. He recommended two surgeons, one in Denver and one in Salt Lake.

"They're both excellent physicians, Mrs. Swenson, but you may want to ask them for the name of someone in Seattle since your older daughter lives there. Could be I'm out of line professionally, since your attending physician didn't consult me, but I strongly urge you to get Kari to a large medical center as soon as possible. Good luck." My throat constricted with panic.

Bob phoned the head of the W.A.M.I. medical program at our university and got the name of a surgeon at the University of Washington Medical School.

During the next three hours I spoke with four chest surgeons who all told me the same thing: "Get her out. I don't care where you take her, just get her to a large clinic as soon as you can get a flight."

I asked why, hoping they wouldn't be able to give me a good reason for moving her. "You're a nurse, right? I shouldn't have to tell you about the risks of empyema in a case like this, should I?" the physician answered. The word threw me into a frenzy of organizing for a fast move.

Kari decided to go to Seattle so she could be close to Johanna. The physicians offered to send the Harborview emergency plane to transport her, but I assured them we could make it on a commercial flight.

"I'm glad we're going. The sloshing sensation is back and my side hurts." She hesitated. "Mom, I'm really scared." I hugged her. I was scared, too.

Paul drove in from the ranch. He and Bob would leave Bozeman very early in the morning, drive to Seattle, pick Kari and me up at the airport, and take us to the hospital. Our friend Denny Lee loaned them his new air-conditioned car because ours needed a new clutch. Paul cornered us before he went to bed and asked, "Is Kari going to die?"

"No, no. We just need a second opinion." Bob's voice lacked conviction and Paul's eyes reflected the fear we all felt.

11

TRAUMA HOSPITAL, SEATTLE, WASHINGTON

Thursday, August 2

Bob and Paul were waiting for us at the airport and hustled us off to the Harborview Hospital. A physician hurried out of the emergency room before we could help Kari from the car and asked, "Are you Kari Swenson?"

"Yes," she answered, startled.

He whisked her off in a wheelchair and left me standing in the warm evening breeze with my mouth open. I scrambled to gather the x-rays and surgeons' notes and found Kari in an examining room where a resident was explaining that she would have more x-rays taken as soon as her blood was drawn. A handsome young resident stepped in, introduced himself, and in a swish of white coattails he and his colleague were gone.

"Gosh, they're sure young!" Kari exclaimed. "If they tell me to take my clothes off, I won't! They aren't much older than me."

I was still laughing when the doctors returned with a wheelchair, dashed her off to x-ray, and directed me to a waiting room, where I found Johanna, her boyfriend, Paul, and Bob. An hour later the handsome resident, pushing Kari on a stretcher, took us to the seventh floor and turned Kari over to the nursing staff.

"Wow! How do you rate, Kari?" teased the nurses.

"What do you mean?"

"Residents never push a stretcher, and rarely, if ever, bring a patient to the floor to be admitted! You must have turned on the old charm, huh?" The nurse wiggled her eyebrows in a parody of Groucho Marx.

Kari blushed and smiled.

"See! There it is! You can't smile at our residents like that!" the nurse grinned. Kari's face turned a deep purple.

"Would it be possible for my mom to stay in the room with me? I still have trouble with nightmares and I don't want to be alone," Kari asked, her shyness relieved by the nurses' humor.

"We usually don't allow it," hesitated the nurse, "but I don't think anyone will mind in this case. Unfortunately, we can't bring in another bed," she apologized, frowning at the only chair.

"The chair is fine," I assured her. "I'm a pro at chair sleeping."

Drooping with fatigue, Paul hugged Kari and told her to stop smiling at the doctors. I walked into the corridor with Johanna, and she burst into tears.

"I'm so scared! Is she going to be all right? Are they going to operate? Will you phone me at work? She looks so skinny!" She sobbed in Bob's arms. I watched them walk down the hushed corridor, hand in hand, heads bowed, shoulders drooping. Johanna looked back and blew a kiss.

"Kari, we can't see anything wrong in the x-rays we took an hour ago," said one of the two residents standing at her bedside.

"Great! Then I can go home in the morning, right?" She smiled.

"It's not that easy," he grinned back at her. "Dr. Maier will want to do a work-up in the morning, then we'll decide about letting you go home."

"Maybe you two could explain something to me as long as you're here. Why do I have the sloshing sound in my chest?"

"Sloshing sound?" Their eyebrows arched.

"Yes. When I turn over or sit up, I can hear and feel it."

They placed their stethoscopes on her chest and back. "Okay, Kari, make it slosh."

She turned onto her side and back again. "See?"

One of them cleared his throat uncomfortably and said, "Dr. Maier will be in early tomorrow and we'll let him talk to you. Is there anything we can do to make you comfortable?"

"No, thank you. I'm sorry I caused so much fuss for all of you and an unnecessary trip for my parents."

"Hey! I think you're jumping the gun on the guilt trip," said the young physician. "Rest. Tomorrow will be a tough day for you."

Kari retrieved the teddy bear she had hidden in her duffel bag, tucked it under her chin, took my hand, and slept.

Friday, August 3

Dr. Ronald V. Maier, the chest surgeon who would oversee Kari's care, arrived early and explained that he'd be in surgery all morning and that he wanted some tests done while he was busy. First, she would go to the ultrasound lab where they would check out her heart, lungs, and abdomen, and then on to the pulmonary function lab for lung-capacity tests.

"The pulmonary tests will be difficult for you," he warned, "but do the best you can. Our team will be going over the CAT scans you brought and we should have some news after we compare them with our test results."

Left alone, I paced the room, upset with myself because I hadn't insisted on going with Kari to the ultrasound lab. I hated not knowing what was happening to her. I looked out the window. Seven stories below, a medical helicopter had landed and was surrounded by an emergency room crew from the hospital. They resembled ants swarming around a dead beetle as they removed two stretchers, placed them in an ambulance, and disappeared into the bowels of the building.

The family arrived and brought me a sweet roll and a bottle of juice. "Hey! This is good," I said. "Are you sure this is juice? It says Orange Wine Cooler!"

Bob read the label and laughed. "No wonder the nurse was staring at you. You just had wine for breakfast."

"The people were great!" Kari bubbled later, tired but excited. "They explained what they were doing and let me watch the screen to see what they were talking about. You know that they have a big screen that looks like a TV, right?" I nodded. "They'd say, 'Wow, look at this! Wow, look at that.' They'd point to something on the screen and explain what part of my anatomy it was. It was really interesting until the 'Wows' turned to 'h-m-m-ms' and 'what's this?' They showed me a large shadow and said it was blood between the lung and chest wall. I guess that explains the sloshing," she said, watching my face carefully.

Oh, damn! I thought, and poured her tea to hide my expression. Her friend John Yurich arrived and visited until they were interrupted by a resident who whisked her off to the pulmonary function lab.

I went with her this time. We were greeted by two pleasant young women who said they were the technologists who would be doing the tests. "This is our baby," said one tech, gesturing behind her. A huge metal machine dominated the room. Plastic tubes tipped with rubber mouthpieces snaked out of it and hung as flaccid and disjointed as the arms of a puppet. An elaborate computer stood to one side of the machine. In one corner of the room was an exercise bike dangling with electrodes, and the walls were covered with posters of the body's organs. A counter along one wall held microscopes, glass slides, syringes, and bottles of different colored fluids that caught and reflected the sun's rays from the large windows. The technologists were cheerful and tried to put Kari at ease by explaining how the equipment worked and talking about Montana. They took blood from her wrist for arterial blood gases, pushed her chair close to the machine, handed her one of the mouthpieces, and the tests began.

Over and over Kari took a deep breath and exhaled as forcefully as she could into a tube. The results were seen and recorded on the computer. I watched nervously as she became dizzy and disoriented from the lack of oxygen and the pain. Encouraging and kind, the technologists were as relieved as Kari was when the hour-long tests were over.

Back in her room Kari collapsed. "Just let me sleep. I'm so lightheaded the room is spinning!" she gasped.

While she slept I walked the corridors with a medical school friend who worked at the hospital.

"Mom! Where have you been?" Kari cried, when I went back to her room. "The doctors were here, but I was so dizzy I didn't understand what they were talking about. One of them said my pulmonary capacity is lousy! They have something else planned for me—I don't know what."

We were interrupted by two residents who looked uncomfortable. "Kari, we have to apologize. The x-rays didn't show the bleeding in your chest, but the ultrasound did. Dr. Maier wants us to try draining it by doing a thoracentesis. I'm sorry."

She groaned, knowing what was ahead, then grinned. "If we hurry maybe I'll get to eat a hot dinner!"

She sat on the edge of the exam table and leaned forward, resting her head on my shoulder and exposing her back. She clasped her trembling hands behind me and burrowed her face into my neck.

"It's very important that you don't move, Kari," explained the physician. "We'll use the ultrasound screen to guide us, but we may have to probe around inside your chest before we find the exact location of the pocket of blood. It's going to hurt."

I gauged her pain by her biceps contractions, the sweat that soaked into my blouse, and the shivers that ran through her body. I whispered encouragement into her damp hair. They inserted the needle several times at different locations and angles but were unsuccessful at draining the blood from her chest. Suddenly Kari moaned and sagged against me in a faint. We lowered her onto the table and one of the technologists tenderly wiped her face with a damp cloth. He handed me a tissue. I hadn't realized I was crying.

She opened her eyes and he smiled at her, "It's all over, Kari. You were great."

"Did they get it all?" she whispered, back in bed, tucking the bear under her chin.

"No, Punkin, but they won't try again."

The blood had been there so long that it was too viscous to be withdrawn, and the clot was walled off into small compartments by fibrous tissue. The small amount of blood the doctors did get would be cultured for bacteria, and the results would be ready on Monday. Dr. Maier wanted to consult other physicians about the CAT scans and ask their opinions about the options open to Kari. He planned to monitor her temperature but gave her permission to leave the hospital each day at noon as long as she was back by seven o'clock in the evening. That cheered her. She hadn't looked forward to lying in the hospital waiting for Monday to come.

That evening we all watched the pre-Olympic programs on TV in Kari's room, and John Yurich brought her a poster of Hawaii to brighten her wall. Later, snuggling with her bear, she said, "I'm glad you brought me here. We'll know exactly what I can and can't do by the time I go home." She was silent for a few minutes. "What will they do about that blood? I heard the physicians in the lab say it was about 300 ccs. That's a lot! Will they operate to get it out?"

"Honey, wait until Dr. Maier tells us what they recommend. It would be a mistake for us to try to guess. Why not relax this weekend and enjoy being with Johanna and Paul?"

"You did a nice job of evading the question!" she laughed. "Is that something they teach doctors and nurses, or is it a prerequisite to getting into school?"

"No," I teased, "that's the jargon mothers learn to use when we don't know the answers to our children's questions."

August 4 & 5

We left the hospital each day just before noon and spent the afternoons with family and friends. After dinner we returned Kari to the comfort of the hospital bed and watched the Olympics with her.

Sunday night she said, "What will I do if they say I need surgery? Darn those creeps! Why? Why did they do this? I told them I didn't want to go with them! Why did they insist on keeping me? If they had let me go Al would be alive and I wouldn't be in this mess! I wish I could forget what happened, but so many things trigger bad memories. When an ant crawled across my foot today, I almost screamed! How long will I be like this?" She twisted the sheet in agitation and her eyes demanded an answer.

"I don't know," I answered inadequately. "I'd like you to see a psychologist if we stay longer. Dr. Maier suggested a woman he thinks you'd like. I can't help you yet because of my own anger, but there are professional people who can. Think about it, sweetie."

She finally slept. I stood at the window watching the rain drops splatter against the glass like smog-stained tears trickling their way to the sill. I closed my eyes and saw the image of Kari lying alone, bleeding, calling for help. Maybe if those men had tried to help her and Al, if they had directed searchers in to help them, I could forgive them. But the thought of them flopping her from the sleeping bag and leaving her alone to die was unbearable. I would never forgive them.

Spanish Peaks

While we were in Seattle the search continued. One morning Bob Campbell and Bob Morton left the trailhead at dawn. It was a dreary day, and the fine drizzle dripped from their ponchos. The trees drooped. Thick fog settled over the mountain peaks and closed around them as they neared Mirror Lake. Morton was uneasy and kept looking over his shoulder or stopping to listen to the sounds from the mist-shrouded forest. Campbell spoke softly to his horse, stopped in the middle of the trail, and dismounted.

"What the hell ya doing?" hissed Morton.

"The hair's standing up on the back of my neck. I think someone's out there watching us," Campbell murmured. "Thought I'd walk awhile, rest the horse, and make a smaller target just in case the Nicholses step out of the fog and take a potshot at us."

"Sometimes you're real smart! Wish this fog would burn off!" Morton dismounted and walked with his friend.

They rode and walked, believing that someone was just out of sight, listening to them, hidden in the fog. They circled the lake, crossed the meadows, and found a fireplace constructed in the three-stone design favored by the fugitives.

"Bob, those guys have used this place recently," Campbell said, his voice strained. "Look at the way the grass is smashed down."

Morton glanced over his shoulder. "Damn fog!" His voice rippled out into the gray mist.

The riders left the high country and headed down the trail. The fog swirled behind them, rolling down the side of the mountain as if pursuing the pursuers. High above them an old man and a younger one noted the passing of the officers. "It was them same two. One on the red horse and the other on the white mare."

Monday, August 6

Dr. Maier, two other physicians, and several residents gathered in Kari's room to tell her that they did not recommend surgery to remove the clot. "Surgery would cause more damage to the chest musculature and nerves, which means it would take you longer to get back to training. Barring complications, the clot should dissolve in three or four months," Dr. Maier said. "The cultures were negative, but you must be aware that there's still the possibility of infection until that clot dissolves. You're lucky, Kari. Everything that could have gone wrong didn't. We'd like to see you again in six months to repeat the pulmonary function tests and see what kind of progress you're making. Any questions?"

"How active can I be? What type of training can I do?"

"Start slowly; let pain be your guide."

"It won't make me bleed again if I train? I can do anything I want to?"

"You shouldn't bleed anymore, and yes, you can do anything."

I laughed and asked if he had any idea what he had given her permission to do.

"Describe a typical training day for me, Kari," he said. When she finished he looked a little surprised and advised her to start as if she had never done a workout in her life. I saw the glint in her eyes and knew I'd have my hands full.

Kari said her goodbyes to the nurses and John, and we went to see Johanna. As we drove away, I looked back and Joey waved, tears streamed down her cheeks. She looked so little, forlorn, and vulnerable that my heart ached. She has a deep need for family and closeness, and this tragedy with Kari had destroyed her peace of mind. Thank heavens for her friends and Aunt Agnes. They would take care of her for us.

The drive over the Cascade Mountains to Coeur d'Alene was horrible for Kari even with the air conditioning. We stayed at a motel on the edge of the lake and walked barefoot along the shore, amused by the gulls who flocked around us until they realized we had nothing for them to eat. The waves lapped at our ankles. I dropped behind Kari and Paul and studied their footprints in the sand. Paul's arch is low, hers high; he toes out, she in; his foot is wide, hers narrow. Foam bubbled around their toes and obliterated the prints. For a split second I experienced horrifying panic—I felt that if the water washed away their prints they would die. I dashed forward, grabbed them, and pulled them back from the waves.

Tuesday, August 7

Home at last, Kari wanted to sleep in her own bed. We arranged the special foam mattress and a pile of pillows on her bed, hoping to make her comfortable, and pulled a mattress onto the floor for me. She had terrible nightmares, and we were up most of the night. Toward dawn she slept, and I sought out my favorite chair on the deck.

The eastern sky was streaked with rose and gold, the meadowlarks sang in the hayfield, and a light breeze rustled the shiny leaves of the aspen trees. I opened my notebook to finish a poem I had started, and a snapshot of Kari and Paul at their birthday-graduation party fluttered to the deck. Their smiling faces were spotlighted by the sun of the new day, and sadly I realized that our lives were changed forever.

Janet and Bob Swenson. *Bruce Pitcher, Bozeman, MT*

Johanna, Paul, and Kari Swenson.
Bruce Pitcher, Bozeman, MT

Paul, Kari, and Stu Jennings at a wedding reception, August 1988.
Janet Swenson

Bob and Kari in Washington, D.C., where Kari was presented The President's Healthy American Fitness Leader Award, September 1985.
Dean Ebel, Ebel Photography

Bob and Vivian Schaap at the Lone Mountain Guest Ranch. Bob's attempt to obtain assistance from the Madison County sheriff's department was thwarted when he was told, "We don't do night searches." *Janet Swenson*

Alan Goldstein at the Lone Mountain Ranch, 1984. "So he did it; he laid his life on the line, and he lost it because the instincts of this defendant were to kill and Alan Goldstein's weren't." *Linda Best, Bozeman Daily Chronicle*

Jack Drumheller, Bob Swenson, and George Tuthill. Jack and George shared in the frantic search for Kari. *Janet Swenson*

Left to right: Brad Brisbin and his dog Bear. Bob Pearson with his dog Skip. Brad and Bob went out on the early morning search for Kari. Brad and Bob Schaap found a bloody bone that was thought to be part of Kari's arm. *Janet Swenson*

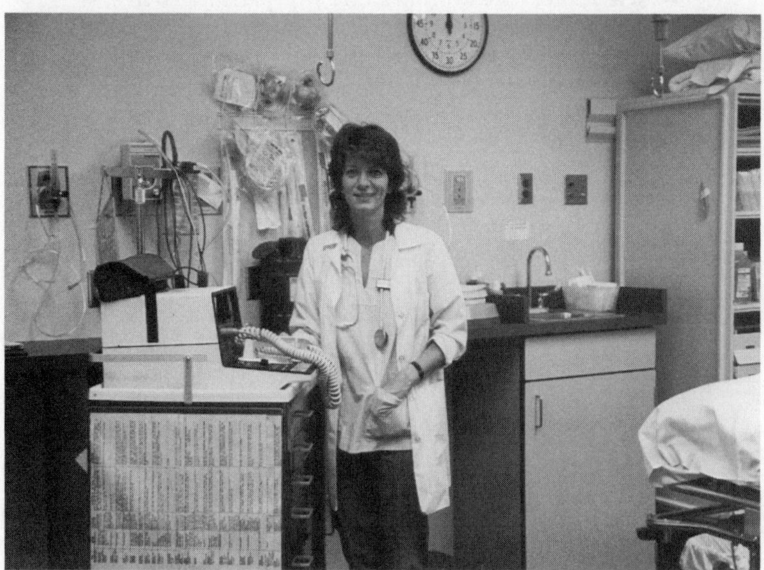

Jennie Nemec, trauma nurse at the Bozeman Deaconess Hospital's emergency room. *Janet Swenson*

Helicopter pilot Murray Duffy who participated in the search for Kari, and delivered Sheriff Onstad and Bob Campbell to the site where the Nicholses were captured. *Paul Swenson*

Sheriff John Onstad of Gallatin County conducted the search for Kari after she and Alan Goldstein had been shot.
Linda Best, Bozeman Daily Chronicle

Lower Ulreys Lake. *Janet Swenson*

Left to right: Bill Pronovost, Don Houghton, and Dave Dunn. The Gallatin County law enforcement officers searched for Kari and assisted in her evacuation from the crime scene. *Janet Swenson*

Kari removing a horse's halter during a hailstorm. Wrangling for the 320 Ranch, 1980.
Linda Best, Bozeman Daily Chronicle

Bob Campbell riding Red, and Bob Morton on Sally, searched the high country in Gallatin and Madison counties for five months hoping to apprehend the Nicholses. They were present and helped organize the capture of the fugitives in December of 1984.
Janet Swenson

Lone Mountain is reflected in Ulreys Lake, the scene of the kidnapping.
Janet Swenson

"We walked into a dense, shadowy forest where the trails were muddy, and each depression was filled with mosquito-breeding, slimy water."
Janet Swenson

Slash pile in the Jack Creek area. Janet looked under each one in her search for Kari. *Janet Swenson*

The old tree fort behind the Swenson's Gallatin Canyon cabin. *Janet Swenson*

Paul, Kari, and Bob. Two days after leaving the hospital, Kari celebrated her twenty-third birthday. Six days later she was admitted to the Harbor View Trauma Hospital in Seattle. *Janet Swenson*

September 22, 1984. Kari and Wister pose after a training run up Wapiti Creek. For the first time since her injury, Kari was able to jog two miles without stopping to rest. *Janet Swenson*

The Labor Day dinner party at the cabin. Left to right: Paul Swenson, Stu Jennings, Kari, Dave Hollier, and Carol Hollier. *Janet Swenson*

Jonathan Jennings and Hunter. Jonathan gave unselfishly of his time, energy, and feelings to help Kari recover. *Janet Swenson*

Bob Naert. Bob's humor and kindness prompted Kari to say, "He makes me feel good about people again." *Janet Swenson*

Kari Anne Swenson, December 1985.—National award winning photograph, **U.S. Biathlon Gold Medalist**. *Bruce Pitcher, Bozeman, MT*

Kari on the shooting range. West Yellowstone biathlon race. *Janet Swenson*

U.S. Women Biathletes Pam Nordheim and Kari Swenson. *Janet Swenson*

Left to right standing: Kari, Pam Nordheim, Peter Hoag, Julie Newnam. Front: Pam Weiss. Peter, Pam, and Kari were the occupants of the "Convalescent Condo" in West Yellowstone at the winter training camp, 1984. *Janet Swenson*

Christmas Eve 1984. Kari, Paul, and Wister. The joy of the holiday was marred by the necessity of giving depositions to the prosecuting and defense attorneys. *Janet Swenson*

Book Two

REHABLILITATION, THE CAPTURE, AND THE GOLD MEDAL

12

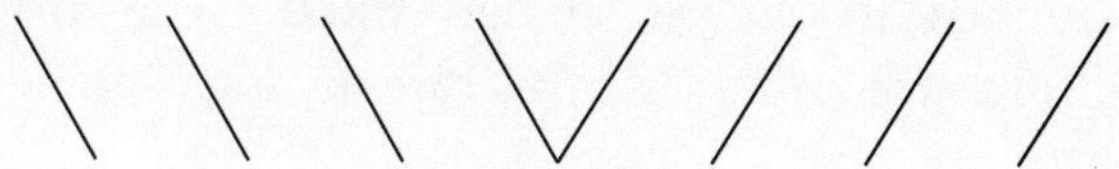

RELEARNING

> "I can't quit skiing. If I do the kidnappers have won, and for the rest of my life I'll be a victim. I won't let them do that to me."
>
> — Kari Swenson

Wednesday, August 8

"Let's go for a walk, Mom. My training log has a lot of empty pages that need filling," Kari said. "Look at this." Wearing the running suit Paul had given her, she did a self-conscious pirouette for me. "This should put me in the right frame of mind."

"How far do you want to go?" I asked, tying her shoe laces for her and smiling at her happy face.

"Oh, down the driveway, I guess. There's no reason to drive to a trail until I can walk farther."

We ambled along and stopped to watch a young meadowlark sitting on the fence. He muffed the last four notes of his song, puffed out his spotted breast, and tried again and again.

"Persistent little cuss, isn't he?" Kari said.

"Yup. Reminds me of a redhead I know," I teased.

She laughed and looked at her watch. "The tortoise and I have something in common. At this rate my log is going to remain empty."

"Ah, but remember who won that race!"

That afternoon's activities set a pattern for many to come. Becky came to visit every day, and Stu stopped by when he was in town. Kari napped off and on during the hot hours of the day, read her mail, wrote letters, read books, and walked around the room or sat on the deck. I was still opening her mail for her and was stunned by the malicious letters from people who had to be mentally ill. Those letters were greatly outnumbered by the ones of support and encouragement from strangers and friends. Books of poetry, philosophy, religion, humor, hypnosis, and even a coloring book came from people all over the world.

A floral arrangement arrived with a card signed Jonathan and Bill. "Jonathan has his own construction company," Kari explained. "He and Bill are building the new log cabin at the ranch."

Jonathan's note said that his coffee consumption had dropped considerably since she wasn't working in the kitchen at the ranch, that he was a good listener if she needed to talk, and if she wanted to get out for a ride he would be happy to take her. Kari chuckled and said, "The kitchen crew gave him a hard time, and Al teased me unmercifully about him." She smiled at the memory. "Jon asked me to go bike riding, but I was supposed to go condo hunting with Pam. Then all this happened." She shrugged her shoulders and a shadow of regret flashed in her eyes.

"What was Al like, Punkin, can you talk about him yet?"

She swallowed hard a few times, picked at the hem on her shirt, and looked up with wet eyes. "He—he was a tease just like Paul and Stu. He had a magnificent mustache, a wide smile, and the most impish eyes you've ever seen! He was handsome, and sweet, and . . ." Her voice broke. She cleared her throat.

"Everyone at the ranch liked him, probably because he took an interest in each person, and he was always cheerful. He had an infectious laugh, and once he got started you couldn't help but join in. Jay told me Al was a blacksmith, that he could shoe horses and was interested in doing some ornamental ironwork." She drank some iced tea and wiped her eyes with her shirttail before I could hand her a tissue.

"I never saw any of his work." Her eyes had a faraway look. "He and Diane were so much in love, it was fun to watch them. That's probably why he kept teasing me about Jon and Jon about me—he couldn't stand to see anyone alone when he was so happy. It's hard to imagine Al in a three-piece suit. Levi's, cowboy shirts, and a western hat fit his personality perfectly, but I guess he was a very successful business man before he moved to Big Sky."

"Vivian told me he helped run the family clothing store with his father and brother in Flint, Michigan. How in the world did he get out here?"

"I guess he came out on ski vacation with a friend, fell in love with our mountains, and decided to move here. Last winter he drove the horse teams for the ranch, and the wranglers say he's as good with horses as he is with people." She fell silent when she realized she had used the present tense. Wister laid her head in Kari's lap and nosed her fingers, begging to have her ears scratched. Absently, Kari stroked the silky head. "He was crazy about wildflowers—the meadows were beautiful this year—I remember him describing a field of glacier lilies to some guests—I wonder if he liked forget-me-nots?" She was far away, seeing the meadows, listening to Al's laughter. She heaved a sigh. "When I was little the books I read said the good guys always won. They lied. The bad guys won this time."

Thursday, August 9

It was hot during our late-morning walk and Kari complained that the sun shining on her chest and abdomen caused more pain. We decided to exercise early in the morning when it was cooler.

Later, elbow deep in bread dough, I watched her reading her mail. "No!" she screamed and struggled out of the recliner.

"Hush, honey. What scared you? What happened?" I asked, holding her tightly.

"That note," she gasped and pointed at a card on the floor.

"I don't understand," I said, reading it. "There's nothing here to upset you."

"Look at the picture on the front of the card!" It was a muted blue and white painting of a unicorn. "I hope I never see another unicorn!" She wiggled out of my arms. "You'd better wipe the flour and dough off me before I go back to the recliner. That was a pretty sticky hug." She grinned and the crisis was over for the moment, but it gave me the opening I needed to bring up the subject of counseling.

"Give me a little more time," she said. "It'll take a lot out of me to talk about those days and I don't think I can deal with it yet."

"Tell me when the time's right. Meanwhile, I'll keep the unicorns out of the house!" I teased, and brushed flour from her hair and shirt.

Friday, August 10

Kari and I walked three-eighths of a mile to Durston Road and back again. It was hardly the type of workout she wanted, but it was a beginning. "Your mom said you made it to Durston," Stu said later that day. "Next week let's walk up Bozeman Creek. Okay?"

"We'll see. What are you doing here? Just a visit?"

"I thought I'd shoot if it won't bother you." The shooting range was located in our backyard.

"No problem," Kari lied. "Come in and have some cookies when you're finished."

"I couldn't pass up that invitation! When you're ready to shoot again I'll help you." He grabbed a cookie from the plate and ran for the door, grinning over his shoulder. "If you need me that is."

Kari watched Stu jog across the lawn. "Would you close the windows and doors and turn up the music?" she asked me. "I guess I'm a sissy, but I don't want to hear him shooting." She sighed. "I'll have to get used to it some day, won't I?"

Monday, August 13

"Let's walk on a trail, Kari, I'm tired of your driveway!" Becky said, waiting for Kari to put on her running clothes.

"Okay, but I don't want to be in the trees," she warned.

Kari was nervous and uncomfortable as the sun beat down on the meadows of Stone Creek. Sweat trickled down her neck, and Becky chattered about fishing and floating to distract her. Becky, tiny and feminine, exuded style even in running clothes. Her thick, dark hair framed a pretty face, and a mole on her right cheek emphasized her green eyes. I was amazed that she had taken over Kari's rehabilitation with such vigor and persistence. She probably sensed Kari's need to be drawn out of herself, forced to face friends, to get back to the old way of life, and she didn't trust me to push her.

Probably the Forest Service checking for fires, I thought when I heard the engine of a small plane. Kari stopped, listened, and picked up her pace. The plane passed over us, then returned and circled overhead. It skimmed the treetops and buzzed lower over the meadow where we were walking. "I have t-to go b-back! I can't s-stand this!" Kari stammered. I grabbed her hand to keep her from running, and Becky took her other one. Kari was silent and withdrawn as we returned to the car with her sandwiched between us.

She rushed into the house ahead of me, and I found her huddled on the sofa. "I was right back in the forest with those two creeps holding me under the trees where I couldn't be seen from the plane! I remembered how they smelled, the feel of their hands, and even the weight of the chain around my waist!" She trembled. "It was all so real again."

Madison County

The Goldstein family was angry that the search for the Nicholses had been terminated when the tracker said they had been so close to them. The FBI was consulted, and it was agreed that the tracker would return to the Cowboy Heaven area with Brad Brisbin, Gary Lincoln, Bernie Hubley, John Onstad, and the regional FBI SWAT team.

John and Bernie were on the crest of a hill at Barn Creek using spotting scopes to scan the area around them. They would be able to spot the Nicholses if they made a run for the low country.

Bob Morton, Bob Campbell, and Dan Bauer closed off one of the Nicholses' escape routes from the high country by riding into the search area from the cowcamp on Cherry Creek. Later in the day, the SWAT team asked the riders to meet them on Red Knob Mountain. The three men rode through thick downed timber and bogs and fought their way through clouds of mosquitoes and flies. When they finally arrived at Red Knob, the foot team wasn't there. Someone had misread the map; they were on a mountain, but it wasn't Red Knob. Morton oriented the team by radio and got them headed in the right direction, but he and his companions stayed on the mountain and continued to scan the area with binoculars for another hour or two. The three friends decided it was too far to return to the cowcamp and rode to the SWAT team's take-out point. The riders were surprised to find the tracker at the base—alone.

"How the hell did you get here? Where's everyone else?" Campbell snapped, brushing the dust from his clothes, wishing for a cold beer.

"I found some prints that looked like the Nicholses' and followed them into the hills. The others couldn't keep up with me, I guess," the young man said. "I don't know where they are."

Hot and dirty, the search team straggled out of the mountains. Humor did not exist by the end of the day, and the tracker did not return for a third try.

Friday, August 17

Kari asked to walk on the ski trails at the Cross Cut Ranch in the Bridger Mountains. It was a mistake—it was hot, and being hemmed in by trees frightened her. On the way back to town she huddled in a corner of the car, eyes vacant with panic, and withdrew into a frightening silence. Her mind created a prison without windows, doors, or sunlight, and she was overcome with depression and fear. She was trapped by her memory and thrust down a path of inner agony that lasted two days.

Kari's nights were miserable. All positions were uncomfortable, and her nightmares were so terrifying that she fought sleep. I suggested that we move back to the family room, but she said she couldn't take the recliner to ski camp, she had to get used to a bed. I still slept on her floor, and my dislike of the fugitives increased with each of her sleepless nights.

About a month after the kidnapping, Kari, Stu, Bob and I met Paul at Big Sky for the Summer Fair and parade. It was cold, gray, and windy—a preview of the early winter to come.

Kari's friends crowded around her, piled jackets over her, pressed hot drinks into her hands, and talked about the ranch, the preparation of the float for the parade, and the care Jay was giving her horse.

Douglas Goldstein was there, and Kari was surprised at his physical resemblance to Al. Anger and grief radiated from him, and he spoke with suppressed rage about the fugitives being free. He asked us what Sheriff France was doing to catch them, and we told him the sheriff had never been in touch with us. He made a comment about the sheriff being too busy fishing to search or to meet with him.

We planned to meet with Al's widow later that afternoon. We had been remiss in our attention to their family by not sending a letter expressing our sorrow until we returned from the trauma center in Seattle. We were wrong in assuming that the family was aware of our grief concerning Al's death—they hadn't read Bob's press release and didn't know about Kari's involvement in setting up the memorial. We hoped meeting with Diane would begin to straighten out the misunderstanding, but at the last minute she cancelled the get-together. Bob gave Doug a letter for her—our apology.

Paul had the day off and stayed with Kari. He had lost a lot of weight, and his sunken eyes attested to his sleepless nights. I asked him to come home. He said he couldn't leave during the busy season, but planned to quit as early as possible and spend some time with his friends in Jackson before returning to the university. He admitted that it was difficult for him to be at the ranch, and I mentally kicked myself for allowing him to return.

After the fair I drove to Jim Schwalbe's to thank him for saving Kari's life. Jim is a wiry, handsome young man with blond hair, a full beard and glasses. His cabin was homey, with a colorful quilt on the big bed and bright cushions on the chairs. A kitten scampered and tumbled on the quilt, amusing us with its antics. San, Jim's attractive wife, served us lemonade, and we discussed

Kari's kidnapping and Al's murder. I was shocked when Jim told me he thought we had been unhappy with him for not staying behind with Kari after she and Al had been shot.

"That's ridiculous!" I said. "If you hadn't escaped they probably would have killed you, too. It took real courage to walk into the camp, unarmed, to help her."

"I couldn't see her at first," Jim said. "She was kind of tucked behind a tree, and when I realized she was chained to a log I knew we were in trouble." He studied his hands. "Was she raped?"

"No."

Driving back to the cabin, I thought, His nightmares must rival Kari's.

"I enjoyed seeing my friends, but I felt uncomfortable," Kari said later that evening.

"Why?" Bob asked.

She swallowed, tucked a strand of hair behind her ear, stalled, and finally said, "I think the residents up there blame me for Al's death."

"Punkin, that's not so! They helped us search for you and know you had no control over the situation," I said. "Did someone say something to upset you?"

"No. It was the way they looked at me. They were uneasy when they talked to me."

"Honey, it's hard for everyone," Bob said. "People don't know how to act because they don't want to bother you, but they want to let you know they care." I phoned Dr. Frank Seitz, a psychologist and friend, explained the situation, and set up an appointment. Kari needed help.

Madison County

Dave Wing cooperated with the FBI in the search for the Nicholses. After the tracker found Dan Nichols's prints in the cowcamp tent, Dave put an electronic tracking device in a box of biscuit mix in the camp tent. Had the Nicholses taken the box, it would have been possible to locate them by following the "bug." The electronic receiver for the equipment, as well as the ones that would be installed in the future, was located in Bozeman at the Gallatin County sheriff's office. There were problems with the repeater, so the signal was weak and erratic and created false alarms.

In late August it was decided the bug should be removed. Sheriff Onstad, Brad Brisbin, Bob Campbell, FBI agent Bernie Hubley, Dave Wing, Sheriff France and U.S. Forest Service District Ranger Virgil Lindsay set out to check campsites frequented by the Nicholses. They checked some abandoned mines on their way. They were empty.

The men formed two groups. John and Dave went to the cowcamp to remove the electronic device and the others rode through the thickly timbered area of the Barn Creek drainage searching for a site known as the Nicholses' "moose head camp." Dave was familiar with the camp; he had checked it years ago while searching for them regarding Dan's truancy.

The officers rode several horse lengths apart and spoke softly when communicating. The lead horse shied, spooked by a grouse that flew out of the brush ahead of them. The men spread out and searched the timber on either side of the trail, wondering what had frightened the bird. They found nothing. Actually, it had been flushed by the Nicholses, who spotted the lawmen, left the trail, dashed downhill, crawled under a pile of dead timber, and stayed there until night. After his capture Dan Nichols told Bob Campbell they had come close to being caught that day.

The pots and pans in the moose head camp were destroyed by the search party. The semi-cave's roof had fallen in, and it wasn't clear anyone had lived in the camp in the past month or so. The posse rode out of the mountains searching for gardens and other camps. Dave Wing and John Onstad rode away from the cowcamp discussing the fugitives and the expensive bugging device they had just removed from the biscuit mix.

Approximately ten days later the cowcamp was raided again.

Gallatin Canyon

Kari and I moved to our cabin to escape the ringing telephone. We enjoyed the quiet, our long talks, and just being together in a place that had always been our haven from the busy world. Kari's friends had given her some new tapes, and the music she played that summer will always evoke memories of those bittersweet days.

My brother Jim, his wife Marsha, and their children Janet and Douglas arrived from Casper, Wyoming, for a short visit. Bob and Paul took us on a fishing trip up Bacon Rind Creek where the walking would be flat for Kari and the fishing would be easy for the children. Bob stopped on the trail, squinted into the sun, and said, "What's that?" He pointed to the far side of the meadow.

"Looks like someone lying on a rock. I'm not sure," Jim answered.

We waited for the person to move. Kari stepped closer to her father, and Paul scrambled up a tree for a better look. "I think it's someone's clothes, but I don't see anyone around," he said.

"Better have a look," Bob muttered. "We'll go on to the creek after we see what's going on." Kari was hyperventilating and told Bob she was afraid the clothes belonged to the Nicholses and they would kill everyone when we got close to the creek. He reassured her before he and Jim jogged across the meadow to check out the clothing. He shouted back that the clothes looked like they belonged to a hiker who had overdressed and had left them on the rock to be picked up on the return walk. We started across the field and Kari stiffened when she saw the patched Levi's, dirty plaid shirt, and socks with holes. She retreated into herself and sat silently in the shade while the men fished. Marsha and I sat beside her, talking, hoping to draw her into the conversation.

Back at the cabin we packed. Jim's vacation was over, and they planned to leave from Bozeman the next day. Kari wanted to see her horse and asked Bob to stop at Lone Mountain Ranch on the way into town. Had we known the impact this visit would have on her emotional recovery we would not have gone.

Kari brushed her horse, talked with the kitchen crew, and went to the office to see Vivian. Diane Goldstein was there. She was pale, thin, and her lovely eyes were heavy with sorrow. It was the first time she and Kari had seen or spoken to each other since Kari's kidnapping and the murder of Diane's husband. We hugged her and talked to her until she unwittingly said that it's not so bad for parents to lose a child because they still have each other, but to lose a husband is to lose everything. Kari's composure crumbled, and she stumbled blindly from the office. Marsha helped me put her in the car, and we left Bob and Jim behind to say our goodbyes. When we got home she closed herself in her room and refused to talk about the incident at the ranch.

Jim and his family left early the next morning, and Kari, exhausted and red eyed, kept her appointment with Dr. Seitz. During the drive back to the cabin she looked miserable and was unusually quiet. I settled her on the cabin porch with her dog, a book, and a glass of iced tea. While I cooked dinner I peeked nervously through the window, hoping to find her reading or playing with the dog, but she sat staring into space.

I carried on a monologue at dinner until she stopped me and said, "It's okay. I have so many emotions to sort out I can't concentrate on what's going on around me. Dr. Seitz suggested ways to deal with this mess, and I'm busy working them out in my head." The haunted look I remembered from ICU was back in her eyes, and I felt helpless—a frustrating emotion for me. She cocked her head and smiled. "Thanks for trying, though."

"Well, I'd better do some training," Kari said the next morning. "I've slipped backward the last few days and I haven't made so much progress that I can afford to do that. Where should we walk today? I don't want to be in the trees!" We decided on Teepee Creek.

Wild grasses rustled and rippled in the warm morning breeze, tickling our legs as we followed the trail along the flat bottom land of the wide drainage. The hills sloped gently upward to the higher timbered areas of the mountains where two coyotes crouched on the surface of a dried pond. We were within a quarter of a mile of them when they dashed into the cover of the trees. Their gray coats could be seen in the shadows of the forest as they continued to watch us. Kari shivered. "I can't stand knowing we're being watched! Talk to me, Mom," she insisted. "I don't care what you say, just talk! I think too much when I walk and I scare myself."

Saturday, August 25

Bob joined us for the weekend, and we decided to take him to the Almart Lodge for a Mexican dinner. Kari wanted Jonathan to join us and made at least four attempts to reach him by phone. She was obviously disappointed that he wasn't home.

Bob and Kari spent the next day together walking, talking, and laughing. Paul joined us for dinner, and they compared the Cinnamon Creek walk Bob and Kari had taken with the past training runs they had done on the same trail.

After Bob and Paul left, Kari phoned Jonathan and invited him to the cabin for a beer. "Oh, my gosh, do we have any?" she gasped.

"Fortunately, yes. After you introduce us I'll go up to Merry Lou's," I said. "Okay?"

"No way! You have to stay and talk with us."

"Honey, you asked him to have a drink with *you*, not with you and your *mother*."

"I hardly know him! We won't know what to say to each other! You have to stay! Please?" We argued. She won.

Jonathan was exactly as Kari described him: soft blond hair, pale blue eyes separated by a straight, narrow nose, a pleasing smile, high cheek bones, and a well-muscled physique. He tried to conceal his surprise when I didn't leave after the introduction, and his eyes questioned me, but I wasn't about to explain the situation. I had to force down a chuckle more than once. Later, Kari walked Jonathan to his truck and returned with the comment, "I asked him to go walking with me in the morning."

My eyebrows arched into my bangs.

"I'd like to talk about the meeting with Diane," Kari said at lunch the next day after her walk with Jonathan. "Something she said really bothers me." Her tears soaked into the shoulder of my blouse while we discussed the loss of a child versus the loss of a husband. I told her how deeply we loved her and explained some of the emotions we had experienced while we searched for her.

"But if I'd died you'd still have had Joey and Paul. You wouldn't have missed me too much." She hiccupped between sobs.

I said that each of them was loved individually, one could never replace the other, and that the loss of a child was the worst pain a parent could suffer.

"The Goldsteins must be having a terrible time," she said, blowing her nose. "What can I do to help Diane? I know she's angry, but I didn't want Al to die!"

"Try to understand her. She didn't mean to hurt you, it just came out that way." Kari put her head in my lap, I smoothed back her hair, rubbed her head, and eventually she slept. We went back to Bozeman for a few days so Kari could talk to Dr. Seitz more frequently.

Kari went grocery shopping with me because she was afraid to stay home alone. She became dizzy at the check-out counter, and I explained that when she stood still, the blood pooled in her legs and abdomen, making her blood pressure drop. She paced back and forth to keep her blood circulating, and the clerk, overhearing our conversation, hurried to sack my purchases. A stranger stopped me as we left the store and said, "This was God's will, you know. He plans our lives." I was too shocked to argue, and I was thankful Kari hadn't overheard her.

Later that summer, a man I had just met said that I should not be angry at the Nicholses, because God had planned this for Kari. He insisted that from the moment she was born God guided her to that trail in the mountains. I lost my temper and said if that were so then every criminal in the world had an excuse—they weren't guilty because God made them do it! He planned for them to be murderers, rapists, and kidnappers, and had thrown their victims in their paths. He answered, "Oh! I—uh—I never thought of it that way, that can't be right."

There came, at last, a major turning point in Kari's rehabilitation. After a walk with Stu, she dashed into her room and reappeared with her rifle.

"I have to try this sometime. Stu will help me." She stopped with one hand on the doorknob and said, "What if I can't do it?" She sighed, gripped the rifle, and walked out to the range. Bob and I stood on the deck watching her and Stu sitting on the ground talking. Kari shook her head, Stu patted her shoulder, she stretched out on her stomach, took aim, fired, and shot for twenty minutes.

"I did it! I did it!" she shouted, hurrying across the field. "I was shaking so badly I missed the target, but that doesn't matter, does it?" Stu stood behind her grinning from ear to ear.

"We don't care if you shot every horse in the pasture!" Bob laughed.

In the mail that day there was a violent letter from a deranged person who threatened Kari's life. I gave it to the sheriff's office and asked them to investigate. Since he signed his name and address they felt he was harmless. I insisted. The name and address were fictitious.

September

Big Sky's fire department sponsored a Labor Day weekend pancake breakfast at the firehouse to raise money for equipment, and Kari, Bob, and I went. Kari became less talkative as we approached Big Sky and reminded me she was still uneasy around the Big Sky people. I promised we'd leave if she was too uncomfortable.

Buck Knight walked up the road to the firehall with us and teased Kari about how jealous his wife would be when she saw him walking with a "purty gal." Kari smiled at him, taken in by his jolly, rascally personality. Buck is an old-timer in the canyon. He's short and wiry, like many cowboys, and has a gift of gab that no one in the canyon can match. His grin and infectious chuckle put Kari at ease before we reached the firehall. Jim Schwalbe was there and Bob introduced Kari to him. We moved down the line exchanging greetings with John Palmer, other firemen, and Neil Navratil, the chef from Lone Mountain Ranch who was cooking the pancakes. Bob Naert waved to me from the end of the line. Bob is a tall, handsome young man. His gentle brown eyes crinkled into slits when he laughed, and listening to the banter between him and the Big Sky people it was obvious he was a favorite. Wrapped in a huge white apron, he was serving coffee at the end of the line, and I introduced him to Kari. He looked a little flustered when she said, "Haven't we met?"

"A-h-h-h, no, I don't think so, but I've seen you around."

We sat at one of the long tables and were soon joined by Steve Gamble from Lone Mountain Ranch, the Schaaps, and other families from Big Sky. Strangers walked over to introduce themselves to Kari and to wish her well. Their friendliness put her at ease, and she began to enjoy the morning. Bob Naert sat down with us, noticed my empty coffee cup, and jumped up to refill it. Kari's gaze followed him across the room.

"I know I've met him somewhere," she said, her forehead wrinkled in concentration.

"Well, he joined the search for you," I answered, "and he helped Jennie when you were brought to the base. He took your blood pressure while she was starting an I.V. In a way you've met him."

"Oh! I remember!"

"Why don't you two come out and go on the hayride?" Steve, who had the horse team hooked up to a flatbed hay wagon, said to Bob Naert and Kari. Kari hesitated, but Bob didn't give her a chance to refuse. He whipped off his apron, pulled back her chair and whisked her out of the building. Later, they sat on the wagon talking about horses, hay, and pack trips with Steve.

"Jim Ritten and I are going grouse hunting up Cinnamon next Saturday," Bob said. "If you'd like to go along I have a horse you can borrow."

"U-m-m," Kari hesitated, "I'd love to ride, but I'm not sure I could stand the jolting yet."

"Well, anytime you want to go, call me. You can borrow Cody, he's a good horse and shouldn't give you any surprises."

"Thanks. I might be able to go in a week or so."

Walking back to the car Kari looked over her shoulder at Naert and said, "He's more handsome in color."

"What?" I laughed.

"The first time I saw him everything was black and white." She grinned. "I'd sure like to go riding. Do you suppose he was serious about going with me?"

13

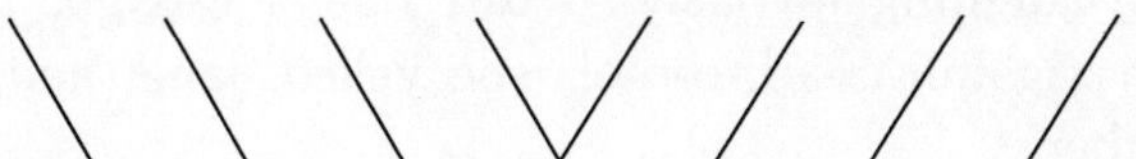

"I CAN RIDE!"

Labor Day Weekend

On Monday the Hollier family and Stu joined us at the cabin for dinner, and Kari was too busy to talk about riding with Bob Naert. Monday evening when the last guest drove away, Kari told me she had decided to try riding her horse the next morning. She phoned the ranch, arranged to ride with her friend Janet Story, and asked Diane Goldstein to go with them because Bob Schaap suggested that the two women should get together and talk. Diane turned down the invitation. Kari shrugged, smiled, and said, "Well, I'll ask her the next time I go." I was proud of her. Calling Diane had been difficult, but she had done it and accepted the refusal with understanding.

Tuesday

I paced nervously and talked to Vivian Schaap while the girls rode. When their silhouettes appeared on the horizon I breathed a sigh of relief that made Vivian chuckle.

"You can't imagine how much fun we had! Do you know what this means?" Kari asked, dancing around Sassy, swinging the reins, laughing joyously. "I can ride! I can get out in the mountains again! Ya-a-h-o-o-o!" she yelled. Janet and I grinned at each other.

Chattering triumphantly, she stopped to see Bob Naert. She said she could ride whenever he had time to take her.

"Is Sunday too soon?" he suggested.

"Perfect! I'll bring the lunches. Do you like bagels? What time should we go? Where should I meet you? Should I bring my own saddle? May we go even if it's raining?" She paused, panting for breath.

"Hold on! One question at a time. I'll pick you up at ten o'clock at the cabin, I don't know where I'll take you yet, yes, I like bagels, I have a saddle you can use, and we can ride in the rain if you want to. Does that cover everything?" He was laughing, caught up in the effervescence of her mood. He shook his head when we drove away.

"I'll bet he thinks I'm crazy," Kari chuckled.

"He probably wonders what he's in for."

She napped, then coaxed me off to the Cinnamon trail, where she tried a new training pattern. She did a slow jog for five minutes, walked, and jogged again. "Hey! I'm getting better at this!"

That evening Kari hummed to herself, wrote letters, tucked the bear under her chin, and slept well for the first time since the kidnapping.

The rest of the week was busy. Jonathan came to dinner at the cabin, we drove into Bozeman for Kari's appointment with Dr. Seitz, shopped, stopped at the ranch to collect the rest of Kari's things, and planned a get-together with some of the ranch crew and Jonathan for Saturday night. Kari rode again on Friday and asked Diane to accompany her. The answer was no.

Friday evening we went to the Almart to make reservations for the dinner party and came face to face with six bearded men in bloody camouflage clothing. Kari stood rigidly clutching my hand and hyperventilating while I made the reservations. The Almart's owner tried to reassure her. "They're just bow hunters blowing off steam. They won't bother you." Kari didn't hear him. She was glassy eyed, withdrawn, and the bar patrons' laughter made her jump as if she'd touched a cattle prod.

"How long will bearded men make me feel hysterical?" she asked when we climbed the steps to the sleeping loft.

"I don't know, Punkin," I answered helplessly. Unable to sleep, we read and listened to the distant thunder as lightning flashed against the drawn window shades. The monotonous patter of rain on the roof finally lulled us to sleep.

Sunday

Bob Naert and Kari returned from their ride joking and making plans for their next trip.

Paul arrived at the cabin about nine o'clock. This had been his last day of work at the ranch, and he planned to visit friends in West Yellowstone or Jackson until classes started at the university.

"The crew gave me a going away party at dinner this evening, and the guests enjoyed it almost as much as I did," Paul told us.

"What did they give you?" Bob asked.

"Oh, some crazy little things, plenty of silly speeches, and topped it off by giving me my favorite bottle of wine. I'm going to miss everyone, but I need time away from this area. Hope the fishing is good in Yellowstone Park," he said, starting a conversation with his father about fly-fishing. I watched the light from the fireplace dance across his face and realized how much weight he had lost in the weeks since Kari's kidnapping. The lines of fatigue were gone, but sparks of anger and sorrow still flashed in his eyes. When Kari wasn't looking I caught him studying her with an expression of tender puzzlement, as if this were a sister he had never known. I felt a deep sadness when I realized that the happy, trusting young man who had gone to the ranch last June had become an angry, guarded, silent man. Kari and Paul popped some corn, and we had a long family talk in front of the blazing fire.

"I had a wonderful time," Kari said later as she bounced on my bed. "It was good to be out, and I didn't have much pain. Sometimes I felt uncomfortable being in the trees, but Bob kept up a running dialogue so I didn't have time to spook myself. I think I'll be paying for my rides with M & Ms and chocolate chip cookies." She settled in her own bed. "Bob's sure nice. He makes me feel good about people again."

The next morning Paul left for West Yellowstone. He grinned and waved until he was out of sight. We'd miss him, but he needed this time to recuperate.

Wednesday

Nailed to a post in the Red Cliff campground was a wanted poster of the Nicholses. Their eyes had been gouged out and their throats slit with a knife. Kari whirled away and gagged.

"Let's get out of here!" I said, putting my arm around her. "We'll walk somewhere else."

"I'll be okay, give me a minute." She wiped her face with her headband, drank some water, and walked toward the Elk Horn trailhead. The path dropped down to the river. Wister belly flopped into a deep, cool pool, and we sat on the soft carpet of squaw grass and talked.

"I'm going riding with Janet tomorrow." Kari hesitated and concentrated on sinking a floating stick with some stones. "I've tried three times to get Diane to go. I can't take her rejection anymore, Mom. It's her problem now."

"I hope this won't keep you from enjoying your friends at the ranch," I frowned, watching her unhappy face.

"It won't. Dr. Seitz is helping me accept what's happening and has made me realize I shouldn't continue to hurt myself to make other people happy."

"What do you mean?"

"It means I'm not going to call her again—not to please the Schaaps, you and Dad, or anyone. It's done. Ended. I can't take anymore."

She tossed one last stone, pulled me to my feet, and we continued the hike.

14

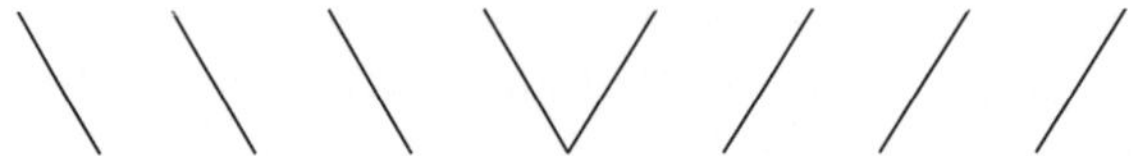

FALL TRAINING

Sunday, September 17

Enormous white clouds edged the deep blue sky, and a warm breeze ruffled the spruce and fir trees. This was my last day of summer vacation, and tomorrow I would return to work at the student health service. Jonathan and Kari had gone for a walk, and Bob and I were on an all-day hike that would take us up the Elk Horn trail, cross-country to Burnt Ridge, down the west face of the ridge, and back to the cabin.

Bob and I ate our lunch in a sunny meadow with a panoramic view of the mountains. With binoculars Bob glassed the cliffs of Rams Horn for mountain sheep, and I studied him. He had aged since July 15. Fine lines around his eyes and mouth had deepened, and there was a sadness that never left his eyes. Al's death haunted him. Would he ever come to terms with the senselessness and violence of that day? It was emotionally draining for him to provide the children and me with the love, humor, and support we needed. Watching our children trying to regain a foothold in their world was taking its toll on him.

Kari's immediate future concerned us, and we discussed it as we climbed the steep ridges and slid down the scree slope of Burnt Mountain. Our friend Denny Lee had offered to let Kari stay at his house just two blocks from Bob's office and the health service. We could be there in a few short minutes if she needed us. She had decided to sit in on a German class to keep herself occupied and to put herself on campus where she would be among students.

"Don't worry about me," Kari said that night when we discussed the situation with her. "I can hibernate in the university library and read or write letters. Lisa Newton is back, and Stu and Paul will be here as well as the ski team. I'll have plenty of company." Lisa and Kari had met on the MSU ski team and the friendship had blossomed because of their common interests: skiing, horses, vet school, and biathlon.

"It'll be difficult for us without each other, won't it, Mom?" Kari said, clearing her throat. "I'll have to relearn independence. It was easy the first time, but now . . ." She struggled with words. "We'll do okay, you'll see." She settled beside Bob, and they finished reading *A River Runs Through It* by Norman McLean.

Paul returned from West Yellowstone looking rested and tanned. For several evenings he joined us for dinner and entertained us with his tales of bears, fishing, and friends. There was an air of reserve about him that was new, and I couldn't pierce the shell he had built around his emotions.

Friday, September 21

Kari and I hurried off to the cabin after work, and I could feel the tension drain away from each of us as we settled in front of the fireplace with a good book and bowls of popcorn. We put a George Winston tape on to play, and I read to her. Eventually, she put her head in my lap and fell asleep. The week had been difficult. She had been afraid to be alone in the house and had spent many hours in the library or with friends.

"Will I always be afraid to be alone?" she asked me last night. "Most of my life I've needed time by myself, and I've walked or run in the mountains for the solitude I wanted. Now what'll I do? I'm afraid to be alone in my own home with all the doors locked! Will I ever be able to go camping? Will a full moon always bring back bad memories? Damn! Damn! Damn!" she cried, and hurled a running shoe across the room.

"Oops!" She looked surprised, shocked, and embarrassed. We laughed, but the fear remained and the questions went unanswered.

Saturday morning Jonathan and Kari drove to Jackson, Wyoming. He had become a regular visitor since that first humorous evening in early September. Bob and Paul had gone to a friend's ranch, and I had the day to myself, so I packed a lunch, took the dog, hiked up Cinnamon trail, and dropped down into Buck Basin. Clouds hung low, obscuring the mountaintops, and a fine drizzle dampened my wool clothing. I felt uneasy and found myself looking over my shoulder, peering into the blurred, mist-shrouded forest. Unable to see more than four feet ahead of me, I turned back and climbed up into the fog that smothered Cinnamon Mountain. Something crashed out of the mist. I screamed as a deer ran across the trail and dashed into the timber. Wister's hackles were up, and she barked and snarled into the swirling white at the side of the trail. My heart banged against my ribs and I tried to run, but I was terrified, unable to move. A figure emerged from the mist and stepped onto the trail in front of us. The man was wearing camouflaged clothes, and his face was smeared with something black. He carried a hunting bow.

"Sorry, I didn't mean to scare you!" he said. "Does that dog bite?"

"Yes! Boy, you scared me! I forgot bow season was still open. Sorry I spooked your deer." My voice was a loud, nervous staccato.

"No problem. I do this more for the walk than anything. Didn't I see you and your daughter in the Almart a few weeks ago?"

"Could be."

"Yeah, I remember, now. The owner told us who you were—no wonder you're nervous. If I meet those guys they won't be seen alive again! I have two little girls, and I think I have some idea of how you folks feel. You want me to walk you back to the trailhead?" he offered.

"No thanks. I'll be okay if I can make my heart stop pounding!" He disappeared into the fog, and I jogged the three miles to the cabin, slipping and sliding in the mud with Wister at my heels.

A hot bath and a roaring fire revived my good spirits. Wister snored on the hearth rug, and I stared into the flames analyzing my motives for going into the mountains. Friends told me my attitude about being alone and hiking in the mountains would affect Kari's recovery, so I reasoned that if I could overcome my fears it would help Kari temper hers. What happened today certainly wouldn't help her, and I decided not to tell her of my fearless trek.

Kari returned exhausted, but talked for an hour about the trip, the wildlife they saw, the visit with Pam Weiss, and the elegant Chinese dinner she and Jonathan had shared.

"Sleep in tomorrow, Punkin. You can miss one day of training," I said.

"Nope. I want to go early in the morning because Bob and I are going riding in the afternoon."

"Your schedule is unbelievable!"

"I'm lucky to have friends who'll spend time with me. I'm not good company sometimes, but they let me be silent and moody without asking questions. They could be with friends who're more fun. How'll I be able to thank them for giving me so much of themselves?"

"Tell them what you just told me," I murmured, tucking the blankets around her shoulders.

Sunday, September 22

We ran up Wapiti Creek because of its sunny exposure and rolling terrain. It was cold, and the rain the day before had frozen in puddles along the road. We wore running tights, warm-ups, sweat shirts, the red-and-black wool plaid shirts from our horse riding days, ski hats, and gloves. Warming up as we ran, our clothing was shed layer by layer and tossed into the sagebrush along the red dirt road.

Today was a first. Kari jogged without walking. It wasn't a fast pace, but it was uninterrupted. Elated, we did a jig. We whooped at the top of our voices and spooked the placid cattle grazing on the wild grass. Wister ran in circles around us, barking and wagging her approval.

While Kari rode with Bob Naert, I had time to review some problems that had arisen. She and Stu had gone roller skiing, and her chest pain had been intense. I phoned Dr. Maier in Seattle and discussed the possibility of using a T.E.N.S. unit to reduce the pain. I had read about the Transcutaneous Electrical Nerve Stimulator and its use in treating post-thoracic surgery patients and chronic back pain. He wanted to discuss the T.E.N.S. with physicians at the pain clinic in Seattle before we tried it, and suggested marcaine injections first.

The theory behind the injections is to block the nerves and interrupt the pain impulse on its way to the brain. The theory behind the T.E.N.S. was the same, using electrical impulses. It was possible the pain cycle would be broken long enough so the nerve would forget how to transmit pain.

September 24-28

"I realize I'm going to have to work through the emotional aspect of this pain if I'm going to ski in December," Kari said, pushing her food around on her plate. "It wouldn't be so bad if the pain didn't remind me of its origin, but every twinge reminds me of the Nicholses, Al's death, and what I went through. I want to forget! I want them out of my life! Maybe I'm being unrealistic about skiing this year, but I can't give up. If I do those creeps have won again!"

Earlier that day a student health service physician had checked her tender, swollen chest muscles. With her finger she drew a line from the exit wound, along the ribs under her arm, to a point just below her right breast and told him that was the route of sharp, shooting pain. He increased the dose of her antiinflammatory medication, insisted that she cut back on the roller skiing and weight lifting, and told her to get started with physical therapy.

Saturday, September 29

Kari and Jonathan toured the Red Rocks Wildlife Preserve. It was late when Bob and I arrived at the cabin because we had stopped to listen to Paul and a friend play their guitars, fiddles, and mandolins. The gate was open, lights were on in the cabin, and smoke rose from the chimney. We expected to hear laughter and music, but instead we found a subdued duo. "Kari, what's wrong?"

"We'll talk about it later, Mom," she hinted gently, so I changed the topic of conversation until Jonathan left.

Bob helped Kari up to the sleeping loft, and she told us the chest pain had started about noon and had become worse during the afternoon and evening. She talked about the trip and was describing the trumpeter swans when she fell asleep in mid-sentence.

Satisfied that she was sleeping, Bob asked questions I couldn't answer. "Is her training causing the pain? Could she be bleeding again? Do you suppose lifting weights ruptured something? That clot hasn't dissolved yet, has it?"

The next morning I had to help Kari dress and braid her hair because she couldn't raise her arm. The pain hadn't improved by the time we returned to town, so I phoned Dr. Maier. His recommendations had been supported by the physicians at the pain center, and they wanted Kari to be in Seattle for several days for extended marcaine injections. Realizing she wouldn't leave Bozeman, they suggested that the surgeon here do the nerve block. They weren't optimistic about the results of a single treatment but advised it as the first mode of treatment.

Several days later she went to the surgeon. Three injections were made to deaden the nerve along the damaged rib and the nerves above and below it. It hurt her. Wiping Kari's face with a damp cloth, I suddenly flashed back to the ICU: to the bleeping cardiac monitor, the gurgling chest tube, and the long sleepless nights. I reminded myself it had only been ten weeks since the kidnapping, and because of her desire to recover she was doing better than we had expected.

Dr. Maier told her to try some form of exercise within six hours of the nerve block, so she decided to go for a short run. We ran two miles and she smiled all the way.

"I'd forgotten running could be fun! Wouldn't it be wonderful if the pain didn't come back?" she panted happily.

The following day the pain was worse. Dr. Maier was disappointed but not surprised. He assured me the increased pain was not unusual and that it might be several days before the pain level dropped to its previous intensity. We made arrangements for him to talk to Dr. Murray at the Olympic Training Center in Lake Placid. Dr. Murray worked with athletes at the center and would obtain a T.E.N.S. unit for Kari to use when she arrived for the dry land training camp in October.

Kari's discomfort remained, but she wanted to go riding with Bob Naert to look for elk. Wrapped in warm wool clothing, they left the cabin at sunrise. Frost glistened on their boots, and puffs of white punctuated their laughter in the cold fall air.

They returned glowing from the sunshine, exercise, and fresh air. We were going to the Almart for dinner, and while Kari bathed, Bob told me about an accident Kari had had with the horses.

"We dismounted to watch a herd of elk, and I left her standing between the horses holding the reins. A twig snapped under my foot and the horses bolted, dragging Kari with them. I ran behind, yelling, 'Let go! Let go!' The horses separated, and Kari was stretched between them. Her feet left the ground, and for a few seconds she was airborne, then she crashed head first into the sagebrush. I ran over to her yelling, Are you hurt? Are you okay?' She had the breath knocked out of her and wheezed, 'I'm fine! I always wear sagebrush in my nose!' She looked pretty embarrassed.

"I said, 'Why didn't you let go of the reins? You could've broken your neck, and your mom would've broken mine!' We could both see your reaction in our minds. I knew you'd skin me alive if she got hurt, but she looked so silly with sagebrush in her hair, and I was so relieved she wasn't hurt, that I had to laugh," Bob said, grinning from ear to ear.

"What's so funny? Are you telling stories again, Bob?" Kari said, stepping into the room.

"Just telling your mom you looked like an old pair of long johns flapping from a clothes line when you were suspended between the horses."

"Wh-h-a-at?" she yelped in mock anger.

"Well, you looked pretty funny! I still can't figure out why you held on so long."

"I thought they'd stop, but I guess *your* horses aren't as well trained as *mine*." She grinned, inviting a protest, and the dueling continued throughout dinner.

Kari was unable to lift weights or run, and the Lake Placid training camp was coming up the next week. She was desperate.

"I'll feel like an idiot if I get there and can't train. I don't want the team to feel sorry for me, and they will if I don't do well."

"Dr. Murray will teach you to use the T.E.N.S., and you'll be able to continue your physical therapy, so the trip won't be a loss. Is therapy helping you?"

"Yes, but it hurts like crazy while they're doing it and for a couple of hours afterwards. The muscles seem more supple, and I can extend my right arm over my head. It's a good thing I started therapy, or I wouldn't be able to diagonal pole this winter. I'd look like a bird with a broken wing."

"Why do the treatments hurt so much?"

"Come with me and see," she challenged.

The therapist started with ultrasound treatments, then applied heat packs to her right chest from the spine to the sternum. After the heat, a lubricant was spread over the skin in the same area. The therapist positioned her fingers on the intercostal muscles, those between the ribs, and, using her full body weight, pressed downward, sliding her fingers along the muscles attempting to break up the spasms, scar tissue, and tightness. Kari blanched and sweat ran down her face.

"I thought I'd learn to do the massage so you could have one every day," I said on the drive home, "but I couldn't bring myself to hurt you like that."

"Softy," she murmured.

Wednesday, October 17

The plane grew smaller and became a dark speck disappearing into the clouds. I was happy and sad at the same time: happy Kari had made it this far, and sad knowing she would soon realize how much she still had to do to "catch up" on her conditioning.

She and Stu were on their way to Lake Placid for the training camp. Kari was excited but anxious about leaving her major support group. Thank God, Stu was with her.

Sunday, October 21

It was a beautiful fall day. I had to take some papers to Bob Schaap at the ranch and decided to combine the trip with a hike since Bob and Paul were out of town. It was hunting season (with rifles), so I decided to hike up Castle Rock where few people hunt.

The snow became deeper the higher Wister and I climbed. At the last switchback I found a bush with dark reddish leaves that reminded me of the color of Kari's hair. Wind tore at the branches, but the leaves held fast. I shivered. I was being bombarded with painful memories of the kidnapping and the first days Kari was in the ICU. I saw the gray blanket, the bloodstained shirt, her unfocused eyes, and the blood filling the container on the foot of her bed. I tried to force away the images, but instead I heard the sucking, bleeping, hissing of the machines. I ran through snowdrifts to reach the summit and looked out over the valley and mountains. I had come to sort out my thoughts, but all I could do was cry. Alone on top of the mountain I yelled, screamed, and cried until my head ached. Two hawks took exception to the noise, left the trees, and spiraled upward on the wind.

Wister's tongue on my face brought me back to reality, and I drank some tea from my thermos. Retracing my footprints, I passed the red bush, and a leaf tumbled off. It looked like a bloodstain against the white snow. I picked it up, carefully tucked it in a pocket, and left the mountain.

Monday night Kari phoned from Lake Placid. She had been fitted with a T.E.N.S. unit and had tried out its effectiveness by roller skating on her new roller blades with the team. It had worked and she was elated.

A phone call later in the week was less positive. She had experienced increased chest pain after removing the unit. "I did too much. Nothing to worry about." Her voice was multitones of cheerfulness, fatigue, hope, and fear.

"Marie Alkire phoned," I said. "She's read about a machine called an Electroacuscope that's being used in sports medicine clinics and pain centers. She thinks you should try it. It's similar to acupuncture, but an electrical impulse is used in place of a needle. Jim Booth, a dentist in town, has a machine. He said you could try it when you get back."

"Great!" Kari exclaimed.

Spanish Peaks

Early autumn vanished, and snow appeared in the high country. Bob Campbell and Bob Morton continued their rides disguised as hunters or snowmobilers. In Ennis Dave Wing and Gary Lincoln frequently checked the mountainous area from a plane. Dave's wife Jerri said the two men left Ennis at 5 a.m. almost every day and returned well after dark. She and Dave cancelled their vacation plans for summer and fall so he could search for the Nicholses with Gary.

November 1, Bozeman

Kari, Stu, Peter Hoag, and Pam Nordheim returned to Bozeman from Lake Placid, spent several days with us while they reorganized, then moved to West Yellowstone for the on-snow training camp. Kari planned to drive into Bozeman every Tuesday afternoon. She would see Dr. Seitz and Dr. Booth on Wednesday mornings and be back in West for a Wednesday afternoon workout. She and Jonathan arranged to see each other on Tuesday evenings.

It was difficult for him to have her attention diverted by her training, but they had both known this situation would arise.

15

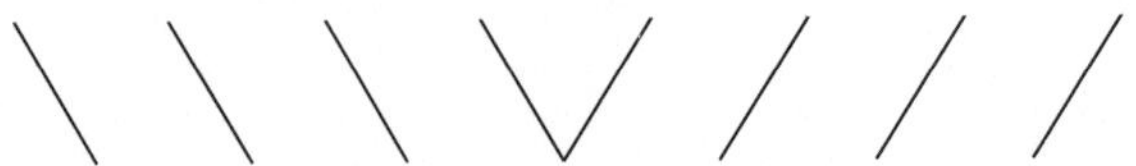

ENCOUNTER

During Kari's absence my husband and Bob Schaap talked to Sheriff John Onstad about the search for the Nicholses. When Bob asked if there was a chance the kidnappers weren't in the Gallatin-Madison area, John told them about the October robberies. Several cabins in Gallatin Canyon, near an area known as Beckman's Flats, had been burglarized, and the thieves had stolen food staples such as flour, pancake mix, Crisco, canned chili, powdered milk, frozen meat, a sheepskin coat, a pair of snowshoes, and several paperback novels. The Spanish Creek Ranger Station was also pillaged, and a pair of Sorel boots had been stolen. Bill Pronovost investigated the robberies on October twentieth and was certain the Nicholses had been involved in the break-ins. A snowstorm following the thefts made tracking impossible. The evidence was circumstantial, but Onstad was sure the Nicholses were in the Madison Range—probably in the area known as Cowboy Heaven.

Bob Schaap asked what Sheriff France was doing to find the criminals. John said he had no idea. Schaap asked what he and the Swenson family could do to encourage cooperation between the Madison and Gallatin officials. He was worried that one of his guests or staff might be lost or injured in Madison's jurisdiction—again—and he didn't want a repeat of last July. Onstad suggested there could be a budget problem hindering the search from the Madison side. My husband and Bob Schaap decided it would be advantageous to talk with Sheriff France and offer to help him find a way to raise funds for his county.

Bob Schaap phoned me a few days before the meeting and asked me to bring any information on search and rescue (SAR) programs I might have to the meeting. He thought Sheriff France would be interested. I decided to take the SAR manual used by the National Association for Search and Rescue and the National Park Service. Thumbing through the pages, I marked several to show Sheriff France. They included the information on how to respond quickly, the importance of searching at night, mobilizing and keeping searchers in the field, and a quote from the manual about night searches.

A cafe in Ennis was chosen by Sheriff France for the meeting. Melting snow had created a puddle that rivaled Ennis Lake in front of the cafe. We skirted it and pushed open the door. The blast of heat, the smells, the voices, took me back to my childhood in a small town, to the homey cafes on the main street of Thermopolis, Wyoming. There was the same odor of coffee, burned toast, hot griddles, and grease. Sounds of people, the clink of coffee cups on saucers, a burst of laughter, and the ring of a cash register. It made me nostalgic.

Johnny France, wearing a Stetson cowboy hat, left a booth and sauntered our way. His face had the leathery, wrinkled look of someone who spent too much time in the sun. He was not much taller than I and appeared to be in his late forties or early fifties. A heavy sheriff's badge pulled at the fabric of his uniform shirt, and on his belt was a holster holding a pearl handled revolver.

We sat at a table in the side room. The sheriff started the conversation by telling us we didn't need to thank him, that he had received his thanks when he found Kari and she had smiled up at him and said "thank you." He said it was fortunate "he" found her because he was certain the Nicholses would have tired of hauling a reluctant woman around and would have killed her and dumped her body off a cliff. He continued for some time telling us details concerning his rescue of Kari. He refused eye contact with me.

"Why wouldn't you come and help us search for Kari Sunday night and Monday morning?" I asked when he paused for breath.

He rested his right elbow on the table, cupped his chin in his palm, looked at the wall behind me, and explained that he didn't believe in doing night searches because "it's impossible to find someone in the dark. Besides," he said, "somebody might fall and get hurt."

I thought I was prepared for his answer, but my heart hammered and I was as breathless as if I'd been kicked in the stomach. I remembered the night searches the Nordic Ski Patrol had done with the Gallatin County deputies and Sheriff Onstad. Most of our rescues were in the winter, at night, with the temperatures as low as minus thirty and sometimes in an avalanche situation.

"Nonsense!" I sputtered. "I've been on night searches with the Gallatin deputies and no one fell and got hurt'!"

His face dropped deeper into his hand. He avoided my eyes and said he wouldn't listen to any criticism of his deputies. I told him as far as I knew only Jay Cosgrove had been involved in the search for Kari. I reminded him that in Montana the local sheriff is responsible for directing and managing search and rescue, and, I said, there could be no blame placed on deputies who didn't have orders to follow.

My husband nudged my foot. It was a signal—back off. Too late; the ball was rolling. The sheriff said that searches were expensive. He had to stay within his budget.

"Wait a minute! Are you telling me that whether or not you search for someone depends on what's left in your budget?" Heads swiveled in our direction. An elderly man winked and nodded his head. Bob Schaap tried to catch my eye.

"Well, I have to stay within the budget. Right now one of my men is gettin' ready to go out and look for a hunter who was reported lost last night." He explained his policy: if the missing person hadn't walked out by midmorning or noon, a search party would be organized.

He studied his fingernails and added that we didn't have the right to go out looking for Kari because we were not law enforcement officers. They were the only ones allowed to organize and carry out searches, he informed us.

Bob grabbed my elbow to keep me from jumping up, but it didn't close my mouth. "You abdicated the right to even *say* that when you refused to help us search for her! What did you expect us to do? Sit and suck our thumbs until you decided to show up? You knew we were reforming at four o'clock in the morning, why didn't you join us?" My trembling hands clutched the coffee cup.

"I've got to watch the budget. I can't go runnin' off every time I get a call about someone being missing." He explained that most calls from parents, upset because their daughters were missing, were false alarms, and if he had gone looking for them it would have been a waste of money. Bob nudged my foot again and said, "This conversation isn't getting us anywhere. I agree with Jan. It wouldn't have been possible to sit and wait for seventeen hours for you to show up. That's water under the bridge. Let's do something constructive so a problem of this magnitude isn't repeated." His voice was calm. Only his pallor indicated his anger.

Schaap's cup rattled as he used both hands to center it in the saucer. He cleared his throat and in a clipped, tightly controlled voice said, "Bob's right, Johnny, you bungled this one, but the future is our major concern."

"You say your hands are tied by the amount of budget you're given," my husband said. "The obvious answer to your dilemma is to find a way to increase your department's finances without raising taxes. Right?"

"Yeah."

"Would you be interested in training your deputies and yourself in search and rescue techniques if you had the proper funding?" Bob asked.

"My deputies wouldn't mind the training."

The discussion of budgets continued with the three men exchanging ideas on raising revenue. A young Madison County deputy joined us. He was a large man with a ready smile and happy eyes. He extended a huge hand, and mine was lost in his grip. He introduced himself as Merlin Ehlers. The discussion now concentrated on SAR, spurred by the fact that Merlin had recently attended Search And Rescue Management classes in Bozeman as a refresher course. He asked me if our Nordic patrol would come to Ennis to instruct the deputies in avalanche rescue. "We have a lot of snowmobilers running around in the mountains, and one of these days they're going to get caught in a slide," he explained.

I said I was sure we'd help, since part of our assigment as a patrol is public education. Sheriff France approved the plans for the training sessions, said he'd schedule it with his men, and would give me three weeks advance notice.

The subject returned to finances. Bob Schaap asked the sheriff for his departmental SAR expenses for the last few years so he and Bob would have facts when talking to people about funding for Madison County.

The sheriff and Merlin discussed a news conference soon to be held by the sheriff as they followed us to the door. Overhearing this, Bob Schaap said, "Why do you keep having news conferences? People interested in helping the Nicholses escape keep tabs on what you're doing by reading the papers! I'd suggest you stay away from the press."

"I can't. I was really burned by 'em once and now I cooperate. Oh, by the way, Mrs. Swenson, you might be interested in a TV program called Victims for Victims." He told me when it would be aired. Everyone shook hands and smiled, but no one looked comfortable.

A three-page document reviewing all points of the conversation we had had with Sheriff France was sent to him. We thanked him for meeting with us, and asked that he send us a letter listing Madison County's search and rescue expenses for the past three years. If we were to help him raise funds, we needed those figures. My husband and Bob Schaap also composed a letter addressed to both Sheriff Onstad and Sheriff France encouraging them to develop an intercounty agreement on search and rescue activities. We received a short letter from Sheriff France dated December 3, 1984, in which he enclosed the expense list. The other letter was never acknowledged.

16

"SOMETHING BIG'S COMING DOWN"

November

One fall day at the student health service the receptionist cornered me in the nurses' station. "There's a very tall, very handsome man at the desk asking for you," she said, rolling her eyes.

"What's his name?"

"I don't know, but he's a hunk!"

Approaching the desk I saw a gentleman who fit Judy's description. His face crinkled into laugh lines when he smiled, and he introduced himself as a member of a national television show. He explained his presence by relating an interesting story. Two days earlier he had phoned the Madison County sheriff and asked if anything was happening with the search for the Nicholses. He was told no. Later, the lawman called him back and said that the TV team should get out to Montana right away because "something big is coming down." He asked what was happening, explaining that it would be very expensive to move his team and equipment to Montana. The answer was "something big is coming down," and if they wanted to be in on it they better get out to Montana on the double. The TV crew arrived as quickly as possible and found that the "something big" no longer existed.

He asked me some questions, and I gave him my angry opinion on the romanticized image of the criminals. He wanted me to speak to that issue on film. I said maybe.

I phoned Bob Campbell at the Gallatin sheriff's office, told him about the television crew, and asked what was going on. He wasn't sure what the other sheriff was alluding to, but he said there were new developments that he, Campbell, couldn't talk about. He explained that discussing certain aspects of the search could jeopardize the whole effort.

My husband and I talked about the network's request. They phoned again and said they would be filming Sheriff France riding in the mountains looking for the Nicholses as well as interviewing Bob Schaap and other people from the Big Sky area. Bob was reluctant to talk to them, but after speaking with Bob Schaap, he decided he'd make a statement. He refused to be interviewed.

Several days later the *Bozeman Daily Chronicle* reported that a hunting guide had met the Nicholses in the mountains, talked with them, and had taken three days to report the incident. This had taken place over a week ago. Now I knew what the "something big" was.

The outfitter was quoted. "I told them that at first there had been an outcry, but that the world had recognized that what had started out as a good idea—trying to get Danny a wife—had blown up in their faces and gotten worse and worse."

Irate, I phoned Bob Campbell, and he admitted he had known about the outfitter when he had spoken to me. He said the man had phoned Bob Morton and insisted on absolute secrecy in exchange for his statement about the episode.

"Then why did he go to the papers for a full-page spread with posed photographs?" I fumed.

"I was told he heard someone was going to leak the story to the press and he wanted to tell it his way," Bob answered.

"What did you do after he told you?"

"Jan, I can't give you particulars, but we are, and have been, doing something."

My brother Bob phoned. He was furious and insisted the outfitter was guilty of aiding and abetting and we should press charges against him. I told him the Madison County sheriff and the Gallatin County sheriff were the ones who should decide whether or not to file charges.

Later, the guide was featured on a "20/20" television program concerning the kidnapping and explained that he understood the Nicholses and their way of life. He said, "Dealing with the powers of the elements definitely changes you. It makes you strong if you can survive it, but I think you develop a disdainful attitude for people who live indoors and don't experience it. I don't condone kidnap. Nonetheless, I can understand Don Nichols. I guess maybe if you live up here long enough and watch the animals mating there's a certain amount of aggression and male dominance involved. And living the way Dan and Don did could have something to do with it."

Madison County

Following the outfitter's statement, six men disguised as hunters rode into the cowcamp in Cowboy Heaven to plant electronic devices in the tent and in food packages. The six were Brad Brisbin, Bob Morton, Bob Campbell, Wally Schumacher, Dave Wing, and Gary Lincoln. They spent a couple of days pretending to hunt while they installed motion and heat sensors and tracking devices similar to the ones used earlier in the fall. There was no game in the area, and the men couldn't risk blowing their cover by pretending to hunt beyond two days. They left behind a substantial supply of food, hoping to entice the Nicholses into their web. The bugs were removed a week later.

Word reached Sheriff Onstad's office that caves located on the Spanish Creek Flying D Ranch could be hideouts for the fugitives. The authorities decided to look for the caves—at night.

The men arrived at the Gallatin sheriff's office at midnight, were issued sophisticated night vision equipment and briefed. Present were Brad Brisbin and his dog, a Jefferson County man and his dog, Gary Lincoln, Bob Morton, Bob Campbell, Bob Secor, Dick Noorlander (Madison County deputy), Sheriff France, Wally Schumacher, Dave Wing, several FBI agents, and Sheriff Onstad.

At the search scene Onstad was issuing last-minute equipment and instructions when they realized the Madison sheriff wasn't present. They saw him disappearing in the distance, walking across a field. The lawmen were concerned because they planned to do the search in teams, and someone going ahead of them might alert the kidnappers—someone could get killed. They continued as planned, hoping Sheriff France's team would catch up with him.

Lincoln, Brisbin, Campbell, Morton, and Secor were assigned to locate and search the lower cave along the creek bank. They found the cave and waited until dawn to send Brad's dog into the cave. When Bear returned, indicating there was no one in the cave, Brad and Gary stripped to a thin layer of clothing and squeezed through the entrance to the cave. The only visible tracks on the sandy floor were the dog's. They explored the dark cavern and realized it would be a perfect place to hide. There were two major rooms with a spring running through the second one and a large "blow hole" in the roof to ventilate the cave.

Later, on the way back to base, Brad's team met France's group, who hadn't been able to locate their cave.

17

COURAGE

Bob, Paul, and I went to West Yellowstone each November weekend to ski and visit with Kari and the other biathletes. It was disconcerting to watch Pam Weiss, Peter Hoag, and Kari as they prepared to go out for a training session. Peter did his stretching exercises, and the girls put ice packs on his back for him while Pam ice-packed her injured knee. Pam or Peter positioned the four electrode pads of the T.E.N.S. unit on Kari's back, connected the wires to the battery pack hanging from a belt on her waist, and wrapped an ace bandage around her chest to keep the unit from slipping while she skied. Peter aptly named their house "the Convalescent Condo."

Kari's friends Todd Boonstra and Marsha Hoem of the U.S. Nordic team were also training in West. They spent hours encouraging and calming Kari when her pain kept her indoors.

November 17-18

The T.E.N.S. no longer helped. Kari and I attached the electrodes in different patterns but were unable to find a placement that would provide relief. Her sense of humor never flagged.

"You should have seen me earlier in the week, Dad," she chuckled. "Peter put the electrodes too far to the right, and I didn't notice the impulses were making the muscles in my arm twitch until I tried to shoot. My shots went every which way! When I realized what was happening, I tried to time my shots between electrical impulses, so it was jerk, pause, shoot; jerk, pause, shoot. Stu thought it was pretty funny and said he was surprised I didn't bring down a duck or a goose!"

November 20

One of Kari's friends phoned to tell me that Kari was in "shocking condition," that she could hardly walk from the living room to the kitchen. I decided to make an appointment for her to see a chest surgeon in Billings. I knew she wouldn't take time off to go see Dr. Maier.

November 22, Thanksgiving Day

By midafternoon the aroma of the turkey provoked hunger pains among those of us in the condo. There were nineteen athletes and coaches coming to dinner, and the kitchen was a beehive of activity. We had a wonderful evening. What made it special for Bob and me was the cheerful camaraderie of the young people.

The next day I told Kari she had an appointment with a thoracic surgeon on November 27. She had mixed reactions. On one hand she needed information about the pain, but on the other hand she was afraid he would tell her to stop training.

Saturday, November 24

Today was the first biathlon race of 1984. It was bitterly cold, and the wind whipped into the range, numbing the faces and fingers of the competitors. It made life miserable for those of us who worked on the shooting range or in the penalty loop. We jumped around, swung our arms, and jogged back and forth trying to stay warm. Paul raced; Kari didn't. She took photographs and cheered the others out of the starting gate with such longing in her eyes that I had to look away. I blamed my tears on the stinging wind. "Yeah," she said brushing at her own eyes, "that's some breeze!" Her hug almost crushed me.

The weather remained foul for the next day's relay race. Kari stood with us and watched Paul. He grinned and waved as he skied by in a sweat-soaked uniform. "I've skied with him all these years and never knew he smiled when he raced!" she laughed.

Tuesday, November 27

The physician in Billings told Kari exactly what she didn't want to hear. He showed her the x-rays displaying the metal fragments that remained in the chest wall and told her he thought the nerve was irritated by the fragments when she strained the chest muscles. He advised her to stop training and give her body time to complete the healing process.

"I can't do it," Kari said as we left the office building. "I have to keep going! If I quit, the kidnappers have won, and for the rest of my life I'll be a victim. I won't let them do that to me! I'll ease off, I promise, but I'm going to ski!" We didn't have time to brood about the physician's advice because we drove into a ground blizzard outside of Big Timber and battled it for forty miles.

The next day Kari went back to the training camp to be with her friends. That weekend she told us she planned to go to Lake Placid to race, and until then she would shoot and ski just enough to stay in shape so she wouldn't hurt herself "going all out" in January. Bob opened his mouth to protest, but she stopped him and gently explained that this was her choice, she had made a decision and would live with the consequences.

"Besides, what have you been encouraging me for if you hadn't planned to let me ski?" She cocked her head and smiled, knowing we couldn't argue with that logic.

Tuesday, December 4

The biathlon team moved to Lone Mountain Ranch to train and participate in the Alan Goldstein Memorial Races. It was a poignant weekend for us, for Diane Goldstein, for the Schaaps, and for the people at Big Sky who had known Al. The week before the Goldstein races, the athletes held a race on the Lone Mountain ski trails. Kari cheered for her friends, but after the last racer finished she sighed, put her arm around her dad, and said, "I used to ski like that."

Later, she discussed her uneasiness. She wasn't sure why she was afraid, but she spent most of her days in a state of tension that was making everyone around her jumpy. The nightmares had intensified, and she was getting little sleep.

Thursday, December 13, Madison County

It was cold when Roland Moore left his ranch house at midmorning to check the water supply for his cattle. It was well below freezing, and he knew he would have to chop through the ice on the stock tanks. On horseback Roland headed toward the tank above Red Bluff. He used an ax to chop through the ice and retraced the prints in the snow. A plume of smoke rising through some timber caught his attention and he reined in. This time of year a fire meant someone was on the ranch without his permission. Could be a poacher, he thought, or it could be the Nicholses.

He urged the horse back to the ranch and phoned the Madison County sheriff's office. The sheriff was not available, so Roland left a message for him to call back as soon as possible. He dashed out, jumped into his pickup, and drove slowly along the highway looking for a parked vehicle or prints in the snow that would tell him where someone had hiked to the ridge. Two days before a snowstorm had raged for twenty-four hours, leaving fresh snow that would have shown prints made since then. There were no prints, so someone had been camping up there for several days. This ruled out coyote hunters who might have sneaked in for a day of hunting.

He crossed the steel bridge that spans the Madison River and drove to the closed Trapper Springs store. From there he used his binoculars to scan the ridge where he had seen the smoke. He focused on a brushy draw, slowly scanned up the ridge, and focused on a man standing in the snow looking back at him with binoculars. Startled, the men stared at each other. The man on the ridge turned and ran toward the shelter of the sparse timber, where he was joined by a second man who had been waiting at the edge of the trees.

Moore sped home and phoned for help again. There was still no sheriff. He was supposedly transporting a prisoner to the jail in Bozeman. The rancher called Madison County Deputy Merlin Ehlers, who was at home in Pony having lunch. Merlin listened carefully and advised him to phone Gary Lincoln at the FBI office in Butte. Lincoln immediately alerted Onstad in Bozeman and phoned the Madison County sheriff's office to tell them he wanted the operation delayed until all forces were in place as planned. This time the assault would be done correctly, without the risk of losing someone in a needless shoot-out. Weeks earlier, Lincoln, Wing, Campbell, Morton, Onstad, France, and several others had formulated a plan later to be named "Barnstorm" by the Madison group. They had decided that while ground teams organized, a helicopter would be used to track the Nicholses. If they had to run them for hours they would, knowing the fugitives would eventually become exhausted and hole up somewhere. Lincoln wanted Barnstorm to go off without a hitch.

In Bozeman John Onstad ordered a fixed-wing plane into the air and sent Bill Pronovost as the spotter for the pilot. He made this decision because Murray Duffy, the helicopter pilot, wasn't available. John was assured that every attempt was being made to reach him.

The sheriff's office crackled with excitement. Bob Campbell, shutting out the noise around him, tried unsuccessfully to contact Bob Morton on the Forest Service radio frequency. Wally Schumacher, in his patrol car, listened to Campbell's urgent voice, toggled his radio mike, and said, "Campbell, this is Schumacher. I'm driving down the canyon and I'll be at the Squaw Creek station turnoff in a few minutes. I'll stop and tell Morton to call in."

Morton had finished lunch and was leaving the house when Schumacher's car skidded to a halt in the driveway and Wally jumped out yelling, "Call Campbell! It's an emergency! It may be the Nicholses!"

Morton ran back into the house and phoned. Schumacher left to get warmer clothing and a rifle, and Morton loaded a snowmobile into the back of his pickup truck and headed at top speed for the sheriff's office in Bozeman. The office was humming with activity: phones were ringing, officers were making calls, deputies were reading a map spread on a desk, and Onstad was shouting orders to the dispatcher. The sheriff made assignments, and Morton and Slaughter ran from the office and drove to the Madison bridge in Morton's truck. Other deputies were assigned duties, and Campbell and Onstad waited for the helicopter to transport them to the Madison bridge, where they would set up base headquarters.

2 p.m.

Campbell was on the phone with the Madison office. He yelled across the room at Onstad, "They say they still can't find France. He told them he was bringing us a prisoner, but they haven't been able to contact him. We haven't been notified about an incoming prisoner—I checked with our jail to be sure."

In three strides Onstad was across the room, grabbed the phone, and shouted, "This is Sheriff Onstad. Get ahold of France! We have something we have to act on immediately, and I want him NOW!"

Sheriff France returned Onstad's call and was told the fixed wing was up and the request was in for the helicopter. France was to meet the Gallatin team and Gary Lincoln at the command post near the steel bridge over the Madison River.

Madison County

France told Merlin Ehlers the operation was go and ordered Ehlers to get to the command post. He said Deputy Noorlander would be patrolling the highway between the bridge and the Montana State University Agricultural Experiment Station in case the Nicholses tried to escape by getting to the road. A call had gone out to Deputy Lee Edmisten to meet them at the bridge.

Ehlers frantically pulled on warm clothes, threw his rifle into his four-wheel-drive vehicle, and sped over the icy roads to the command post.

2:45 p.m.

Morton and Slaughter arrived at the bridge just as Ehlers, Highway Patrolman David Schenk, and Deputy Edmisten drove up. Schumacher was already there. Word came that Campbell and Onstad were driving to the bridge, where the helicopter would pick them up when it was available. The officers were told Lincoln was on his way from Butte. The men watched the fixed-wing plane circle over and over the area. Bill Pronovost reported from the plane that there were no people in sight, that the fugitives were probably holed up in a clump of timber just below one of the ridges because that was the only good cover available. The speed of the plane made it difficult to pinpoint the prints in the snow, but Pronovost said they would continue to fly surveillance and keep the men pinned down. If anyone attempted to move across the open areas, they would be seen. If they could just get the helicopter out!

3:15 p.m.

Sheriff France's car skidded to a stop, and he joined the other law enforcement officers. He was briefed on the whereabouts of Onstad and Campbell, the reports from the fixed wing, and who was available to assist in the search.

"Lincoln's on his way," Bob Morton said to the sheriff.

"Whose snowmobile?" France asked, pointing to the truck and ignoring Morton's remark.

"Forest Service's," Bob answered.

"Think I'll use it to scout this first ridge and see where those footprints go," said the sheriff.

"If you want to do that we should go together," Morton protested. "It'll be safer that way."

"Nah. I'm just gonna check right up there." He pointed to the ridge and started the snowmobile. "I'll be right back!"

Ehlers turned to the surprised men staring after France. "Come on! We'd better head for that high road that takes off across the meadow. We have to keep an eye on Johnny—back him up if he needs it. We'll be on the ridge!"

"What the hell you talking about? He said he'd be right back," snapped an officer.

"Yeah. He's said that before!" scoffed a deputy.

"Who wants to go with me?" Ehlers shouted, starting the motor of his vehicle. Slaughter volunteered and the two men disappeared up the road. They climbed quickly, ramming the four-wheel-drive truck through snowdrifts, and listened to the communications from the sheriff.

Bob Morton watched Merlin's truck disappear and listened to France's voice telling them he had changed his mind and thought maybe he'd follow the men's tracks for a while.

"Shit!" sputtered one of the deputies. "Lincoln will be pissed!"

Morton and Schumacher scrambled into Morton's truck and drove slowly along the highway, paralleling Johnny France's progress on the snowmobile. They advised the sheriff of their position. Onstad and Campbell arrived at the command post at the same time as the helicopter and took off immediately.

France told Morton he had hit a fence and was now on foot continuing his pursuit of the men. The sheriff was out of breath, and his labored breathing obscured most of his words. The last transmission from France was, "I think they're in the timber about six hundred feet away."

Bill Pronovost watched France's progress from the airplane and listened to the garbled messages. He shook his head; one man off on his own wasn't in the plan.

Gary Lincoln was upset when he arrived at the base and found out what was happening.

3:45 p.m.

Bob Campbell sat in the front seat of the chopper with Murray Duffy. Onstad was in the back. The engine noise made it difficult to hear the radio communications from the other officers, and they strained to interpret radio messages from the ground. They saw Ehlers and Schumacher standing on a ridge. A message came in from Bill Pronovost and was lost in the noise. It sounded as if he were trying to give them directions. They saw the abandoned snowmobile. Duffy realized they must be going in the wrong direction and turned back to follow the fence in the opposite direction. They passed over a clump of trees, and Campbell thought he saw someone. He tapped Duffy's shoulder and pointed. They banked and returned for another look.

"There they are!" Campbell yelled, pointing, but Sheriff Onstad couldn't hear from the back seat. Duffy saw the men and gestured to Onstad.

"I got a couple guys down here who need a ride." Johnny France's voice was muffled and chopped.

"We can't read you!" Onstad shouted, toggling his radio.

"Why, I've got Don and Dan Nichols down here," France shouted into the radio.

Murray landed the chopper on a ridge about fifty yards from the Nicholses' camp. Onstad and Campbell jumped out and ran downhill, floundering through the snow, and found France holding his rifle on the fugitives. When they walked into camp, Dan was saying to France, "You better clean the snow outta yer barrel." The law officers seized the fugitives' rifles. Don's was loaded and a shell was in the chamber; the safety was off. Dan's rifle was also loaded—no shell was in the chamber and the safety was on. So, thought Campbell, the old man was going to blow Johnny away. I wonder what changed his mind? They searched the men for other weapons and read them their rights.

Murray Duffy sat in his chopper wondering what was taking so long. Surely they'd take the fugitives out in his chopper, one at a time. He saw France running up the ridge carrying an armful of guns. He dumped them in the chopper, hopped in, and said, "Let's go! Drop me at the snowmobile. Onstad and Campbell are going to walk them out—down that draw." He gestured at the steep ravine. Murray followed directions and asked if he should stay around. Johnny told him he could leave, so he flew to his hangar east of Bozeman and wondered what to do with the weapons France had left with him.

4:25 p.m. Bozeman

Bob was talking with the executive director of the Chamber of Commerce about setting up a reward for the capture of the Nicholses when a reporter from the *Chronicle* dashed in and interrupted their conversation.

"What do you think about the capture, Mr. Swenson?"

"What capture?"

"The Nicholses were captured about a half hour ago. Do you have a statement?" pressed the reporter.

"No, I don't have a statement, and I won't have one until I verify what you've told me. How did you know about this?"

"We have a scanner and monitor all the police and sheriff's calls."

Someone pushed a phone across the desk to Bob. While he was looking up the sheriff's number, dialing it, and waiting for the under sheriff to come on the line, he made some strong statements about the Nicholses. He didn't notice the reporter, standing aside, scribbling on a piece of paper.

"This is Bob Swenson," he told the officer. "Have the Nicholses been captured?"

"I can't give you any information on that."

"What are you talking about? Have they or haven't they been captured?"

"I'm sorry, I can't give out any information."

"Damn it! Kari is at Lone Montain Ranch. I don't want her to hear about this on the radio or TV. If it's true, I have to call the ranch, arrange for the Schaaps to tell her and stay with her until we get there."

"Well, it's against . . ."

"You've told me that five times! Doesn't the victim of this affair deserve some consideration?"

"Okay! We've received a report, still unconfirmed, that they're in custody. I can't say anything else."

"Thank you! Sorry I yelled!"

He phoned Vivian Schaap, who promised to find Kari, tell her, and stay with her until we arrived. In spite of being asked to leave, the reporter listened to all of the phone conversations.

"Do you have a statement for the press, Mr. Swenson?"

"Since their capture has not been confirmed and I have more important things to attend to, no, not at this time."

"But, the public . . ." Bob dashed out of the building before the reporter could finish.

Bob called Paul, who said he'd come to the ranch as soon as he finished his final exam the next day. I phoned Jonathan. He had talked to Kari and was on his way to the ranch. He said he'd stay with her until we arrived.

Madison County

John Onstad and Bob Campbell decided not to handcuff the Nicholses. The sides of the ravine were steep and slippery and they didn't want their prisoners to fall—wouldn't do to bring them in with cuts and bruises. They radioed Morton and Schumacher, who were parked on the highway at the base of the ravine, and asked them to have handcuffs and a car ready to take the kidnappers to Virginia City for arraignment.

Gary Lincoln drove to the foot of the draw in his van and waited. The prisoners were brought out, searched again, handcuffed, and hustled into the van.

"What did you do with their guns?" asked Bob Morton and Lincoln simultaneously.

"Johnny's taking care of them. He put them in the helicopter," Sheriff Onstad answered.

The prisoners were escorted to the courthouse in Virginia City by Lincoln, Onstad, and Campbell while Morton and Schumacher followed behind in Morton's truck. Deputy Noorlander led the cavalcade, and notified the dispatcher to alert the county justice of the peace to be ready for the arraignment.

"Where's France?" someone shouted from the crowd gathered in the courthouse. John shrugged and shook his head.

Dan and Don Nichols talked nonstop from Virginia City to the jail in Bozeman. The younger man joked about the sheriff's rifle barrel being jammed with snow. Dan repeated the story several times and talked about their stay in the mountains until his father told him to "shut up."

The older Nichols said he could have killed Sheriff France anytime he wanted to. When asked why he didn't, he said if he had been alone in the hills he might have, but he knew they were surrounded and the law would hunt Dan down and kill him like a dog. He didn't want that to happen.

"Besides, he didn't seem like enemy," Don said. "He called me Don, friendly like, didn't seem like enemy." Don wrote in an April 1986 article, ". . . I had the drop on him, not the other way around. My body was shielded by a tree two feet in diameter and Johnny had hopped behind a very straggly bush. I could see him plainly and had my gun all ready to shoot him if need be. He knew better than to even point his gun in my direction. Rather than shoot him I decided to go down and spend a few months in jail. . . ."

At the Gallatin jail the prisoners were photographed and allowed to shower and shave. They were in excellent condition, belying the news reports that they had suffered severe cold injuries of the hands and feet. The reports stemmed from a reporter thinking their soot-blackened hands were the eschar of deep frostbite.

Dan Nichols said that during the warm months, Bob Morton and Bob Campbell had kept them on the run from one range of mountains to the other and back again. He hadn't had time to eat well, but after the snow set in and they didn't have to run as often, he had gained about eighteen pounds. The Nicholses told Campbell and Morton that they had seen the lawmen in the mountains often enough to have named Morton "the white knight" because of the white horse he rode.

The Nicholses were placed in a single cell. Criminals are usually not housed in the same cell, but as Bob Campbell put it, "We were trying to be humane." Another deputy explained, "Everyone was concerned that the old man might go nuts if he weren't allowed to be with his son."

In the midst of the excitement, Murray Duffy phoned the Gallatin sheriff's office. "What do you want me to do with these rifles?" he asked.

"What? What rifles?" shouted a startled officer.

"The Nicholses' weapons are in my helicopter where the sheriff left them."

"Hang on a minute." They put him on hold. Then, "I'll send Deputy Cashell to pick them up immediately. Leave them in the helicopter. Don't move 'em! Thanks, Murray."

Friday, December 14

The morning after the capture I volunteered to replace Diane Goldstein in the ranch office. National TV reports had referred to Al as Kari's "boyfriend," which upset everyone, especially Diane and Kari. Kari went to the shooting range with the other biathletes, then sat in the recreation room knitting and talking to friends. She avoided being alone.

The phone rang constantly. Most of the calls were from news media personnel asking to speak with Kari, Bob, me, or Bob Schaap. My husband and Bob Schaap were in the back office making their own calls. Intuition told them certain people would make every effort to capitalize on this event, and they feared something might be done to jeopardize the case. At their request, I phoned our friend Denny Lee and asked for the name of an attorney they could talk to. Denny consulted as an expert witness with several outstanding attorneys in the state, and he gave us two names.

A reporter from the *Chronicle* phoned for my husband. He said he wanted to check the statement Bob had made the night before. I told him Bob hadn't made a statement and asked to what he was referring. The reporter had taken down every word uttered in the chamber of commerce office and was going to publish it as a statement. Bob phoned the paper. I'd never seen him so angry. The "statement" was not published.

Saturday and Sunday

The Alan Goldstein Memorial Races were held on a cold, stormy weekend at the Lone Mountain Ranch. Residents from the Big Sky area, some of whom had helped search for Kari or had been Al's and Kari's friends, swelled the ranks of the workers and observers. Paul raced on Saturday and on Sunday Kari joined her injured friends, Peter and Pam, for the relay race. It was her first attempt at competition since the kidnapping.

The weather deteriorated, and by the time Kari started it was bitterly cold. She grinned at me from the starting gate, and her face glowed with happiness. This was her world. I draped my heavy coat around her when she finished, and she leaned on Bob panting and laughing

"I was slow, but I did it!"

18

CONFLICT OF INTEREST

Monday, December 17

The day began with a call from a reporter who wanted to write a story for a national magazine on Kari's rehabilitation as an athlete. News media people phoned at the rate of several an hour.

Tuesday, December 18

The Nicholses' formal arraignment was held before the Honorable Judge Frank M. Davis in the district court, and defense attorneys were assigned to them. Steve Ungar would represent Dan Nichols, and Donald White would defend the father. Judge Davis issued an order prohibiting law enforcement officers, court officials, and witnesses from discussing details of the case outside court. The order did not restrict statements about the Nicholses' arrest or release of information in public court documents.

The *Bozeman Daily Chronicle* quoted Mr. Ungar as saying, ". . . I don't think we'll have continuous publicity on this case but it has romantic western aspects." Before, during, and well beyond the trials, most newspapers and magazines perpetuated the romanticized "mountain man" myth. In a speech before the Montana Criminal Law Institute on October 4, 1985, Mr. Ungar said he worked to create sympathy for his client by "manipulating" the media. It was a clever move, and the media fell for it.

Wednesday, December 19

I talked with Madison County Attorney Loren Tucker and asked him about the "gag order" issued by the judge. I was concerned that an article in the magazine might violate the order, but he assured me the article would be all right. He said he was representing Sheriff France's interests for book and film contracts and he knew what could and couldn't be done.

"Did I hear you correctly? You're the sheriff's private attorney?" I was dumbfounded.

"Yes."

"But you're the prosecuting attorney. Can you do that?"

He assured me there was no problem and made an appointment to take Kari's statement/deposition. He phoned back later in the day. "Kari has to meet with the defense attorneys before she leaves for the tryouts in Lake Placid," he announced.

"Why can't they just read the statement she gives you?" I asked.

"The law says she has to meet with them and answer questions. If she doesn't cooperate, they'll subpoena her, then we'll have to get a court recorder to take notes. It'd be an added expense."

"When do you get to question the Nicholses?"

"The prosecution doesn't have that privilege."

"Well, let them subpoena Kari! I don't like this!"

"Now, Mrs. Swenson, we want to keep this friendly."

"What are you talking about? I don't know what being friendly with the defense attorneys has to do with anything!"

Mr. Tucker said he was acquainted with the defense attorneys and they all agreed they should go about this case in a "cooperative manner." I was so shocked I couldn't respond.

That evening's *Bozeman Daily Chronicle* carried this headline and related article: "France: A Star is Born." Loren Tucker said he had fielded calls from producers and agents supposedly stationed in New York, Los Angeles, Canada, and even Mexico City. "If the best of the offers come to fruition, France could be a rich man," Tucker said. "He'd have enough money to buy a bunch of cattle and a place to put them on and still have enough left over to buy a bigger place."

Friday, December 21

Loren Tucker and Jefferson County Attorney John Connor arrived at our house to take Kari's statement. John had been a defense attorney in Missoula, Montana, and was a personal friend of Mr. Tucker, who felt John would be helpful because he would know what tactics the defense might use in the Nicholses' case. John was a slim, attractive man in his mid-thirties. A hint of gray showed in his hair, and laugh lines accentuated his generous mouth. Later we would realize his quiet demeanor was a disguise for an intelligent, sensitive, witty attorney whose hobbies included writing ballads.

Loren was tall, with a pleasant face dominated by a square lower jaw. He wore a western-cut sport coat and trousers, and western boots. He spoke with nervous rapidity as he explained the statement process to Kari, and assured her the statement was private and would be used only by the attorneys. He was loading a pocket-sized tape recorder with a blank tape when Bob arrived from the university and expressed our concern about a conflict of interest. He told Loren he was unhappy about the article in the previous night's paper.

"I don't see any problem with a conflict," was Loren's response.

"Maybe you don't. We're worried that your sheriff will use the trial to promote his movies and books, and we won't stand for that!"

"While we're talking about publicity, we'd like you to ask the judge to ban TV and still cameras in the courtroom," I said.

He looked surprised. "I can't do that."

"Why not?"

"The press has the right to be there."

"Our understanding is that the judge can determine if he wants them there or not." I insisted. "It's his decision, and we want him to know that Kari and her family are not in favor of cameras in any form."

"He won't grant such a request," the attorney shrugged.

"At least ask that he allow only one television camera—other networks can use those tapes," I said uneasily. "There is no reason why Kari and Jim Schwalbe have to share their grief with the evening news if they don't want to."

"We'll see," he answered, turning away. "We'd better get on with this, Kari; it'll take quite awhile."

Kari was withdrawn when the meeting concluded and excused herself after being told she had to meet with the defense attorneys on December 26. They had requested that Bob and I not be present in the room while they questioned her. My response to Mr. Tucker was simple.

"Then they'll have to subpoena her, and our attorney will see that she doesn't attend without us, him, or Dr. Seitz. It's unthinkable!"

"I'm sure Don and Steve will see it that way. We want to keep this friendly," he assured me.

Bob spoke up. "I want you to consider this conflict of interest question, Loren. We can't make a mistake that will let the Nicholses go free."

"I've already asked Ungar, White, John here, and the judge about it and they said they didn't see a conflict of interest," Loren answered shortly.

"I don't know much about the law," I said, "but if I were their attorneys I'd say that now, then if the verdict didn't come out in favor of my client I'd scream conflict of interest all the way to the Supreme Court!"

An attorney friend phoned Bob, urging us to hire a lawyer to protect Kari's rights. Bob said he thought that was the prosecuting attorney's job, and the friend pointed out that Mr. Tucker represented the state, *not* Kari. He thought we might be running into some "problems." Pressing him, Bob asked, "I don't understand what you mean."

"The whole setup feels wrong, and the potential for error due to a conflict of interest is real. Several of my professional friends and I discussed it, and we all agree that you should get Kari an attorney. After you choose one have him immediately file a civil suit against the Nicholses, preventing them from profiting from their crimes."

It was our first hint that in criminal matters the defendants have attorneys (often provided at taxpayers' expense) and the state is represented, but there is no one protecting the interests of the victims.

19

THE GOLD

December 24

The pungent scent of the newly decorated spruce tree filled the house while we prepared the traditional Christmas Eve dinner: Swedish meatballs, lefsa, and lutefisk. It was bitterly cold outside, but the kitchen and family room were cozy and resounded with the children's music and laughter. Kari baked Bob's favorite cookies and was helping make the Christmas morning cinnamon rolls. She punched, slapped, and thumped the mound of sticky dough with unusual vigor. Paul and I grinned; she made a silly face at us and returned to the dough. There was no need for words—we each knew what the other was thinking. Discussion of past Christmases made us miss Johanna, so we phoned her. She was spending the holiday with friends but she cried because she wasn't home making a mess in the kitchen with us.

Paul and Kari began their Christmas Eve weaseling to open a gift. It had been an expected mode of behavior for twenty years, and after a certain period of teasing, prodding of larger packages, and shaking of smaller ones, they were allowed to open one. I missed Johanna, who was the Christmas Eve weaseling expert.

Of the three children, she was the most sentimental about traditions, but I noticed Paul and Kari were going out of their way to make sure everything was done the way their father liked it. He had been strong for all of us in the last five months, and they were determined to repay him in subtle ways. They kept the woodbox full, his favorite foods and cookies were in plentiful supply, his skis were waxed, and they made sure he had time to spend with them.

Paul and Kari woke us up early and the Christmas Day rituals began. By midafternoon the house was filled with the aroma of the baking turkey. Bob Naert arrived bearing a huge pot of hot wassail. Behind him came the Mussehl family, Peg, Tom, Marsha, and Judy, with Bob's favorite pies.

December 26

Kari met the defense attorneys in a conference room that reeked of stale cigarette smoke. Sunlight filtered through the unwashed windows, and the gloomy atmosphere amplified Kari's apprehension. Steve Ungar, his assistant, and Don White arranged themselves on one side of the large table with Kari facing them—alone. Loren Tucker sat at one end of the table. Bob took in the seating arrangement, frowned, and moved to sit beside her. She swung her foot nervously and clutched Bob's hand under the table. I sat on the sofa in a corner of the room and took notes. Mr. Ungar asked a series of questions, and the direction of his defense for Dan Nichols became clear. He repeatedly asked questions relating to his client's behavior after Kari was kidnapped. Had Dan been ordered about by his father? Had he been hysterical? Passive? Scared? Mr. White asked a few questions and concluded the meeting.

Kari's hands trembled as she zipped her coat and pulled on her mittens. "Mr. White will be harder on me on cross-examination," she said, "but Mr. Ungar is going to be difficult.

He'll try anything to get his client off. You just watch! Becky and I overheard some lawyers talking in the restaurant a few days ago, and they said the "kid" would get off with a suspended sentence because of his age. A kid, baloney! They should've been there!"

"He won't go free, honey, the prosecutor will see to that," Bob said.

"The lawyers talked about the problem of a conflict of interest with the prosecuting attorney. They said the Nicholses could get off."

"We'll worry about that, and you worry about ski races. Rest and get packed to leave tomorrow," Bob said gently.

December 27

Kari, Stu, and Brian Wadsworth were ready to board the plane to Lake Placid for the U.S. Championships. I whispered to her, "You can make it on your own now. You can get to Europe. Remind yourself of that every day before you ski."

"I hope she won't hurt herself," I said to Bob, watching the plane lift into the air.

"She'll push herself beyond her limits, you know that, but this is what she wants. This is what she has been working for since the first day in the hospital. Did you see the happiness in her smile?" I nodded.

January 5, 1985

Kari phoned and told us the team was leaving for Valcartier, Canada, for the championships because there was no snow in Lake Placid. Stu and Brian were both sick with colds.

"When are your races?" Bob asked.

"Monday, Wednesday, Thursday, and Saturday. They'll take our three best races and figure the points on them. I'm scared. What if I don't do well?"

"It's enough that you're there, skiing. You don't have to win," I answered.

"But I'll disappoint everyone."

"Now, wait a minute," I said. "You won't disappoint anyone I know! Who do you think you'll disappoint?"

My ears buzzed in the extended silence. "Me," said a wistful voice.

She phoned again Wednesday and was upset because she hadn't raced well Monday and had placed fifth today.

"Fifth place is great!"

"It won't get me on the team! The pain is worse than I thought it'd be."

"Have you talked to anyone about it?"

"I don't want to complain to anyone. I'm nauseated most of the time and I'd like to curl up somewhere and cry. Instead I hide in a corner with my Walkman and knitting."

"I've got a suggestion," I offered. "Don't try so hard. Relax. Let it flow and just enjoy the race. Okay?"

"Can't hurt. I couldn't do any worse," she moaned.

Thursday, January 10

The health service emergency phone rang at 5:25 p.m. I was alone working the 9 a.m. to 6 p.m. shift.

"Congratulations! She did it! She did it!" Pat Oriet, friend and colleague, shouted in my ear.

"What are you talking about?" In the background I heard someone yelling and whooping, and Pat shouted, "Bill, be quiet! Jan can't hear me!"

"What's happening, Pat?"

"She won the gold! Kari won the gold medal in the race today!" Bill continued to shout in the background. "We just heard it on the TV. She won! Say something!"

"Are you sure?" I yelled back, afraid to hope.

"There's no mistake! Bill and I are going to toast her victory with a glass of wine."

"Drink some for me!"

My hands shook as I dialed our home number. "Have you heard the news? Has Kari phoned?" I asked Bob.

"What news? No, I haven't heard from Kari," he answered.

"Pat said the TV news announced Kari as the winner of the five kilometer gold medal!"

"You're kidding! Do you suppose it's true?" he shouted excitedly.

I jumped in the air, clicked my heels, and shouted at the top of my voice as I ran down the carpeted halls. I would have done the same thing had the emergency area been full of patients.

I drove home as fast as I could, slipping and sliding down our long, snow-drifted lane. Before I could park the car, Bob ran from the house, jerked the car door open, grabbed me, and swung me around and around yelling, "She did it! She did it! She just phoned. She'll call you in the morning before you go to work." He swung me again.

Friday, January 11

"It hurts to sit, stand, walk, or breathe, but it's worth it," Kari exclaimed. "I can't believe it! I took your advice and went out easy. The more I relaxed the faster I went. I shot one penalty prone, and people started shouting that I had a chance at first place. I thought they were kidding, but I skied faster. Standing, I missed one, and Peter went nuts, yelling, 'You've got it, you've got it! Go for it!' A group of people skied out on the course with me and cheered me on. I've never been so excited or scared!

Everyone forgot about my chest and hugged me and pounded on my back." She paused for breath. "If I finish in the top four Saturday I'll make the team that goes to Europe. I'll soak in a hot tub and load up on aspirin. Maybe I can pull it off." Her voice lost its cheerfulness when she told me Stu and Brian were ill and didn't ski well.

Saturday, January 12

Bob and I paced the family room—waiting. When the phone rang I dashed to pick up the extension and heard Kari shouting, "I made the team! I finished fourth. That puts me in third place overall. Pam Nordheim, Pam Weiss, and Julie Newnam are going, too." She paused for breath. "I'm returning to Burlington where I can get physical therapy. A week of that and maybe the pain won't be so bad." Her excitement disappeared. "Stu and Brian were sick and just couldn't make it." The sadness in her voice conveyed her disappointment for her friends.

Kari and Janet, 1988. *Paul Swenson*

Kari riding Sassy and Holly Flies on Cody explored the high country with their friend Bob Naert. *Bob Naert*

Bob Naert, Kari, and Holly Flies set out on an all-day ride into Buck Basin. *Janet Swenson*

Johanna, Bob, Paul, and Hazel Bowman at Paul's graduation, June 1986.
Janet Swenson

One of the Jerome Rock lakes. *Janet Swenson*

Kari and Becky Lohmiller at the airport as they prepare to depart for San Francisco, where Kari received an award from the Women's Sports Foundation. *Janet Swenson*

Begun in 1876, the Madison County Courthouse was completed in 1887. *Paul Swenson*

The Honorable Frank M. Davis. "There have been tears shed in this courtroom, but not by the defendant." *Perry Backus, High Country Portraits*

Jefferson County attorney, John Connor. John prosecuted two men for the 1987 murder of Patrick Duffy's parents. *Janet Swenson*

Marc Racicot, assistant attorney general. "Two thousand years ago a Greek legislator said that justice will only be achieved when those who are not injured feel as indignant as those who are." *Eric Wordal*

Judy Browning, assistant attorney general. Judy represented the state in all of the Nicholses' appeals before the Montana State Supreme Court.
Janet Swenson

David (left) and Douglas Goldstein at Don Nichols's trial. "Dan and Don Nichols are pure criminals. Justice was done." Quote from David.
Courtesy Bozeman Daily Chronicle

Don White (left) and Steve Ungar were assigned to defend Don and Dan Nichols. *Linda Best, Bozeman Daily Chronicle*

Dan Nichols and his father, Don Nichols. "This is not an epic story of two mountain men. It is an insult to the image of mountain men." Statement by Marc Racicot. *Albert Dickson, Bozeman Daily Chronicle*

BOOK THREE

THE ATTORNEYS, THE TRIALS, THE AWARD

20

THE PROSECUTION'S ROCKY START

> Two thousand years ago a Greek legislator said that justice will only be achieved when those who are not injured feel as indignant as those who are.
>
> —Marc Racicot, Prosecuting Attorney

Late December 1984

While Kari was competing, the judge appointed a man to "evaluate and diagnose" Dan Nichols's mental and emotional condition. I asked about the man's qualifications and was told he was not a licensed psychologist in Montana. Statute 37-17-102 defines the practice of psychology, and the man didn't qualify under that statute. He was actually a therapist or counselor. By accepting the appointment by Judge Davis, he held himself out as legally competent to do the testing and diagnosis of Dan Nichols, skills which fall only within the purview of a trained and licensed psychologist. My friend said that a group of psychologists, shocked at the appointment, planned to discuss the situation with their professional board.

The chairman of the Board of Montana Psychologists wrote to Loren Tucker and informed him that the therapist was not qualified to accept the position and suggested that the court replace him with a qualified psychologist. Loren sent a copy of the letter to Steve Ungar, Judge Davis, and Kari's attorney, Larry Moran. I was told that Mr. Ungar was furious, because he had suggested the therapist's name to the judge.

Larry told Loren that the appointment of the therapist had probably created an unqualified witness and raised the problems inherent with disqualification of him as a witness at trial, and potential case error. Believing the letters from the board and Larry would prompt the court to rename a qualified psychologist or psychiatrist, we relaxed.

January 1985

All of the attorneys, the Madison County sheriff, even the judge continued to have interviews with the press, which appeared to me to be a violation of the gag order. The judge, commenting in an article about the appointment of the attorneys, was quoted by the *Bozeman Daily Chronicle* as saying ". . . it's a fairly simple case outside of the romantic Western aspects of it."

"Damn it!" I sputtered. "Even he refers to this crime as 'romantic'!"

"Calm down!" Bob said. "Maybe he was misquoted. When did you start swearing so much?"

"Okay, give him the benefit of the doubt. I started swearing when I found out the Nicholses are being treated like celebrities at the jail. I questioned Larry about those two being allowed in the same cell and found out it usually isn't done. There's a steady stream of people walking in and out of jail. Not official business, you understand, just to visit. Some visitors have asked the younger Nichols to draw pictures for them. I wonder if he does unicorns and naked women on request?"

"Quit wasting energy on things you can't change."

After Kari's win at the U.S. Championships, I phoned Mr. Tucker's secretary and told her that Kari would be leaving the country and asked if there was anything important Kari needed to know before she left. The secretary said it was imperative that Kari sign the statements she had given the defense and prosecuting attorneys. They would rush their copy to us as soon as it was transcribed from the tape. We received Mr. Ungar and Mr. White's copies first. I was shocked because the transcript was full of omissions. Words or entire sentences were missing.

Loren Tucker's deposition arrived replete with blanks, but it was not as unacceptable. Bob made copies and sent the originals to Kari in Lake Placid. Enclosed with it were Loren's instructions and a request for her to release to him all of her medical records. That made us uneasy. We were apprehensive about his involvement with the sheriff's book and movie ventures and weren't interested in her medical history ending up in his book. Bob and I were convinced there could be a problem if Kari signed the incomplete statements, so we made an appointment to talk to her attorney.

Larry Moran's office smelled of books and leather and was decorated with photographs he had taken. Some were of his sons, who were Johanna and Kari's ages. Larry walked across the room and I studied him carefully. He was of medium height and build, and his thick dark hair showed no signs of gray. He was wearing a beautifully tailored navy blue suit. A gold-and-blue striped tie was neatly knotted beneath a white starched collar. His pleasant, intelligent face split into a mischievous smile when he shook hands with us. He removed his reading glasses and placed them on the desk. He played with the ear pieces, bending them back and forth, while we talked. Pushing the glasses back on his nose, he studied the documents from the attorneys.

"You're right," he said. "Kari shouldn't sign these."

"We were concerned that the defense could fill in the blanks somewhere along the line or use them to confuse her later when she may have forgotten her complete answer," Bob said.

"I'll write a letter informing all three attorneys that I have advised my client not to sign the documents." We talked about Kari, and I decided I liked Larry and his deep, comforting laugh.

Later that evening we realized that Jim Schwalbe would be receiving similar transcripts. I phoned him and said he should consider talking with his attorney before he signed them. Jim told me that there would only be one statement because both the prosecution and defense attorneys took his statement jointly. He said Tucker, Connor, White, and Ungar came up together and did one questioning session. The only other statement was the one Jim had given immediately following the incident in July.

Larry went to the prosecutor's office on January tenth and asked to review some of the files possessed by the county attorney. Eight days later he wrote to Loren Tucker saying that the current status of the Nicholses' case presented several matters of grave concern to him. He discussed the dual representation role of Loren and pointed out that caution must be taken to avoid any legal error allowing for Supreme Court reversal of convictions that could release the defendants under double jeopardy concepts.

He said he felt that the situation fell within the pronouncements of *Sinclair v. State*, 278 Md. 243, 363 A.2d 468, (Maryland, 1976), wherein the court held (paraphrased):

> If the prosecutor has, (or it appears to reasonable persons with knowledge of pertinent facts that the prosecutor has), any pecuniary interest or significant personal interest in a civil matter which *might* impair the obligation in criminal matters to act impartially to both the state and the accused, then the prosecutor is, on the basis of

public policy, disqualified from *initiating* or *participating* in prosecution of that criminal case.

Larry told Loren that if he insisted on seeking Judge Davis's ruling on the conflict issue, he wished to appear at the hearing and present Kari's position on the matter.

He addressed the therapist's involvement in the case, then went on to the problems of the statements and medical releases. He advised the attorney that we remained concerned that personal information provided to him might be used by his other client, so he had told Kari not to sign the medical release forms or the statements. He viewed the depositions as providing significant ammunition to the defendants for use in cross-examination at the trial for the express purpose of confusing and misleading one of the primary witnesses.

Larry also said he was displeased at the manner in which Jim Schwalbe and Kari were "interrogated" by the defense attorneys and said there should have been a certified court reporter at the interviews so there would have been a verbatim transcript.

"It's my belief this prosecution is off to a rocky start," Larry said to Bob at our next meeting, "and exhibits some clear possibilities of substantial difficulties at trial and on appeal."

January 25

Larry went to Virginia City and filed a complaint and motions for a civil suit against the Nicholses. A woman reporter from the *Chronicle* phoned Larry at his office five days later and said that the judge "was livid about our complaint." It violated his gag order, she said. Larry was surprised, because the phone conversations between himself and Judge Davis that same day had been gracious. The judge was concerned about the depositions being made public at a civil trial, but he thought they could be "sealed" to protect the Nicholses' rights in the criminal case. Larry explained that we were not interested in having the civil case heard before the criminal one.

January 30

Larry understood that the judge would enter an order freezing all of the Nicholses' assets until conclusion of the civil case. However, on February second Larry received an order staying further proceedings in the civil case and requiring that he show cause why the stay order should not be in effect until conclusion of the criminal case. He was to present himself at a hearing in Dillon at 1:30 p.m. on February eighth. Taken aback, he had three conversations with the judge, who was angry and said he would do anything to avoid more publicity. Larry told him a show cause hearing played right into the hands of the press.

Larry learned that an agreement between the judge and the defense attorneys had been made related to the story rights. After the trial someone would negotiate or sell the rights to the Nicholses' story, and the proceeds would be used to defray trial costs and attorneys' fees.

I was furious as I paced the floor in Larry's office. "Is that legal? What about the rights of the victim? Why should the Nicholses make money from the horrors they perpetrated?" I sputtered. "If their attorneys negotiate for books and movies, they'll get a commission on top of their defense fees! It stinks!"

"Larry, does the judge understand that we are only interested in seeing that criminals don't gain either notoriety or monetarily from their crime?" Bob asked.

"I clearly and unequivocally explained that what the plaintiff wanted at this time was an order that would freeze the defendants' assets as security for the civil case. He refused to commit himself to granting an order as requested."

"It doesn't sound as if he realizes that we don't want the civil case heard until after the criminal case. Does he understand?" Bob asked.

"I believe so, but the concern is who's going to pay the tab."

"I don't give a darn if it costs Madison County an arm and a leg!" I said through clenched teeth.

"I'll do my best to straighten this out. I'm upset, too, Jan. You swear, I'll smoke," Larry grinned, and lit a cigarette.

We had ten days from the date of filing the civil suit to disqualify the judge, only a few days left.

Larry contacted Judge Davis and asked that they meet in Virginia City on February fifth and sign an "enlargement order," not only staying the proceedings but freezing the collateral assets until the civil action was over. Larry was told that he could mail the proposed order for the judge's consideration, but he avoided answering whether or not he would sign it. We were confused and concerned. It looked as though we had made an enemy of the judge before the criminal matter had gotten off the ground.

"Let's sit on it this weekend and see if anything turns up by Monday," Larry said with a reassuring smile.

Kari phoned from Lake Placid. Her voice was tight as she explained what had happened with the story for the magazine. The writer had agreed to stay away from her at the tryouts, but the day she won the gold medal he and the photographers moved in. She refused interviews or photograph sessions until later. After she returned to Burlington, she phoned the writer and they set up a date for the interview. A week later in Lake Placid he called her and said a car would pick her up at the Olympic Training Center the next day. Kari was puzzled and asked him who was picking her up and where they were going. It was her understanding that the interview would be done at the training center and the photographs would be taken on the biathlon course at Lake Placid.

"He told me they had rented a cabin in the mountains and planned to do the picture session and interview in front of a roaring fire in this rustic cabin. They even bought me a red-and-black wool plaid shirt to wear!"

"What?" Bob yelled.

"I know, Dad, that was my first reaction. I told him no way. This was supposed to be about my skiing, and I wasn't going to dress up in their version of 'mountain woman' clothes and go to a cabin with them. He got awfully mad at me, told me they had spent a lot of money to rent the cabin, and when I still refused he hung up on me."

"That's it! You have no obligation to do this story," I blurted.

"Peter Hoag found me in tears and took the next call from them. He laid down the ground rules. He said everything would be done at the training center and he was going with me. If he didn't like the way the interview was going, he'd stop it."

"Thank heavens for Peter! What happened?"

"The photographers didn't take any pictures, so Peter, the writer, and I went to a restaurant and drank cocoa while we talked. I'm so glad it's over I don't care what they write." She burst into tears. "I can't sleep and the chest pain is driving me crazy! I've been so upset about this article I've let too much tension build up. I wish I were home!"

Peter took the phone from her and filled in more details of the past forty-eight hours. He assured us that Kari would be all right. "'She needs sleep, though, a lot of it."

Monday Bob and Larry decided to disqualify the judge from the civil case. "It makes sense that the criminal trial judge shouldn't hear the civil suit," Bob said to me that night when neither of us could sleep.

"I don't understand the system," I yawned. "I always thought the court and prosecuting attorney were there to protect the victim, the innocent one. Is this a special case or are we naive?"

"You know as much as I do," Bob answered. He punched his pillow and continued. "There's still the conflict of interest problem. If the Nicholses go free I'll take everyone to court!"

"You can't. Members of the justice system are protected from law suits. Pretty neat, huh? The criminals have a variety of rights for appeals, but if the justice system makes a mistake and the criminal goes free, the victim is out of luck."

"Thanks, honey, I'm sure I'll sleep better now!" He punched his pillow again, turned over, and faked sleep.

21

CHANGING PROSECUTING ATTORNEYS

We waited for Loren Tucker to respond to Larry's lengthy letter and for the judge to set a trial date. The local paper rather than the justice system was our source of information. It reported that the Gallatin County sheriff was looking for another jail to house the Nicholses because of overcrowding and a security problem, and that May sixth had been set for Dan Nichols's trial.

Larry showed us the letter from Loren Tucker that indicated he was not going to remove himself from the case.

"What do we do now?" I asked.

"Ask the attorney general to make a ruling. If there's no conflict, fine, we can get on with the case," Larry said. "But I'd still hesitate to have Kari sign those medical releases until we know if the judge will allow medical evidence to be introduced at the trial. The longer you delay, if it doesn't hamper the prosecution, the longer Kari's privacy is insured." Larry fixed us with his gray-blue eyes and toyed with his glasses' stems. "The judge told me the conflict of interest problem was none of our business, that it was up to the defense attorneys to object if they thought there was a conflict."

"It is our business!" Bob insisted. "Kari and the Goldsteins have a lot to lose if the trial is thrown out." He took a deep breath, "Get in touch with the attorney general."

The next article in the *Chronicle* surprised us. We thought the court had replaced the therapist assigned to Dan Nichols, but Mr. Ungar said the counselor had elicited information from Dan that was "indispensable to his defense," and he requested state funds "to further develop relevant psychological evidence about Nichols." The request was granted, and the therapist remained on the case.

February 11

Following an interview with the attorney general, Loren Tucker was removed and Marc Racicot, a special prosecutor from the attorney general's office, was appointed to the case. Loren was quoted by the local paper as being bitterly disappointed, and Sheriff France said the state was "sticking its nose in where it doesn't belong."

Madison County commissioners told reporters they didn't believe a conflict existed but went along with the decision because they "were concerned about the possibility of a retrial which would cost Madison County taxpayers more money."

About the same time the Nicholses were moved to the Beaverhead County jail in Dillon.

Marc Racicot phoned to say he was frantically reviewing the case file turned over to him by Loren Tucker. "If you have any questions, any at all, call me," he said. That statement was the sweetest we had heard in months.

"You've got the best," Larry said, referring to Marc. "He doesn't go in for courtroom theatrics and has a reputation for winning difficult cases because he's thorough, efficient, and hardworking. He does his homework, is a stickler for detail, and overturns every stone in an investigation. Attorneys have a great deal of respect for Marc and his knowledge of law. Besides, they like him."

"You mean he won't be interested in making a circus out of this trial?" I asked.

"You can depend on it," Larry said with a happy sigh.

March 1, 1985

Kari returned from the World Championships in Switzerland bearing gifts of chocolate, Swiss knives, candles, and beer steins. She hadn't placed well in the races but was determined to return in 1986 to capture a medal for the United States.

"Why aren't you going to the North American Championships next week, Punkin?" I asked.

She kept her back to me as she folded her laundry into neat piles. "There's no way I can ski with this chest pain," she said, tugging at a towel. "I may have to give up skiing."

I turned her around and studied her face. The familiar knot of worry twisted inside me.

"Last fall Dr. Maier suggested that you have a workup at the pain clinic in Seattle. Do you want to go now?" I watched her eyes for the spark of defiance that had accompanied her recovery last autumn. I saw fatigue and doubt.

"I'd like to rest for a week or so and see if it improves."

That night Bob told her he had made an appointment for her to meet Larry and that Marc wanted to see her to go over her statement.

She met Larry, phoned Marc, rested, and decided to go to the pain clinic. Dr. Maier set up an appointment for her with

Dr. F. Peter Buckley, associate professor of anesthesiology at the University of Washington hospital.

We drove to Seattle during the university's spring break and stayed with Johanna. Kari and I waited nervously in the examining room at the hospital. Dr. Buckley walked briskly into the room, introduced himself and his assistant, and asked about the sport of biathlon. He was a short, wiry, energetic man, with a British accent and a quick smile. He talked about playing rugby to put Kari at ease, and she described the pattern of her pain for him.

"While I check another patient, Kari, slip out of your blouse and put on this silly gown. I'll be right back." He whisked from the room like a whirlwind and returned as if blown in by a storm. "Sorry, I'm busy this morning," he grinned. He had Kari stand, facing away from him, and did a visual check of her back.

"Mrs. Swenson, you can see that the musculature of the right back is prominent," he said, pointing at Kari's back. "Are you interested in a lesson in anatomy?" he asked her.

"Sure."

"Very well." Tracing the muscles with his fingers he said, "Your trapezius, rhomboids, levator scapulae, latissimus dorse, and the serratus anterior are more prominent than the same muscles of the left side. They're tender, aren't they?" She nodded. "Yes. Well, the spasms in these muscles have pulled the spine to the right. It's a mild scoliosis, but it's obvious," he continued as he ran his finger down her spine.

"Please sit on the exam table and close your eyes." Using a sharp pin, he began a systematic pricking of her back and chest and asked her to tell him if the pinpricks felt sharp, dull, or if there was no sensation.

"You have an area of decreased feeling or sensation from behind your arm, traveling along these nerves under your arm to your midabdomen. That's about the same area that you said you have sharp, shooting pains, right?"

"Yes."

"Lie down, please. On your stomach."

The physicians palpated the muscles of her back. "There are a lot, aren't there?" the assistant said.

"Kari, he's referring to the knots we can feel in the muscles. These are trigger points, so to speak, for the muscle spasms. They feel like little peas or marbles to us. Does it hurt if I press on them?"

"Ouch!"

"Good answer," he laughed. "Didn't you say that the pain increased with the inactivity of the past two and a half weeks?"

"That's right," Kari answered.

His assistant smiled and the two physicians nodded an "Ah-ha" look at each other. "You're lucky you followed your own intuition and kept in shape by training for your sport," the assistant said. "When these muscles aren't conditioned, they spasm more easily. That's why you're in more pain now that you're inactive."

Dr. Buckley said, "If you hadn't trained you'd be a mess, young lady. All right, sit up and let's discuss this." He helped her up and explained what he thought was the origin of her pain. "You may have a neuropraxia or a neuronotmesis of the intercostal nerve, somewhere between the posterior division and the lateral division. I don't think you have a neuroma at either the entrance or exit wound areas, but I'm going to get some x-rays to be sure. You've developed a myofascial syndrome affecting all the muscles we talked about earlier, and I'd like to inject most of those "hot spots," or trigger areas, with lidocaine to see what effect it has on your pain. If the pain goes away, we can be pretty sure of our diagnosis."

He took a deep breath. "I'd also like you to see Dr. Schoene, a Harborview chest physician, for a pulmonary function workup. According to your records you had pulmonary tests when you were here in August of 1984, and I'd like to see what has happened since then. I'll tell the secretary to set up an appointment for tomorrow. Any questions?"

"Are you going to do the injections now? Should I come back to see you tomorrow? Will the pain go away in a few more months? What can I do when I get home to improve the situation?" The questions tumbled over each other, and she looked embarrassed when she said, "I'm not sure I understood my diagnosis."

He laughed, pulled up a chair, answered her questions, and explained her condition in lay terms. "We'll do the injections as soon as I check another patient, and you should phone me tomorrow so I can question you about the results. Now, there's no way I can guarantee when, or if, the pain will go away. There's a chance that it will—someday—because you are motivated to help yourself. I'll speak with a physician in our sports medicine clinic and then make some recommendations for intensive physical therapy. I want you to consider biofeedback to help you deal with the pain. If you were staying here for treatment we'd use a combination of injections, acupuncture, physical therapy, and biofeedback. In Bozeman you can use the last two, and you'll see a definite improvement. Continue to train, but remember to start slowly and work up since you've taken several weeks off." He smiled. "I'm warning you because you probably have a tendency to overdo your training."

She laughed and glanced at me out of the corner of her eye. "Will my spine straighten itself?"

"Yes. It'll be corrected faster if we can get the spasms under control."

Dr. Buckley injected marcaine in at least twenty trigger spots, x-rays were taken, and an appointment was made for the pulmonary function tests. In Dr. Schoene's written report, he suggested an operation known as "a pulmonary peel" if the other modes of treatment were unsuccessful.

22

PRETRIAL DIFFICULTIES

"France's Questions Violated Nichols' Rights, Lawyer Says"

This *Bozeman Chronicle* headline greeted us on our return to Bozeman. The report said that the sheriff had questioned Dan Nichols about the kidnapping and Al's death while transporting him to the jail in Dillon. Nichols's attorney claimed that the questioning violated his client's constitutional rights. The article also reported that the defense attorneys had filed for separate trials for the Nicholses.

After a lengthy phone conversation with Marc, Bob said to me, "Well, the sheriff did interrogate Nichols. Not only that, but he 'confiscated' his papers, diary, and letters, and made copies of them. Let's hope that what was done won't get the trial thrown out for violating Nichols's rights."

"My God! Could that happen?" I gasped.

"It's possible. Marc's going to a hearing March twenty-fifth and expects the defense to ask that murder charges be dropped in both cases. He said Steve Ungar will ask to have the kidnapping charge set aside because he claims his client didn't willingly or knowingly kidnap Kari."

"What?"

"Don't get upset! Marc says this is routine and he expected it. He's going to ask that some charges against the Nicholses be dropped. Too many trivial charges have been filed, and Marc's afraid the jury could get so busy deciding on the little things that they'd forget the main issues of kidnapping, homicide, and the use of a weapon in the commission of a felony. On the twentieth Marc will go to something called a "suppression hearing." As I understand it, both sides will argue what evidence can and cannot be used at the trial. He said something about Don White being upset because of the way the crime scene investigation was done. Anyway, he'll call and tell us what happened at the hearing."

Marc phoned. "Janet?" His voice was quiet, tense, almost a whisper. "Don White asked for dismissal of the charges against Don Nichols because of the inadequate crime scene investigation." He sighed. "We were lucky Judge Davis denied the motion. There's a problem with measurements, photographs, sketches, et cetera. This will really make your day: the sheriff lost, or misplaced, the .22 and .222 cartridges from the defendants' guns."

"Lost them?" I sat down abruptly as if I'd been slapped.

"Yes. It's going to make this case more difficult to prosecute without accurate crime scene information." Marc's voice was clipped, irritated.

"You said something about photographs. What's that all about?"

"The sheriff used Jim Schwalbe's camera and took several rolls of film of the crime scene and Alan's body. Only three pictures turned out, and they're inadequate for trial use. Read the transcript of the proceedings if you want the details, but it's going to make you mad!"

March 20, 1985, The Suppression Hearing

The following information and quotes are from the transcript of the suppression hearing and from interviews with Sheriff Onstad, Bob Campbell, Bill Pronovost, and Ron Cutting.

Don White, attorney for Don Nichols, questioned Bob Campbell and Bill Pronovost about their professional education as law officers. Through their interrogations he established several facts for the court:

1. After injured victims are removed from the area, the crime scene should be sealed off with a special yellow tape that says "Sheriff's Line, Do Not Cross" to prevent people from walking into the area to be investigated. Bob and Bill testified that the tape was available the day of the crime scene investigation and could have been used. They agreed that law officers formed a protective perimeter around Kari and the crime scene area until after Alan was removed.

2. After a scene is secured, it should be measured, photographed, and sketched. Evidence that is collected should be put in special bags, labeled, and held under the protection of a law officer until it is turned in to the evidence locker.

3. A 35mm camera with special lenses is used for taking photographs of fingerprints, footprints, "and just about anything you'd want to photograph." Color film is recommended by crime investigation schools because it depicts the scene more realistically. The professional camera was available at the base.

4. On the day Kari was rescued, the Gallatin County sheriff had all the equipment needed (at the base) to do a proper crime investigation, but it was not used by the other sheriff.

Mr. White asked Bill, "Have you ever picked up a camera that was left, dropped at a scene, and used it to investigate the scene?"

"No," Bill answered.

"Have you ever heard of that being done?"

"I've never done it. I've never heard of it being done."

"Have you had it recommended to you by any school you've ever attended?" White pressed.

"No."

Mr. White called Sheriff France to the witness stand and asked him to relate what type of schools he had attended. He said he had gone to at least twenty-one or twenty-two basic, intermediate, and advanced classes. Four or five of the classes involved crime scene investigation, and he had successfully completed the courses.

White clarified that the sheriff had used Jim Schwalbe's camera to photograph the crime scene. The sheriff said he exposed two rolls of film and admitted that most of them "didn't develop." The attorney asked if France had rushed the exposed rolls of film to Bozeman for one-day processing. He said no, but he knew that option had been available. France said he returned to the crime scene the next day and took press people with him, but he didn't include anyone from law enforcement with their photography equipment.

"Did you request the photographers to bring colored film?" White asked.

"No, sir."

White asked if the sheriff had contacted the media or vice versa.

"They were available, believe me!" the officer responded.

"They were, in fact, crawling all over you to get to the crime scene, were they not?"

"That's correct."

"They wanted to go to the crime scene themselves, photograph it, and send these photographs to the newspapers later on?" White pressed.

"Yes, sir."

"They were more than happy to accompany you back to the scene, were they not?"

"Yes. I was in agreement that they bear in mind that they—that they—that they were wanting to get back to the crime scene, and I wanted to take some more pictures. Being professional photographers, I felt that there would be a good opportunity to obtain good pictures."

"But they were taken in black and white?" Mr. White asked.

"Less shadow."

"Well, it's common procedure, is it not, to do your crime scene work with colored photography?"

"True."

Sheriff France said the professional photographer gave him sixty-three copies of the black-and-white pictures approximately three weeks after they had been taken, and he, at some point in time, gave them to the Gallatin County sheriff's office to be held with the rest of the evidence. He testified that he hadn't asked to have measuring devices flown in with the rolls of film, but that he "stepped the distance off." Those figures would be important at the trials, he said, and attempted several days later to record the measurements on a sketch of the crime scene.

"What was that distance, if you recall?"

"Approximately forty-six feet," the witness answered.

"Okay, and you recorded that someplace?"

"In my mind, at least."

"In your *mind?*"

"Yes, sir."

Johnny France said he placed the .222 and .22 spent cartridges in an envelope with a pair of glasses, and kept them himself. He said he presumed that he had given them to Sergeant Cutting but knew they were no longer available.

"They were lost somewhere along the line?" White asked.

"Yes, sir."

Don White continued his interrogation by pointing out to the court that memos from the defense attorneys asking the sheriff for his complete files on the two criminals had been ignored.

He provided the court with copies of the requests dated December 1984 and March 1985.

"I thought, as I recall, I had a memo of about ten days ago asking me for copies of all my documents concerning Dan and Don Nichols," Sheriff France said.

"Those documents were the ones you just produced to us about an hour ago; is that correct?" White asked.

"Yes, sir."

During Marc's cross-examination, Sheriff France said that he controlled the search from the beginning and was directing ground forces while he was flying in the helicopter. He testified that he had sheriff's tape flown in to flag the path leading out of the crime area, but he hadn't thought it was necessary to flag off the entire crime scene even though he agreed with White that it is usually done as a matter of routine. He told Marc he was developing a model of the crime scene based on his measurements and photographs. Once again he said he had placed the spent cartridges in an envelope.

"I guess what you're saying," Marc said to France, "is there's a possibility, considering where you had been throughout the day and the terrain that you'd been involved with, that those could have at some point dropped out of that envelope, or that they were lost by Gallatin County when they were turned over to them?"

"That's possible," the sheriff answered.

"So on the seventeenth you were satisfied thinking that the pictures you had taken the sixteenth would accurately reflect what had taken place. And with the crime scene sketch and the evidence you had retrieved, you felt that the situation was in hand?"

"Yes, sir."

Marc's arguments saved the case but angered the Gallatin County law officers.

"When he tried to pin the loss of that evidence on Ron Cutting and us, it was too much!" Bob Campbell fumed. "We got together—

me, Onstad, Cutting, and Pronovost—and wrote up a statement of what really happened and went to Helena to see Marc. We gave a copy of that statement to him, the attorney general, Ungar, and White. It's not legal for us to let you read it, Jan, but it tells the truth about what was and wasn't done at the crime scene investigation. Mad? Yeah, I guess you could say we were mad!"

Ron added, "After the capture I was worried about the cartridges everyone told me the sheriff had picked up, so I phoned Loren Tucker and voiced my concern. He said not to worry about it, that Johnny had sent them to the state forensics lab in Missoula. Merlin told me the same thing, so I forgot about them until I heard what had been said at the suppression hearing. The cartridges weren't turned in to me and they weren't on the evidence inventory list."

23

THE PROSECUTING ATTORNEYS

Judge Davis granted separate trials for the Nicholses. He ruled against the defense's motions to dismiss deliberate homicide charges against the father and son, prompting Steve Ungar to tell reporters that Montana's felony murder rule was unconstitutional. This rule states that if in the commission of a felony a death results, all parties to the felony may be charged with homicide.

The judge approved a request by the defense to spend up to $2,000 for psychological evaluations of Dan Nichols, by a psychologist this time, and said he was undecided whether or not the prosecutors would be allowed to see the resulting reports before the trial.

The day Marc came to talk to Kari, she received a letter from the Women's Sports Foundation informing her that she had been selected to be honored as a recipient of the foundation's "Up and Coming Athlete Award." The foundation would fly her to San Francisco on May eighteenth in time for the Bay To Breakers festival, and the black tie award ceremony would be on the twentieth.

"With my kind of luck, the trial will be scheduled about that time," Kari said. But the thought didn't dampen her enthusiasm as she read the names of the athletes who would be attending the award weekend.

Marc arrived accompanied by Judy Browning, an assistant attorney general, who was also assigned to the case. Marc's youthful face was accentuated by a gentle mouth, intense blue eyes, and a romanesque nose. His brown suit complemented his trim athletic physique, and his western-style boots were polished to a mirror shine. The gentleness of his expression when he talked to Kari endeared him to me immediately. It was apparent he wasn't thinking only of the details Kari was discussing but was considering her as a human being and was moved by her ordeal. Intuition told me this man was special.

Judy's quiet elegance and restraint complemented Marc's restlessness. She was blonde, tall, and slim, with blue-gray eyes that flashed with humor and intelligence. Her blazer, skirt, and blouse were both professional and feminine.

Marc was discussing the media coverage of the case with Kari. "Well, you've been wise to avoid the press as much as you have. The interviews the law enforcement officers gave right after the incident are going to make this a difficult case to prosecute."

"Why?"

"The remarks comparing Don Nichols to a grizzly sow protecting her cub, that the Nicholses were Daniel Boone types, and that they were probably harmless, gave them a defense before they were apprehended. The news media loved it. 'Mountain men' has a romantic ring to some people. I won't have anything to say to the press nor will anyone else working on this case with me."

Kari explained the sports award and asked about trial dates.

"I'm not sure of the date for the father's trial—probably early June," Marc told her.

They collected their notes and shook hands with us at the door. "We have to drive to Virginia City on the way home to have a look at a model of the crime scene the Madison County sheriff is putting together. He wants us to use it at the trials," Marc said. "Once more, Kari, you're sure of the distances you gave me? The ones at the crime scene?"

"Yes. Why?" I hadn't told her about the suppression hearing arguments concerning the distances quoted by Jim Schwalbe, the sheriff, and herself.

"Well, they don't agree with the sheriff's figures."

"Oh. I could only estimate the distances, but from all my target shooting I have a good idea how far fifty meters is. Did he measure with a tape?"

"No."

"I'll bet I'm not off by more than a foot or two. I had a long time to look at the area." She gave the prosecutors a lopsided grin.

"We'll soon know how accurate you are," Marc grinned back at her. "I've asked Sheriff Onstad to ride in to the crime scene to do the official measurements for me. He was one of the first men to get to you and knows where everyone was. We can tell where you were at the time of the shootings. The chain left a scar on the fallen tree."

Kari frowned. "Don't quit smiling, they're not worth it," he said gently. "Oh, by the way, John Connor will remain on the case with Judy and me. He'll be a real asset."

The model the sheriff made was so far off scale it wasn't used at the trials.

The April fourth *Bozeman Chronicle* ran this headline:

Judge Tells Sheriff to Give Back Dan Nichols' Papers

A court order filed by Ungar charged that France had violated Nichols's constitutional rights when he confiscated and duplicated Nichols's papers, artistic work, diagrams, attorney's notes, logs of conversations, and research memoranda. He allegedly questioned each of the Nicholses while transporting them to the jail in Dillon.

Judge Davis's order called for the return of any papers or copies and prohibited the prosecution from using "any said items or the fruits thereof at the trial." He also ordered that any statements the older Nichols made during his transportation to Dillon could not be used by the prosecution. This ruling comes under one of the most controversial doctrines facing prosecuting attorneys—the exclusionary rule. The rule states that constitutional violations can best be avoided by denying prosecutors any benefits illegally obtained. The rule is meant to stop improper police conduct.

The article said, "When contacted today, France said he performed only a routine 'inventory' of Nichols's property during the move from Gallatin County jail in Dillon with 'no intent of using any of that inventory in court.'"

24

THERAPY

"What is the worst, the absolute worst thing you can think of that could happen to you at the trial?" Dr. Frank Seitz asked Kari.

There was a long silence, she shook her head and said, "I don't know."

"That's not good enough. You said you're worried. About what? Are you afraid they'll hurt you again?"

"No. I just—I just—I don't know." Kari picked at the hem of her bright yellow shorts and avoided our eyes.

"Jan, can you cast any light on the problem?" Frank said. Kari had asked me to go to a session with her, and I found myself sitting with her and my long-time friend in his office. His prematurely silver hair was immaculately groomed, and his handsome, gentle face showed concern. I thought to myself that the phrase "he'll grow old gracefully" was coined for Frank.

"I may be off base," I said, "but I'll tell you what I think. Kari's always been a private person, tucking away her hurts and fears to think about in her own good time. Now she's being asked to share the most traumatic event in her life with the public.

This has been a private terror, and she'd like to keep it that way." Kari squirmed in her chair.

I sighed and continued. "I can give you an example. When she was ten or eleven she was learning to show a horse at halter during a 4-H horse training class. She was kicked in the thigh by the horse in front of her and refused to be carried out of the arena. She made us prop her up against a light pole where people couldn't see her and wouldn't leave until she could walk out without help, without tears. She didn't want anyone to see her cry or to know that she hurt. I think she feels the same way about the trials."

"Well, Kari, is your mom right?"

"She usually is." We knew by her grin that I had hit the mark.

"Then I'll ask again, what is the worst thing you can think of that could happen at the trial?"

"I'm afraid when I see him I'll vomit!"

"That's acceptable. Ask Marc to have a wastebasket close to you."

"Oh, no!" she moaned.

"Seriously, Kari. If you think you might get sick, be prepared for it, turn your back to the courtroom, and do what you have to. There's no shame if your fears take a physical form. Now, what's the second worst thing that could happen?"

"You'll think I'm silly, but I'm afraid I'll start to cry. If I do I'll run behind the drapes and refuse to come out."

"Nope, that isn't acceptable," he smiled. "Can't you see the judge begging you to come out?" They laughed at the thought.

"What'll I do?"

"What do you think would be acceptable?"

"I suppose Marc could ask for a recess until I get myself back together, but I don't want to cry! I'd like to do this with some dignity, and I want you to help me do it my way. Can you do that?"

"I'll try. It's all right to cry, you know."

"Not with the cameras shoved in my face! If they weren't there it wouldn't make so much difference, but . . ."

"We'll work on it," Frank assured her. "How's the biofeedback going?"

Kari had made arrangements with physical therapist Joan Van Natta to start treatments for her muscle spasms and had set up biofeedback sessions with Dr. Robert Morasky, chairman of the psychology department at the university. He brought the equipment to the student health service and worked with Kari several times a week. She was taking a genetics class and working part-time for veterinarian Sid Gustafson, but she juggled her schedule to get the therapy she needed and continued her psychological counseling with Frank as well.

After a few biofeedback sessions Bob Morasky met with Bob and me and said, "I can get her to relax, but the moment I mention anything associated with the kidnapping, the muscles in her back and chest immediately spasm. It's going to take hard work, but she told me she needs all the help she can get to make it through the trials."

One evening Bob came home from work and stuffed the evening newspaper in his briefcase. "I won't let either of you read it until after dinner," he said to Kari and me.

Later, we opened the *Chronicle*. The headline was accompanied by a photograph of Virginia City's Mayor.

Virginia City Hopes to Cash in on Trial

The article said the Nicholses' trials would cost Madison County thousands of dollars, but Virginia City residents were hoping to recoup some of that when the media and the curious descended on the town. Restaurants, taverns, and other businesses were gearing up for the trials by opening early.

" 'A lot of people are saying this will put Virginia City back on the map,' said the woman mayor. 'It's gotten lost in the last couple of years. The business people are hoping to get some money back. The Tavern people were talking about maybe having a "Hangman's Special" or something.'

" 'It's great for business,' owner of The Tavern said of the trials. 'From what I hear, people are excited about it. It fits with the mountain men and the old West.' "

I choked back my fury and looked at Kari's pinched face.

"The circus has started, hasn't it?" she asked, tossing the paper into the fireplace. "Maybe they could set up a barker, popcorn vendors, and a cotton candy booth on the courthouse steps!" She watched the paper curl, turn black, and flash into flames with a whoosh that disturbed the cat sleeping on the hearth. The only sounds in the room were the fire and the wind whipping the April rain against the windows.

Bob changed the subject by asking Kari about the dress I was making for her to wear to San Francisco. Marc Racicot phoned to tell me he was furious about the article. He had been contacted by a group of people who wanted permission to sell buttons and T-shirts with pictures of the Nicholses, Kari, or Al on them. His rejection of the request was vehement. "I told them they'd have this office to answer to if they tried such a stupid stunt! I've also heard rumors that a bar in Ennis is going to sponsor Alan Goldstein and Don Nichols look-alike contests before Don's trial. We'll stop it if we can."

"Thanks, Marc. Has Judge Davis ruled on your request to keep cameras out of the courtroom?"

"Unfortunately, he turned us down on that score and also decided we couldn't see the psychological reports on Dan Nichols before the trial."

"How in the world are you supposed to guess what the psychologist and that therapist reported? Did you tell the judge how Jim Schwalbe and Kari feel about the cameras?" I rushed on before Marc could answer. "What if Don Nichols's attorney goes along with the cameras for Dan's trial, then tries to get the old man off because there was too much publicity at the first trial?"

"White can't have it both ways. He has to object to the cameras now or forget it."

"I'll bet you a gooey chocolate treat that White protests before his client's trial!" I said. "The camera decision makes me sick. If the judge is serious about limiting publicity he should have granted your request."

"Calm down, Janet. I'll request that any witness who doesn't want to be photographed can ask to have the cameras shut off. He might agree to that because he knows Kari and Jim feel their rights are being ignored. John Onstad went in to the crime scene and did the measurements for me, and a forensic photographer went with him to get color photographs. He knows his business, and we finally have the professional photos we need to use in court. We'll come to Bozeman next week because I want Kari to see them."

"Anything else?" I sighed.

"Don't get discouraged, we have a few tricks up our sleeve. We've had investigators checking out Dan Nichols's past in White Sulphur Springs and Three Forks and I'll have some interesting news for you by next week." His voice was cheerful as if he relished matching wits with the judge and the defense attorneys.

I laughed, "The plot thickens, huh?"

The next week Marc and Bob talked about our concerns involving the trial. Kari was distressed by the rumor that some people felt the Nicholses were good old boys who shouldn't have been caught or punished.

"She's afraid some other self-styled mountain men who sympathize with the criminals might appear at the trial and threaten her. It may seem farfetched, but she's genuinely afraid," Bob said.

Marc decided to make arrangements for her to be escorted by a plainclothesman to and from Virginia City and to have her protected during her testimony. He said a reporter from our local paper was delving into his own background, education, and record with the attorney general's office. Marc had phoned the editor to try to stop the article because he didn't want anything in the papers from the prosecution's side that the defense attorneys would claim was damaging to their clients. They ignored Marc's request, and the headline read:

Marc Racicot: State's Man in Nicholses' Cases

Marc's peers, both prosecutors and defense attorneys, gave their opinions of him, all positive. Timor Moses, a prominent Billings criminal defense attorney, called Marc one of the most competent prosecutors in Montana. "He's one of the most formidable opponents. I like to deal with him. He's up-front. His pattern is unchangeable and very effective."

In a related article we read that Judge Davis had denied Marc's motion to ban cameras in the courtroom. He said he'd reverse his decision if the media "is reckless in covering the trial."

"Good grief, Bob, read this!" I handed him the paper, and he read out loud.

"In a related matter, Nichols's attorney has asked Davis to limit the use in court of graphic photos of Kari Swenson's injuries and Alan Goldstein's death," Bob read. "Steve Ungar said that since the aggravated assault charge requires only proof that 'bodily injury' occurred, extensive testimony and photographs of injuries would unfairly influence the jury."

The phone rang in the middle of my angry response, and I jerked the receiver from the wall. "Hello!"

"Oops, you've read the paper," Marc said.

"The story about you was good," I assured him.

"I still don't like it. To write something like that, knowing how strongly I objected to it. . . . Oh, well, it's done and I still think our low profile is the best way to go. It must have been Ungar's request that upset you. It will be granted, but we have ways of getting across what she suffered. I'm certain Judge Davis will allow a physician to testify and will approve some of the pathology photographs. We'd like to take Kari to Virginia City toward the end of the month, let her sit in the witness chair, and prepare her for the small size of the room. She'll be more comfortable if she knows exactly where everyone will be sitting.

"Tom Adamo, the plainclothesman who'll drive Kari to and from the trial, is coming with us. They should get to know each other before the trial. Tell Bob to relax, his daughter will be well taken care of."

"Thanks, Marc. That's one less thing for her to lose sleep over."

"Is there really a possibility she might vomit at the trial?"

"Yes."

"She better not! I have a weak stomach, and if she vomits so will I. Guess I'd better make sure there are *two* wastebaskets handy." Marc continued, "They've moved Nichols to Missoula for his evaluation by the psychologist. Since we can't see the report, we are asking to have him evaluated by a forensic psychiatrist who is excellent, knows his business, and won't be easily fooled. I'm positive the judge will allow our request. He's a good man and is doing everything he can to insure that the defense can't come back after the trial and accuse him of misconduct, or get a retrial on a technicality. I know to the victims it seems lopsided, but that's the way the system is set up."

"It's not right, though!"

"Don't lose faith in Judge Davis, he's just doing his job."

"The fact that you say that, after all the problems you've had, makes me feel better."

25

VIRGINIA CITY

It was a day in late April when Marc, Judy, and Tom Adamo arrived at our house. Kari and the two prosecutors looked at the photographs of the crime scene. Marc asked her to lay out the pictures and explain the scenario to him, asking her to tell him how far it was from point A to point B, C, and so on. When they finished, he grinned and told her about the measurements.

"You remember the bet you had with me concerning the dispute between the distances named by you, Jim, and the Madison sheriff?" Marc asked Kari.

"Yes."

"You win. Johnny's model was so far off it can't be used in court."

"I don't remember what we bet, do you?"

"Sure. We bet that if *you* won you'd buy *me* something with chocolate in it." They laughed as he recited a list of his favorite chocolate desserts. Tom looked at his watch, cleared his throat, and said it was time to leave for Virginia City.

The mountains were free of snow, and the fields were green with winter wheat. The Madison River hosted ducks and geese on their return north for the summer, and fishermen in their waders stood waist deep in the river, casting upstream, enticing the trout with hand-tied flies. The weather had been hot and dry, and drought threatened our crops, but today the countryside was too beautiful to consider the long, hot summer that lay ahead.

We bypassed Ennis and drove over the long, steep sagebrush-covered hill that dropped abruptly into Virginia City. In the 1860s more than 10,000 gold miners lived in the gold-rich Alder Gulch area. Today it is a quiet town of about 200 people.

The courthouse is built on a side hill. An expanse of wide cement steps leads up to the white double doors, which are capped with a graceful arched window and an overhead balcony supported by four white pillars. The walls of the rustic brick building are punctuated with tall, narrow, arched windows.

We stepped into a spacious hallway where a carpeted stairway curved upward. The wooden floor of the second story, shiny with age and wear, creaked under our feet. To the left were double doors leading out onto the balcony over the entryway, and farther down the corridor to the right was the courtroom. Marc opened the tall doors, and we entered a cool, hushed, dimmed room with eighteen-foot-high ceilings. Another door leading from the room lay ahead of us across the small courtroom.

On our right, the west side, were rows of wooden pews for observers. The east side of the room was partitioned off with a beautiful golden oak banister. Rising two steps above the floor within the oak enclosure was the judge's presidium, and to the right of it, from our perspective, was the witness chair. It was also of antique oak, had armrests, a slatted back, and the seat was mounted on a swivel. The windows were almost as tall as the ceiling and were draped with cascades of rich crimson velvet. Several windows were positioned in the wall behind the judge's bench and witness chair. The same number interrupted the wall behind the spectator's section.

"I could certainly hide behind *those* drapes," Kari said, squeezing my arm. Our voices seemed loud in the small room.

"Do you want to sit in the witness chair, Kari, or would you rather sit over here in front of the jury box with your parents?" Marc asked.

"I might as well sit where I'll be during the trial. The room is so small! I'll get sick if I'm too close to the defendant!"

"Think positive! If you get sick, so will I, and I hate to throw up!" Marc made an unpleasant face.

Kari hesitated, stepped up to the witness platform, turned, and sat down with an audible sigh.

"Where will you, Judy, and John be sitting?" she asked Marc.

"Right here." He indicated a table set off to her right and about ten feet in front of her.

"Where will Nichols be sitting?"

Marc pointed to a table farther to her right and to the left of the prosecutor's table.

"I'm afraid I'll lose it when I see him!" Beads of sweat collected on her upper lip.

"That's why Dr. Seitz and Dr. Morasky have been spending so much time with you. You'll do it your way," Marc smiled. "Don't be afraid. John and I won't let him close to you, and since Steve Ungar is going to present him as a weak, dominated little boy, he wouldn't dare demonstrate any of the aggression he showed you in the mountains."

Marc walked to a point ten feet directly in front of her. "I use a podium that'll stand here, so you won't have to look at anyone but me. I'm going to ask that the front row in the center of the room be reserved for your parents. If you want to look at them during your testimony, just look over my shoulder."

"That's great!"

She was distracted by Loren Tucker, who stepped into the courtroom.

"Hi, Kari," he said.

"Hello, Mr. Tucker."

He offered to let the prosecuting attorneys use his office during the trial since the only conference room had been delegated to the defense attorneys. Sheriff France entered, said hello, and joined the men who were discussing reserving the benches. Meanwhile, Judy spoke to Kari, reassuring her.

"It's arranged. The reserved signs will be posted on the first two rows in the middle," Marc said after Loren and the sheriff left.

"Why two rows?"

"Well, Doug and Diane Goldstein have been thinking of coming, and if your Mom and brothers come, Janet, we'll need that much room."

"I had no idea the Goldsteins were thinking of coming," I said, surprised.

"When I talked with Diane and Jim Schwalbe about the pathology report, she said she might come. It would be helpful if the jury had someone from the family to identify with Al, but I can understand their reluctance to attend two trials." He turned to Kari.

"Do you have any other questions?"

"No, but I think I'd like to sit here alone for a while."

"All right. We'll wait in the hall with the door open in case you want us."

We paced the ancient creaking floor, and Bob peeked into the courtroom.

"The pathologist's report must have been awful for Jim and Diane," I said to Marc.

"It was. Why weren't you surprised by it?"

"Last summer a medical friend told me about the autopsy report. I didn't want Kari, Paul, or Bob to know the details, so I kept it to myself. I told Kari about it when you met with Jim and Diane. She took it hard, and the guilt about his death came up as fresh as if it had never been discussed and laid to rest."

"What was in the report?" Tom asked.

"Ah-h-h, it's so damn sad!" Marc said, taking out his pipe. "When Al was shot he fell on his back and aspirated blood from the wound." Anger sparked in his eyes. "If the Nicholses had checked on him and turned him on his stomach, he might, just might, have had a chance to live. Kari couldn't have turned him over even if she could have inched that far. Does she realize that?"

"Of course, but it doesn't make any difference," I murmured.

Kari walked from the courtroom into the corridor. The strong light filtering in from the balcony picked up the shadows under her eyes and the tension lines around her mouth.

"This is a beautiful building, isn't it? When was it built?" She asked questions while she read the captions under the photographs hanging on the wall. "Wasn't there a Sheriff Plummer who was hanged here as an outlaw during the gold rush days? Was he the sheriff of Bannock?"

The conversation dwelt on the history of the area as we drove over the hill to Ennis.

26

\ \ \ \/ / / /

PRETRIAL ACTIVITIES

"When Dan Nichols was fourteen he terrorized a family of young children with a knife," Marc told us after we had returned home. "The parents were gone for the evening, and he chased two of the little girls, ages nine and eleven, around the house with a knife trying to find their thirteen-year-old sister."

"Did he find her?" Kari asked, astonished.

"The girls said he chased Laurie into the house. She hid behind a chair, and when he ran past she dashed upstairs to tell the other children to lock themselves in their rooms. Her older sister wasn't upstairs, so Debbie went back down with Laurie to search for her. Nichols ran out of a room and scared the younger one so badly she fainted. When she came to he was sitting on her chest threatening her with his knife. Her sister tried to help her, but Nichols demanded to know where their older sister was, and the two girls told a convincing lie. They said she'd gone into town to some teenage hangout. Just as he was leaving, the girl he was looking for came into the room. She said hello, thinking he was a friend, and when he turned with the knife she ran into a bathroom and locked the door. He chased her, yelling, "You're the one I want, you're the one I want!" Marc puffed on his pipe thoughtfully.

"Those kids must have been scared to death!" Kari said.

"Well, he didn't get the girl." He squinted at Kari through the pipe smoke. "The irony is that her name was Carrie."

"You're kidding! Was he caught?"

"He was arrested later in the summer by John Onstad, who turned him over to the proper authorities. He was given probation and a psychiatric evaluation."

"If he was sick, why didn't someone help him then?" Bob asked.

"I don't know all the particulars yet. About that time Dan decided to go to a foster home because he was angry with his parents. He went to school regularly, played sports, joined a religious group with an active teen program, worked on the foster parents' ranch, and obeyed the laws of society. A year later he went back to his mother's house and continued to go to school until May or June of 1983."

"That sounds like a normal life to me," Bob said.

"It was, with one exception. He was having an affair with a twenty-eight-year-old married woman."

"What?" I sputtered. "How did that happen? Did his parents know?"

"His father was furious and did everything he could to get him away, but the harder he tried, the more determined the kid was to stay. As a matter of fact, he didn't join up with his father in Jackson Hole until the woman had terminated the relationship. When she did, he left school, found out he didn't like washing dishes in Jackson, and agreed to live in the mountains with his dad."

Marc chewed on the stem of his cold pipe. "There's more irony here, Kari. The woman's name was Sue, and you told them your name was Sue."

"This is bizarre!" she exclaimed. "What should I do at the trials? I can't sit on the witness stand and call them by their names as if I'd known them for years."

"You're right. I don't want anyone to get the impression that this trial is old home week. You may call them Mr. Nichols or the defendant."

"The defendant will do."

" 'The old man' conjures up visions of a gray-haired, aged man. How old is he?" Bob asked.

"He's fifty-four, hardly an old man," Judy answered.

"Changing the subject," I interjected, "will the incident with the young girls help our case?"

"It was a juvenile offense; I can't use it unless Ungar gives me the opportunity. If he uses the defendant's past to try to establish good character, I'll have an opening. It'll be tricky. We'll have to hope Ungar opens it up for us, and that Judge Davis will allow the testimony of the girls. Judy's done an excellent job of researching, so we're primed if we get the chance we'll be looking for."

"Mr. Ungar will be surprised!" I said.

"No, he won't. I have to turn in a list of all possible prosecution witnesses at least ten days before the trial starts. The minute he and his client see those names they'll know what's coming, and Ungar will submit a brief arguing against hearing their testimony."

"Does he give you a list of his witnesses?" Kari asked.

"No."

"The balance of justice always seems tipped in favor of the criminals! Isn't there anything we can do that's a surprise?" Bob asked.

Judy, Tom, and Marc laughed at the look on my husband's face and explained that the state wasn't allowed to spring surprises.

The Women's Sports Foundation public relations agent called and asked to which paper she should send a press release. Kari didn't want the kidnapping referred to in the announcement of her award, but the editor of our local paper refused to do the press release without recapping the tragedy. I explained that the award had nothing to do with the incident; it was for her performance at Chamonix before the kidnapping. He held his position on the matter, I lost my temper and said, "There must be an editor in Montana with some sensitivity, and I'll find him!" I was not sure I was correct.

I spoke to the editor of the *Billings Gazette*, explained the award, the press release, and the problem I was having.

"It's time we allow Kari to be a person again," he said. "She shouldn't have to have her name constantly linked with the Nicholses. Have the Sports Foundation send the release directly to me, and I'll see that it's printed properly. Patty Spurgin, the shooter from Billings, is receiving the award, too. It will make a great article." He kept his promise.

"Judge Davis has ruled that witnesses who don't want to be photographed will have their request granted," Marc said excitedly when he phoned. "The media isn't pleased, but they'll go along or risk getting kicked out of the courtroom. This ruling shows Davis's interest in protecting the rights of the victims as well as those of the press. He put off this decision until the last minute, realizing the media would probably try to get an injunction against his order and hold up the jury selection. Tell Kari that the judge has done us right, so she'd better not vomit on his floor!" He was still chortling when he hung up.

Paul wanted to know about the plea-bargain that Mr. Ungar had offered. When I told him they wanted the homicide and kidnapping charges dropped in exchange for a guilty plea to misdemeanor assault, he exploded.

"How long would he serve?"

"Two years, but he'd be out sooner if he behaved himself."

"Two years!" His face flushed. "I don't understand! Where's justice for Kari, Al, and Jim?" He paced the family room venting his anger for the first time since Kari had been kidnapped. "Will Kari be all right? She's so thin and nervous."

"And you're not? Yes, she'll be all right after she testifies, but it's going to take its toll. She didn't want Marc to accept Ungar's offer, although it would have saved her a lot of grief. It's a gamble, because the jury may let him go, but she and Marc are willing to take a chance."

My mother, who had arrived two days earlier, came into the family room to see what the fuss was about. One look at Paul's face told her. She took him out on the deck for a glass of iced tea. They sat in silence, listening to the evening song of the meadowlarks until darkness and the mosquitoes chased them inside to play cards with Kari and me.

27

DAN NICHOLS'S TRIAL

Tuesday, May 7, 1985

I sat on the deck at dawn remembering last summer when I sought isolation out here with the sunrise. The air was still and hot. Mother joined me, and we sipped coffee without speaking. She is a tiny, attractive woman with a cap of thick brown hair and enormous blue eyes. She has the energy of a thirty-year-old, and people are attracted by her vivaciousness, humor, and kindness. I worried that the trial might be too much for her. She and Paul didn't know all the details, and I suspected they would be shocked when Kari testified.

"Maybe you'd rather stay home and read about the trial in the papers, Mom," I suggested.

"No! I was gone when you and Kari needed me last summer, and this time I'll be where I can help." Her lips compressed into a stubborn line. "Marc didn't know how long Kari would have to stay at the courthouse, so I'll sit with her in the prosecutor's office. She can study and I'll take along a book to read."

I knew it was selfish, but I wanted her with me if she could endure the tension. We discussed last week's meeting between

Kari and Marc. The prosecutors had arrived to tell Kari what arrangements had been made to get her to Virginia City. I wondered why Marc and Kari hadn't had a drill session (they had discussed the deposition in March and only the progress of the pretrial motions and problems since then), so I asked Marc about it.

He grinned at Kari and tamped tobacco into his pipe. "I think we'll make a better team if it's spontaneous, don't you, Kari?"

"Yes, but what if I forget something important?"

"You won't. Judge Davis won't allow long narratives, so I'll ask questions and you answer them. If you forget something important, I'll back up and ask a question that'll bring it out. During the cross-examination listen carefully to the question and ask Steve to repeat it if necessary." He lit the pipe, taking his time, then said, "Kari, I don't want you in the courtroom when I give my opening statement. It'll upset you. Tom'll take you to the courthouse after I've started talking, and the reporters will miss you completely."

"Sneaky! Will Tom and I leave Bozeman after my parents?"

"No, you'll leave much earlier and we'll hide you away. A family in Virginia City offered to let us use their home during the trial, and we jumped at the offer. It will give us a place to go for lunch, and if you need privacy, there's plenty of room to go off by yourself. No one can approach the house without being seen, so that solves the media problem.

"We'll meet you and Tom at the house early Tuesday morning, and you two will arrive at the courthouse fifteen minutes after court has convened, slip in the back door, and up the back steps to the county prosecutor's office, where you'll wait until I ask Tom to bring you in. He'll escort you to me so you won't be alone for a second. He'll be sticking to you like glue except when you're on the witness stand. Deputies will guard all the entrances, but I'll alert the one at the back door to let you in."

"What about Jim Schwalbe? Will he go with us?"

"No. He'll meet us there. Your mother asked his wife to sit with her and your dad while Jim testifies so she won't be alone."

Bob had gone to Virginia City the day before for the jury selection. "The courtroom was an oven," Bob told Paul during dessert, "and everyone was irritable by midafternoon. It was a long arduous process, but Marc thinks they have a pretty good jury."

"Ungar didn't ask for a change of venue, and that worries me," I murmured.

Mom and I stayed on the deck as long as we could, reluctant to face the day. We talked about the family reunion we were planning for August. Johanna was coming from Seattle, and, for the first time in years, all the cousins would be together. During a moment of silence I thought about Dan Nichols's mother and pitied her for the ordeal she faced. However, I sympathized more deeply with the other three mothers—Mrs. Goldstein, Diane's mother, and my mother.

Immediately after breakfast Tom and Kari left for Virginia City. He delivered Kari to Marc and stationed himself to watch the driveway for uninvited guests. Judy, John, and Marc were cheerful, but under the veneer Kari felt their tension. Marc paced, fiddled with his pipe, put it back in his pocket, and carried on a conversation, but it was obvious his thoughts were somewhere else.

John thumbed through notes, then walked about with both hands jammed deep in his pockets. A frown of concentration pulled his eyebrows toward his nose. Judy wiggled in her chair and tugged at the sleeves of her suit jacket.

Marc glanced at his watch. "We'd better go. Tom, you know when to arrive with Kari." He smiled at her. "It'll be all right. Pretend you're having a conversation with me, and blot out everyone else."

Bob parked our car in the shade of a small tree close to the courthouse, and we walked up the steps to the entryway. The beauty of the double doors was vulgarized by a hand-scrawled sign: "If you are carrying any guns, knives, or other weapons, please remove them before you enter the courthouse. You will be searched upon entering the courthouse."

Inside, a deputy directed us through a metal detector borrowed from the airport. Overkill, I thought to myself. Paul walked up the curved staircase with my mother. Tall Paul and short Mother looked like Mutt and Jeff. I laughed. The deputy looked startled, then smiled back.

The television crew was taping microphones to the judge's presidium and the podium. A microphone stood beside the witness chair, and the velvet drapes behind the bench were pinned shut to dampen the glare on the camera lens. Electrical cords snaked across the room and were taped to the floor. The television cameraman and his equipment were perched on an elevated platform to my right. Seated behind him were reporters with their notebooks and cameras. The atmosphere crackled with tension and excitement. I felt sick. John Connor entered from the door next to the TV camera and beckoned to Bob, who joined him and disappeared into the hallway.

Bob and Vivian Schaap, Jay Schreck, and Karen and Debbie Frauson arrived from the Lone Mountain Ranch and sat with us. The Goldsteins had not come, and my brothers couldn't leave their jobs, so there was plenty of seating available. I introduced my mother to the new arrivals, and we watched the room fill with curiosity seekers. Two older ladies who sat behind us brought cushions, a cooler of soft drinks, Tupperware glasses, and sharp tongues. They twittered like sparrows, staring and pointing at Nichols's family and ourselves as if we were a sideshow.

Bob returned, and the attorneys for both sides filed into Judge Davis's chambers, where they remained for five minutes. The jurors entered the room and were seated along the wall close to the witness chair. They were a cross-section of society—young and old, fat and thin, men and women. Dan Nichols was escorted to the defense table by several deputies. Marc had been correct when he assumed they would emphasize his boyishness. His thinning blond hair had been cut to clear his collar and stylishly covered the tips of his ears. He was wearing corduroy slacks and a long-sleeved shirt under an argyle vest. His clean-shaven face was sullen and arrogant. I glanced at the jury. A woman juror cocked her head thoughtfully and followed his progress across the room with a maternal expression on her face. My heart sunk. She looked like a benevolent aunt.

Marc presented an eloquent and moving opening statement, depicting the kidnapping and wounding of Kari and the murder of Alan. Mom clutched my hand.

Mr. Ungar insisted that his client was so dominated by his father that he was unable to reason for himself. He said Dan would not deny "restraining" Kari nor the fact that it was his pistol that wounded her.

Judge Davis ordered a five-minute recess, and Marc, John, Judy, and Bob hurried to Kari and Tom in Loren Tucker's office. Bob returned and sat next to Paul, who was deathly pale. He patted Paul's shoulder and said, "She's okay, what about you?" Paul shook his head and shrugged.

The judged returned, folded his hands, pushed his glasses up on the bridge of his nose, and gazed sternly at the news media gallery.

"All right. Court will be in session. I have just been informed, ladies and gentlemen of the press, that this next witness does not want to be photographed or filmed while she is testifying, so after she gives her name, there will be no cameras. That's my order. It's pursuant to our guidelines." He nodded at Marc, "Call your first witness."

"We call Kari Swenson, Your Honor."

Kari stepped through the door with Tom and two other plainclothesmen accompanying her. She was wearing comfortable old clothes: tan slacks, white blouse, and a teal-green vest. Her long hair hung loose, pulled back from her forehead and temples with a barrette. Marc smiled and told her where to stand to be sworn in. She looked vulnerable as she raised a quivering right hand.

Marc showed her photographs of the Nicholses, taken at the time of their capture, and asked her to identify them. She related the early events of July fifteenth, running around the lake on the left shore to avoid a "fisherman" she saw on the other bank, and on to the confrontation with the Nicholses.

"Were these men moving around, Kari?"

"No. They were standing very still."

"What about the expressions on their faces?"

"No expressions. Just staring at me."

"Did you surprise them as you ran up on them?"

"No. They looked like they had been waiting for me."

She repeated the information from her statements concerning the weapons they possessed and the threatening stance of the defendant with one hand on his gun and the other on his knife. Her voice quivered.

"Now as you turned to leave, what happened?"

"Uh, he . . . grabbed me by . . . both wrists." The sentence ended in a sob. Paul's hands knotted into white-knuckled fists.

"Do you want to take a moment?" Marc moved toward Kari. She shook her head, drank the water offered by Judge Davis, and said she could continue.

"I know it's an ordeal for you," the judge said kindly, "but the jury has to hear your story, so try to compose yourself and give your testimony as best you can."

She nodded at him and replaced the glass on the edge of his table. The muscles in her jaw worked with the effort of quelling her emotions.

The questions continued, and she answered as if in a trance. Marc brought up point after point that proved the defendant was acting independently by urging his father to get farther back in the hills, by leading the way, pulling Kari along with him, and by stating he wanted to keep her when she begged to be released. She said the older Nichols was not always present, and the defendant, since he had a key to the lock, could have freed her.

"Did the defendant ever express his feelings about whether or not they should take or keep you?"

"Your Honor, I'd object. Leading," said Ungar.

"What? Well, it's somewhat leading, but I'm going to permit it."

"Well, when I had asked him to please let me go—'You don't want to get involved with anything like this,' he said, 'No. Let's keep her.'"

The testimony covered important details such as the dropping of her headband and watch, and the threats made by the defendant and his father about shooting anyone who tried to rescue her.

"Were you informed by anyone or apprised by anyone of the defendant's artistic ability?" Marc asked.

"Yes. The old man said that the defendant was quite good at drawing, and he persuaded the defendant to show me some."

Kari identified the drawing of the naked woman Dan had shown her, and Marc said, "And does that appear to be in the same condition as when you saw it on July 15, 1984?"

"Yes, it does,"

"I move for admission of State's Exhibit 6."

"Your Honor, I would object that the photograph [it was a sketch, not a photograph] is irrelevant, and whatever slight relevance it has is outweighed by its undue prejudice under the circumstances," Mr. Ungar argued.

"The objection is overruled. It will be admitted." The naked lady of Kari's nightmares was shown to the jury.

She testified she had heard people yelling, that she was told to keep quiet, and she related the threat to shoot anyone who walked into camp. Questions brought out the manner in which the kidnappers dragged her from tree to tree like a dog on a leash when they heard the airplane. She told the jury about her request for warmer clothing because she was cold.

Marc did not dwell on the long, cold hours of the night, but went directly to the next morning, the shooting of the squirrel, and moving to a new camp location.

"Did he ask you how old you were at any point in time?"

"Yes. He had asked me the night before. When the young man had gone off hunting, he asked me how old I was, and I said I was twenty-two. And the old man said, 'Oh, well, that's a little young. I was hoping for an older woman for my son.' "

"And when he said he wanted an older woman for his son, what did you say?"

"I said, 'Well, then, why don't you let me go if I'm not what you wanted?' And he said, 'No. We'll keep you, and you can decide on one of us.' "

The elderly ladies twittered, whispered, and wiggled on their bench.

Kari talked about the amused, smirking attitude the men had taken in the morning when the father said, "Well, let's go see how your woman is doing this morning. Let's go see how your woman fared the night."

"Now, when you were in the sleeping bag and they were having this discussion, did anything happen?"

"Yes. The old man told me to take my shorts off so he could take them and camouflage them. He said that the bright red color was too obvious." Her face flushed.

"And did you resist that?"

"Yes. I didn't know really what was on their minds, so I . . ."

Kari said both men insisted she take off her shorts, and she felt that she had no choice but to comply. She related where the old man went and what he had done with her shorts.

"And where did the defendant go, if anyplace?"

"He was still tending the fire, trying to get it going."

"So he was in the same area you were?"

"Yes, he was not very far away—couple of feet."

"What did you try to do at that point?"

She told the jury how she had cried and begged Dan Nichols to release her and what his responses had been.

"Did you beg him more than once?"

"Yes, I did. I begged him over and over, and I even started crying. I thought, you know—I just broke down. And it didn't seem to phase him at all. He just kept saying, 'No. I want to keep you. You're pretty. I want to keep you.' "

"And what was he doing while he was telling you, no, he was going to keep you?"

"Just sitting by the fire, putting more sticks on it."

"How many times would you estimate you asked him to please let you go?"

"Oh, I don't really remember. Six, seven."

"Was his response the same each time?"

"Yes."

"Did he ever waver?"

"No."

"Did he ever show any emotion?"

"No. No."

Tears slipped down Mom's cheeks. Dan Nichols flipped a pencil back and forth in his fingers, his face expressionless.

The questioning progressed to Alan Goldstein's approach to the camp, and Marc presented a photograph to Kari that she identified as the scene of the second camp. She pointed out to the jury where she was sitting chained to a tree. It was admitted as State's Exhibit No. 3, as was No. 4, which was a photograph of the area where she saw Alan kneeling.

The judge talked to the attorneys, then called a lunch break. He turned to Kari. "You may step down, dear." Tom met her and whisked her from the room, placing himself between her and the cameras.

Jim and San Schwalbe joined us at the house for lunch. Paul sat beside Kari, his eyes still bright with anger, while she pushed some fruit around on her plate. She relaxed when John and Marc entertained the group. They teased Judy for hanging her suit jacket outside to "dry," insinuating that she had been nervous enough to "perspire a little."

The afternoon session continued with Kari's testimony. She told the court that when she first noticed Alan, the defendant pulled his pistol and aimed at Al, who knelt in the grass and remained still. She said she screamed over and over for him to run for his life.

"Was there any conversation between either the defendant or the old man and Al Goldstein?"

"Yes. The old man said, 'Is this the girl you're looking for?' and Al said, 'Yes.' "

"At any point in time, did the old man say anything to the defendant?"

"Yes. He turned to the defendant and said, 'Shut her up.' "

"And what did the defendant do?"

"He turned and walked towards me."

"Did he have his weapon drawn?"

"Yes, he did."

"How was he holding the weapon?"

"Like you would if you were going to shoot someone—had his hand around the pistol stock and everything." She was breathing rapidly, and the color drained from her face.

"How far away did he get from you?"

"He was standing directly above me."

"And did you see whether or not he raised the weapon?"

"No, I was still, at that point, watching Al."

She described the positions she had been in before and after the bullet entered her chest. Mom was squeezing my hand so hard it was numb.

"Was there any hysterical comment on the part of either one of them?" Marc asked, referring to the Nicholses.

"No."

She testified that Jim Schwalbe entered the camp and assured the defendant and his father, who had their guns trained on him, that he didn't have a weapon. She said the old man alternately pointed his rifle at Jim and Al.

"Was anybody ever able to do anything to help you?"

"No."

"Did Jim Schwalbe kneel down at any point in time?"

"Yes, I think he did."

"And at that point, did anything happen between the old man and Al Goldstein?"

"Yes. The old man raised his rifle, aimed, and shot Al."

Marc questioned her about Jim's reaction, the defendant's position, and what happened after Jim ran from the camp.

"Did either one of them, as far as you could see, go over to check on Alan Goldstein?"

"No."

"Did they come over to where you were?"

"Yes. They came over, and they just looked at my wound but didn't try to help me at all."

"Was the defendant convinced you were going to die?"

"He asked his father, 'Is she going to die?' He said, 'No, I've seen wounds like this before. She'll be okay.' "

"So they continued packing?"

"Yes. They unchained me from the tree and took the chain with them and just started packing up their stuff."

"What kind of shape were you in at that point?"

"Well, not real good, I guess, after being shot. I was still in shock. I thought I was going to die."

"Did you ask them to leave anything behind?"

"Yes. At that point I was getting cold and asked them if they could leave the sleeping bag with me."

"And what was said?"

"They said they were going to take it with them, and they just kind of picked up the end and flopped me out on the ground."

"Both of them?"

"Yes."

Paul was grinding his teeth. Most of these details were new to him.

She explained that the defendant pulled up her shorts, then ran after his father, leaving her in the dirt on the forest floor. The description she gave of crawling to the fireplace and trying to start a fire, the attempt to get to Alan, and opening Jim's pack, rekindled the fury I had felt when she first told me those details. The defendant sat passively, his face expressionless. He had his elbow on the table, chin resting in his palm, looking as if he were listening to a boring teacher.

"When the defendant shot you, the comments he made, did they in any way indicate panic?"

"No."

"Kari, you were with the old man and the defendant for almost eighteen hours?"

"Yes."

"During this eighteen hours, did you have occasion to discuss with the defendant and the old man whether or not they had planned and waited for you before you arrived?"

"Yes, I discussed it with the defendant. I had asked him, 'Well, if I had been ugly or fat, would you have let me go on by?' and he said, 'Yes. I stopped you because you were pretty.' "

"And did you ask him whether or not he had seen you prior to the time you got where you were abducted?"

"Yes. He said that he had watched me from across the lake and told his dad that there was a pretty woman running along, that she was coming around the lake and that he wanted to see me."

"Did the defendant ever—throughout the whole time that you saw him, through the eighteen hours—ever appear threatened, coerced, or intimidated by the old man?"

"No. Never."

Marc asked for a three-minute break so he could talk to Kari. While he was talking to her, the skin on the back of my neck began to prickle as if someone were watching me. I looked up—directly into the eyes of Dan Nichols. We stared at each other, our eyes locked. I broke out in a sweat and shuddered. I had seen that look when I was a child. The neighborhood bully had drowned a little kitten in a rain barrel and was in the process of drowning a second one when my girlfriend and I found him. They were her kittens. She screamed, pushed him away, and grabbed the live one from his hands. She fell to the ground sobbing, the kittens in her lap, and the bully had stared at me with the same mocking challenge I faced now. I had yelled at him, "You're awful! Evil!" He had smirked, walked away without comment, and later doused another cat with kerosene and set it afire.

Nichols looked away, breaking the spell when Judge Davis said, "All right. Mr. Racicot?"

"We have no further questions, Your Honor."

"Cross-examination?"

"Your Honor, we have no questions," Ungar said.

After some further discussion, Judge Davis said, "All right, dear, you may step down." Tom and the other investigators hurried her out of the room, and Bob and Paul followed them. Tom brought the car to the back entrance of the building, and Bill Duncan, one of the plainclothesmen, hustled the children out the back door. Several photographers and reporters were there, and one yelled peevishly, "Ah, come on Swenson, you're going to have to talk to us sometime." She ignored them, knowing there was too much at stake to risk any comments.

Jim Schwalbe's Testimony

Jim was called as the state's next witness, and he asked not to be photographed. He explained that John Palmer had phoned him about two in the morning to search for a lost girl. He put food, a camera, and some medical supplies in his backpack and teamed up with Al when they got to the parking area at the lake. Jim said they had been assigned to search the upper Ulreys Lake area and the forested hills west and northwest from the lake. He testified that Bob Schaap had seen a grizzly bear in the lake area, and there was some concern that Kari might have accidentally run into it.

Al took the portable radio and they separated for a brief time. Al searched along the trail while Jim bushwhacked through the underbrush, and they met again at the upper lake at approximately 7 a.m. From there they headed uphill, in a westerly direction, calling Kari's name and looking for clues as they walked.

He described the terrain and said they were frequently out of sight of each other but met every ten to fifteen minutes to discuss which direction to search. The last time they met it was decided that Al would go uphill and Jim would search downhill as they continued in a westerly direction.

"Okay. Now, at some point did you hear anything that alerted you to trouble?" Marc asked.

"Yes. I was walking down, and I heard a shot and a scream or a yell at the same time."

"What did you hear the woman say? Could you make it out?"

"The yell at first, and then I heard the men say a few words. And then Kari started saying, 'Help me. I'm shot. Help me.' "

Jim said he walked into camp, but he couldn't see Kari and shouted, "Well, where is she?" He couldn't find her and yelled "Where?" again. With his rifle aimed at Jim, the old man escorted him to Kari. The younger man trailed behind, pistol in hand.

"When we got to where Kari was, I set my pack down. The defendant set his gun down. We walked over. I said, 'Well, where is she shot?' and the defendant said, 'Here,' and tried to pull her shirt up. And then I realized there was a chain around her." He said Kari's shirt was bloody. The father told Dan to get the chain unlocked. Jim watched the defendant fumbling with the lock, looked down the barrel of Don Nichols's rifle, and shouted to Al to radio for help.

"Did you see what he did in response to that?"

"He called on his radio, and then reached into his pack and ran over towards a tree." Jim said he knew Al had something in his hand, but he didn't know it was a gun. The defendant was still fumbling with the chain when the old man shouted at Al, "Do you have guns?"

"And what was Al's response?"

"Yes, I have a gun. You can't get away. . . . Give yourselves up; you can't get away. You're surrounded by two hundred men."

"Now, when the old man started to turn toward Alan, did you do anything?"

"I jumped up to grab his gun."

"And what happened at that point?"

"He pointed it back towards me."

"And what did you do?"

"I said, 'Everything is cool. Nobody is going to get hurt. Just put your guns down.' And then there was some rustling, and Kari was saying something. So I looked back, and the next thing I heard was a shot and a thud."

"So Kari diverted your attention away from the old man?"

"Yes."

"Did she say something?"

"It was like she was in pain, like maybe the defendant was pulling very hard on the chain."

Jim said he didn't see the shot fired but heard Al fall. He said he jumped up, looked, and yelled, "Oh, my God!" The old man swung his rifle toward Jim again as he ran to his fallen friend.

"Was Al behind a tree?"

"He was laying on the side of a deadfall, by a tree."

"After you saw Al, was he lying on his back?"

"Yes." Jim's face was pale, his lips compressed into a thin line, and the volume of his voice dropped.

"Did you think he was dead?" Marc asked softly.

"Yes." The word was a whisper.

"So what did you do?"

"I ran . . . I ran by him and looked, and I didn't see any movement of his chest, and I didn't see any movement at all."

Mom handed a tissue to Karen, whose tears dripped off her chin. Dan Nichols sat as before, chin in hand, expressionless.

"Jim, how long would you say it was from the time that you entered that camp—when you first met the defendant and the old man until you had run into the woods a hundred yards away?"

"A minute, two."

Marc showed Jim the photographs marked Exhibits 3 and 4 and asked him to identify the tree where Kari was chained and to identify the tree behind which Alan had stood. Marc asked detailed questions concerning which side of the tree Al was on to eliminate any doubt as to where Al was located. Jim said that Al was not a hunter and was not a crack shot with a pistol.

"When Alan Goldstein was standing behind that tree with the weapon, who was he pointing the weapon at?"

"In the direction of the old man."

"Was anybody standing between Alan Goldstein and the defendant?"

"I was right there."

"You were between those two?"

"I might not have been exactly between them, but I was real close."

"Had to be a heck of a shot to miss you if it had been fired at the defendant."

"Yeah."

"Your Honor, I object. Leading." Ungar interrupted.

"Well, he's already answered it. Overruled."

Steve Ungar started the cross-examination in a condescending tone of voice. Jim squared his shoulders, his chin came up, and his cheeks flushed. He said he remembered making statements to law officers on July 16, 1984, and to the four attorneys on January 11, 1985. Mr. Ungar had confused the dates and Jim corrected him. The attorney referred to the statement Jim had made immediately after the kidnapping and murder. He quoted Jim as having said, "The kid was talking the loudest. He was somewhat hysterical."

Jim said he remembered making the statement, and when Ungar asked him to describe hysterical, Jim replied, "Nervous, scared. Scared, I guess."

"Do you think that Danny recognized that she needed help?"

"I would say so."

"Did he seem able to render any aid to her?"

"Yeah. I couldn't see why he couldn't—"

"But you said he was hysterical—"

"He was scared. He wasn't really shaking or anything."

"Okay. But when you use the word 'hysterical' and he kept repeating the same kind of thing, 'I can't believe it. I can't believe it,' you were implying he was just a little more than scared. He maybe lost control of himself; isn't that true?"

"I won't go so far as 'losing control.' He knew he was walking toward me. He knew he had a gun in his hand. He laid it down."

Jim said he had walked into an armed camp hoping to convince the kidnappers to leave and let him help Kari. When Mr. Ungar attempted to make it sound as if Jim felt safe going into the camp because the men weren't threatening him, he failed. Jim testified that he was surprised Al had a gun, but insisted he aimed at Don Nichols, not Dan, Kari, or himself. Ungar asked if Jim believed that Al was protecting him and Kari by pulling the gun. Jim said, "In his mind, yes, he was protecting us." Jim insisted Don Nichols had never put down his rifle, not at any time.

"Do you recall making a statement that—that Al complicated the situation?" Ungar asked.

"I believe I made that statement."

"And this was done by introducing another gun into the situation?"

"By another person being there altogether."

"Thank you. I have nothing further."

In his redirect Marc asked, "Jim, did you realize when you made that statement—or at the time—that Alan Goldstein had been there before you and arrived before you?"

"No, I didn't."

"So you didn't realize he had seen Kari Swenson shot?"

"No."

"Or that he had weapons trained on him?"

"No."

"Or what he was observing when your back was to the old man?"

"I thought he walked in as I was bent over Kari."

"So he had seen a lot more take place than you had at that point?"

"Yes."

"We have nothing further," Marc concluded.

The judge excused Jim and called for a recess. The length of Judge Davis's "five-minute" recesses were unpredictable. He joked about them.

Witnesses for the State

"What did those x-rays reveal to you?" Marc asked Dr. William Newsome, who was the next witness. He described Kari's collapsed right lung and the considerable amount of blood and tissue injury present in the chest. Dan Nichols lounged back in his chair, pressed his fingertips together in steeple fashion, and stared at the ceiling. Mr. Ungar objected to Marc's line of questioning, but after a session in chambers, the judge allowed Marc to continue.

Dr. Newsome said a general surgeon was called in to insert a tube between the lung and chest wall to drain the blood from the chest cavity; that the bullet entered about an inch below the collar bone and exited at the lower tip of the shoulder blade. He described the angle of the bullet wound and said the bullet narrowly missed the subclavian artery.

"Had that occurred, would that have changed her condition?"

"Your Honor, I object," Steve said.

"Yes, sustained."

Marc gripped the podium and asked, "Did the fact that Kari was in good shape assist her in her ability to deal with this wound?"

"Your Honor, I object. Irrelevant," protested the defense attorney.

"Your objection is overruled."

"I think definitely the fact that she was in the physical condition she was in improved her chances of surviving this wound," answered the physician.

There was no cross-examination. Bill Pronovost testified to verify that the crime had been committed in Madison County, that an autopsy had been performed by Dr. Rivers on July 17, 1984, and that the suspects had been apprehended on December 13, 1984.

Dr. Ronald Rivers, Montana Medical Examiner, testified next. His credentials were numerous and impressive. The doctor explained the difference between "pathology" and "forensic pathology," the latter dealing with injuries and what may have caused them. He said he had performed over 10,000 autopsies.

Marc told the court that he had previously marked autopsy photographs as State's Exhibits 7, 8, and 9, which he intended to offer and have the witness identify. He also had autopsy Exhibits 10 through 24, but he didn't intend to enter them as evidence. Mr. Ungar asked for permission to approach the bench, and they had a discussion in chambers, where Steve argued to suppress the three photographs. Dr. Rivers told the judge they were necessary to explain his testimony, and Judge Davis allowed them to be admitted.

Back in the courtroom, Dr. Rivers used the photos to explain the process of the autopsy. The wound was caused by a high-velocity weapon and was a straight-on wound from front to back, perpendicular to the head.

Dr. Rivers said he did an extensive search for the bullet, including a series of x-rays. He concluded that the bullet had either come back out of the mouth at the crime scene or had been dislodged during transportation. He gave a graphic description of the wound. I tried not to listen.

Marc asked for his opinion of cause of death, and he answered that Alan had died from a gunshot wound to the head that caused massive bleeding.

Ungar objected to any further evidence concerning Alan's death, and Marc asked to be heard in chambers on the matter.

"All right, Mr. Racicot," said the judge, "what do you offer to prove by this witness now?"

"My offer of proof consists of the fact that the doctor will say that the actual mechanism of death is that this man died of asphyxiation—essentially drowning in his own blood. He won't say it that way, but—and I want to get to the final cause of death, which is caused by the bullet inflicting massive bleeding and causing the man to quit breathing; and that he would have lived had he had medical help; and that he probably died within five minutes. That's it." The testimony was allowed.

The state rested its case, and Mr. Ungar moved for acquittal.

"Well, the motion will be denied," Judge Davis replied, "and you're going to have half an hour to get ready to put on your first witness." That person would be the defendant, and since the testimony would be lengthy, court was dismissed until the following day.

Leaving the courtroom, Mom and I found ourselves standing next to Dan Nichols's mother. "I know you're suffering too, and I'm sorry," I said. She looked startled and didn't answer.

On the hot drive home Mom had a lot of questions, since much of this was new information to her.

"You're going to have trouble with that jury," she said after a long silence.

"What?"

"I watched them carefully. They resent Kari."

"Oh, Mom, come on!"

"You wait and see. I've lived a long time, and I know people. You're in for trouble. They've already made their decisions."

I resolved to watch the jury more closely.

Kari and Paul had iced tea ready for us, but none of us wanted dinner. Kari said she was not going back to the trial because she had too much homework and was busy with her physical therapy and counseling sessions. Paul had to go back to classes, too, and we were relieved the children would be busy and away from Virginia City.

Dan Nichols's Testimony

Dan Nichols sat as placidly in the witness chair as he had at the counsel's table the day before. He admitted he was "involved with Kari Swenson's restraint," and that it was his pistol that shot her. Mr Ungar guided Dan through the history of his background, starting at age four and ending at age eighteen in the Madison Mountains on July 16, 1984. He forgot to mention the incident in Three Forks when Nichols had chased the little girls with a knife. Ungar presented "Danny" in a manner that made him appear young, confused by his parents' divorce and his mother's alcohol problem, and by his parents' conflicting values.

Nichols said his father took him into the mountains for weekend trips as frequently as he wanted to go, and on two occasions kept him there for approximately two months. He said his father was arrested for that act and spent two months in jail for kidnapping.

He contradicted himself several times, saying that he planned to finish high school and go to art school. In the next breath he said he didn't like going to school, that he enjoyed learning about the mountains and how to live there. He preferred his father's teachings. "Living in the mountains was a natural way of life," he said. "That's where you'd—everything is—like, in society, everything is—you go to work and you have—and you get money to get your food. Up in the mountains you go and get your food. You don't go through the machine of society, or whatever. It's all basic and you follow your instincts. You don't have to get up and go to work every day. You get up when you want to, and you make it on your own and you don't—down here you don't feel like anything is really real."

I was adding up the months Nichols spent with his father over a period of fourteen years, and the total came to about 9 percent of his life. His attorney kept speaking of "all those months" he had spent in the mountains "under the dominating influence of his father."

At age eighteen, in the summer of 1983, Nichols moved to Jackson Hole, Wyoming, and got a job washing dishes. He said he planned to return to school in the fall to finish high school, but during the summer he decided to go live in the mountains with his father.

"At first I didn't want to, but after I worked there all summer, I could—I didn't feel like I could—I could become a steady worker, you know, get a steady job. I just didn't feel that was for me."

I squirmed in my chair, mentally ticking off the summer jobs my children had held: scrubbing dorm rooms and bathrooms, washing windows, mowing lawns, staining houses, digging gardens, playing "sanitation engineer" at a camp, which meant scrubbing the showers, cleaning the toilets, and hauling the garbage to the dump, waiting tables, and washing dishes. Even the summer Kari spent as a wrangler was hot, hard work.

The defendant admitted that for years he and his father had discussed kidnapping a woman. They thought they would have to use a chain, because women weren't interested in going into the mountains with them—and women had been invited, he testified.

Finally, the testimony focused on the day they kidnapped Kari.

"I was wrapping some fish line around a stick, and I see somebody running through the trees on the other side of the lake," Dan said.

"What did you do then?"

"I went back and told Dad there was somebody coming up the trail. I didn't know if it was—I didn't know for sure if it was a girl or not. I thought—I thought it was probably a girl. I thought it might be an old lady. I thought it could even be a guy. I didn't see real good." The defendant swung the chair from side to side on its swivel and wiped his hands on his trousers.

He said when his father stepped in front of the girl and grabbed her by the wrists he was surprised. "We had talked about the type of girl that would be good for the mountains, you know. And I thought she was—she looked like a college girl, and she looked like she wasn't too mixed-up. I just didn't think he was going to grab her. I just thought she was too—well, society—looked too—societyized or too—like she looked like she knew what she wanted and stuff. And so I thought we was just going to let her go by."

He corroborated Kari's testimony concerning the manner in which she was grabbed by the wrists, struck in the face, the struggle on the ground with his father, and the way he (Dan) got the rope from the backpack and tethered her wrist to his own. He denied he was threatening her with his hands on his weapons. He was just leaning his elbows on them, he said.

He told Ungar his version of the watch incident.

"We stopped and—to sit down to rest. And she looked cold, and I asked her if she wanted a shirt or something to put on, and she said yes. And so we got a shirt out, and we had to change hands so she could put the shirt on. And in doing that I had to take off her watch, and we laid it down on the ground. And when we got up to go, she forgot it. I just picked it up and gave it to her. I said, you forgot your watch."

Bob whispered, "You bet! She asked for a shirt on one of the hottest afternoons in July!"

He denied sneering or snickering at her during the incident, stating that she was so scared she might have misread his expressions and intentions. He said he didn't feel he could let her go because it would be "betraying Dad or going against him." Nichols said they weren't going to rape, kill, or harm Kari, just keep her for a while. When asked why he hadn't made sexual advances or suggestions to Kari, he said he knew she was scared and he didn't want to scare her more. When asked if he wanted to turn her loose that night, he replied, "Kind of." He insisted his father was in charge of the situation, but that he (Dan) led the way into the mountains because he always led the way. Steve introduced into evidence the drawing of the unicorn and Kari's horse drawings, but didn't mention the drawing of the naked woman.

Nichols talked about the morning when they got Kari up and moved her to the new camp.

"We moved her over to the tree where the incident happened. And Dad told her that—well, me and Dad kind of had an argument about whether or not to darken the shorts. I thought she could just put a ground cloth around her." Steve interrupted but was ignored as Dan continued, "And Dad asked her and told her to take off her shorts and—and I think she got the message. I was trying to tell her she could just wrap a ground cloth around her. She didn't have to darken her shorts. I don't think she caught it."

The pleading on Kari's part was remembered, but he didn't recall saying he wouldn't let her go or that she was pretty and he wanted to keep her. But he might have said something like "I couldn't. . . . Because I felt like it would be betraying Dad, I guess, like, it wasn't my—my choice to let her go, like I felt it was kind of Dad's thing, you know."

Nichols admitted that he pulled his pistol and aimed at Alan Goldstein because they never allowed anyone to walk into camp and catch them at a disadvantage.

He began to talk about shooting Kari in the same bland, unemotional voice he used to talk about washing dishes. I knew I was going to be sick. Panicked, because I knew there were no bathrooms close by, I jumped up and dashed for the door. The startled deputy acted quickly, and I was through the door in a second, running toward the balcony. I vomited over the side of the banister, staining the old brick. I retched and sobbed, my forehead resting on the rough stone, until someone hugged me. I tried to control myself for Vivian, but months of tension and anger bubbled up and I couldn't stop shaking.

Bob Schaap came out to relieve Vivian. A deputy said, "Come on, Mrs. Swenson, let's find you a cup of coffee." He led us down the staircase to the main floor and into a small office. I was startled to hear Nichols's voice issuing from a large machine in which tape reels were rotating, recording the testimony. Sheriff France turned, gave me a surprised look, and handed over a cup of coffee.

In the courtroom Nichols continued to testify.

"Okay. Let's say the fireplace is here okay? I was bent over. I got up, and the guy was out there. And I was still looking over there, and she screamed, watch out; they've got guns. And my gun was right here. She screamed, and when she screamed, I looked at her and that's all I did.

"I just looked at her because she screamed. I didn't—I wasn't going to tell her to shut up or anything because it wouldn't do any good. She always screamed. I looked at her, and after—after she screamed and I was looking at her, I still had my gun over here because I had no intention of even threatening her with it. And I heard something behind me, which was Schwalbe, and I turned around to look because I heard—and I turned around real fast. And I—and I pulled my gun around with me, and it had a hair trigger on it. And when I turned around, it went off. I wasn't even looking at it when it went off. Is that good enough?" He looked at Steve Ungar for reassurance.

He said he was hysterical, in shock, and asked Schwalbe to come into camp even though his father said no. His version of where people were standing didn't correlate with Jim's and Kari's testimony. He had prepared a sketch for his attorney, and Mr. Ungar used it as a diagram to show the jury everyone's position at the time of the shooting of Alan. Marc objected to having the drawing admitted into evidence because the drawing was not to scale. He said the state would accept it for illustrative purposes.

"This is his recollection," Steve insisted, and the state was overruled.

Nichols said he had removed the chain from Kari, again contrary to Jim's and Kari's testimony, and was trying to find the wound when his father shot Al. He looked around in time to see Al fall. His father told him to pack up, "let's get out of here."

"Now, were you aware that she was hurt badly?"

"I was aware that she had been shot through the upper chest. I knew she wasn't shot fatally through the lungs because if she would have been, she would have been spitting up blood and wouldn't have been able to scream or anything. And I knew she wasn't bleeding hardly at all at the time, and I thought she would be okay."

He said he took the sleeping bag away from Kari as gently as he could and left her there to wait for someone else to find her.

Ungar asked him for his frame of mind for the first few days after the shootings.

"I couldn't—I couldn't shoot anything after that. It was hard. I missed everything I shot at. I worried constantly whether or not she had made it or not."

"Now, if you could think back to July 15 and place yourself in the same situation near Ulreys Lake, except your father wasn't there, what would you have done when you saw Kari Swenson?"

"Objection, Your Honor!" Marc said.

"Sustained."

"Are there any other comments that are relevant to this case that you'd like to make at this time?" Steve asked.

"We'll object, Your Honor, that's not a question."

"Sustained."

The cross-examination would begin after lunch.

Cross-Examination

Marc began his questioning of Dan Nichols, who denied that he had gone to Ulreys Lake looking for a woman and said he hadn't told his father that a girl was coming around the lake. He frequently contradicted his morning testimony. I watched the jury, trying to read their faces, wondering if they recognized his inconsistencies.

"You just told us you discussed the possibility of taking her, that she might be the right one?"

"It was possible."

"And yet you said you weren't waiting for her? Wasn't that at least part of the reason why you were there?"

"Well, yeah. But I wasn't there like I was going to jump out on her or something."

"So you weren't waiting there. Were you looking around to see if anybody else was around?"

"Not at that time. I already knew nobody else was around." He said he had checked because he didn't want anyone walking up on them while his father restrained Kari.

"And that's because you knew that was wrong, didn't you?" asked Marc.

"No."

"You didn't know that was wrong?"

"Yeah. I basically knew it was against the law, maybe, but I didn't want—I didn't want somebody jumping in there, and I didn't want somebody getting hurt."

"So you knew it was wrong and against the law from the very beginning?"

"Theoretically."

"Theoretically? Wouldn't you say that because of your actions, that you obviously demonstrated that you did not want anybody to see you and that you knew it was wrong?"

"I was pretty confused on it right there."

"Has this state of confusion bothered you before in the past?"

"Something like this in the past hasn't happened before—a lot. This major of a thing hasn't happened in the past."

I gripped the edges of my chair, held my breath, and prayed that we had been given the opening needed to introduce the knife incident.

"You wanted a woman up in the mountains just like you wanted your gun up in the mountains or your knife, it was something to have that made your life a little easier up there?"

"No."

"Why did you want one?"

"Because it's awfully lonely up there." The twitterers murmured.

"Now, did you see your father strike Kari Swenson?"

"Yes."

"Saw him knock her to the ground?"

Nichols said Kari dropped to the ground after being hit by his father, and "he just went with her."

"So Kari must be mistaken then about that? That's the way you saw it?"

"That's the way I saw it."

"She must be mistaken about what you said, too, about sometimes girls lie to you?"

"She was pretty scared. She could be."

"Now, when your father had her down on the ground with his arm around her neck and was twisting her head, you were going to get the rope?"

"Yes." He described how he got the rope, pulled Kari's right arm from underneath her, and tied the rope around her wrist.

"And you knew it was against the law, didn't you?"

"Yes."

"And you knew it was wrong?"

"Kind of."

"Excuse me?"

"Kind of." He glared at Marc and swiveled the chair from side to side.

"Kind of. You didn't know it was against the law?"

"I knew it was against the law," he said in a so-what tone.

"But you went right ahead and tied that wrist?"

"Yes." He glanced at his attorney.

"Did you have a lot of time up there to sit around and think and discuss this?"

"We had no more time than any of you people would going to work every day," he answered sarcastically. The mask slipped, and for a second or two the boy was replaced by the man Kari would recognize.

"Now, what were you thinking as you were tying Kari's wrists and she was screaming and had been hit, and was on the ground, and you had to forcefully remove her arm out from underneath her, this girl you didn't believe, that you thought was pretty."

"What was I thinking?"

"Uh-huh. If you were so concerned for her?"

"I was thinking that I didn't want to do it and be too mean with her, and so I was trying to be as gentle as I could."

"And still get the job done?"

"Yes."

Nichols explained what being a "mountain man" meant to him. "Just being—just depending on myself and living in the mountains. I liked the mountains a lot, too."

"Everybody likes the mountains."

"Well, okay. So I like the mountains; that's the main reason I was up there." Dan glared at Marc.

"So this was an incident where you treated another human being the same way that you did everything else up there. If you wanted it, you took it. You shot people's animals; you shot out of season; you broke into places; if you wanted something you took it because it was free up there, as far as you were concerned, and there were no holds barred?"

"Took it if we had to."

The defendant denied he had said he wanted to keep Kari when she appealed to him to let her go just after tying her wrist. He said to her that he believed in what his father was doing, "or something like that." He had hoped in time she would learn to like them and their way of life.

"And you thought that even if you may have violated the law at the beginning, that there would come a time when she saw the same beauty as you saw up there, and enjoy the same kind of carefree life-style as you enjoyed up there, that anything else would be forgiven?"

"It was possible, yes."

"So you were really willing to cross the boundaries of the law at the beginning because you felt that at some point it would make no difference?"

"Yes."

Marc asked about the watch and headband incidents. The defendant couldn't make up his mind if he had taken off her watch, as he had testified, or if she had removed it. He was confused as to why it had to be removed in any case, and frequently contradicted himself.

Marc folded his arms across his chest and walked slowly back and forth between the podium and the jury box. With the toe of his boot he traced the taped-down extension cord running to the television microphone.

"Now, there were numerous occasions, you testified this morning, where Kari begged you to let her go?" Marc said, looking at his boot.

"Yes."

"She pleaded with you, didn't she?"

"No. She just asked me, 'Why don't you let me go?' "

"Why don't you let me go?"

"Yeah."

Marc stopped pacing, slowly raised his head, and looked at the defendant. He repeated the words in the monotone Nichols had used.

"Just kind of like, 'Why don't you let me go?' "

"She put a little more emotion into it." The defendant's voice was surly, and he swung the chair more rapidly from side to side as Marc asked him why he didn't just untie the rope and let her go. He said it might make his father "pretty mad," so he refused her requests, and, yes, he "kind of" wanted to keep her and he knew what he was doing was wrong . . . "kind of."

Marc took Nichols to task for his "kind of's," pointing out that it was obvious he knew what he was doing was wrong and against the law. Otherwise he would not have hidden Kari from the search plane and rescuers.

Marc commenced pacing the taped cord, arms folded, head down.

"Now, Kari voiced her fears to you about being raped or killed, didn't she?"

"Yes."

"And that probably wasn't an unreasonable thing for her to talk about, was it, under the circumstances?"

"No."

"You thought that that was a fairly normal thing for somebody to think at that time?"

"Yes."

"And the reason you thought that was because you were familiar with the ways of the world and what somebody, a young woman like that, might think under the circumstances?"

"Yes."

"So you tried to convince her by being as nice as you could and trying under the circumstances, while still confining her, to be as decent as you could?"

"Yes."

Marc stopped pacing. "It was an incredible plan, wasn't it?" he said softly.

"What do you mean?"

"It was dumb, wasn't it?"

"No."

I looked at the jury. Two of them were dozing, their chins resting on their chests.

Marc asked about the chain, who did what, and it was obvious Nichols had assisted his father without evidence of coercion.

"And both of you had a key?"

"Yes, I was given a key to it."

"So you, at least, had the physical power to release that lock at any time?"

"Yes."

"And you don't think your father would have hurled his knife at you or shot you, do you? If you'd done that?"

"Probably not."

The subject of the evening camp came up. They talked about the defendant's artwork and his father's pride in his son's accomplishments. There was an abrupt change, and Marc pointed out that however nice they thought they were being, they still had Kari chained up and knew they couldn't let her loose because she'd run away.

Nichols talked about the shorts incident, tripping over what he had testified to in the morning and what he was saying now. When Kari began to cry and pleaded to be released, he testified that he said, "I can't." His voice was devoid of emotion when he said she cried too hard to talk. Inside my head I was screaming at him, Damn you, damn you, damn you!

I had missed part of the testimony. Marc asked how Dan's father had punished him when he had walked out on him several years ago.

"He didn't talk to me for three years."

"He didn't talk to you?" Marc stopped pacing and faced the defendant. "So that's the reason that you wouldn't turn loose this girl who was frightened and scared and crying? Because your father wouldn't talk to you?"

"No. It's hard to say. When you're in a situation like that, you don't know how you feel."

"When you're nineteen years old and you know it's wrong?"

"Put yourself in a situation like that. How would you feel?"

"If I saw that?" Marc's voice was low, inviting further comments.

"Yeah. Well, I know you know everything that's right, but I was a little confused," snapped Dan. The judge leaned forward to look more closely at the defendant.

"You were a little confused because you had wants that you confused with what you knew was right?"

"I had—"

"You had desires that you wanted to satisfy?"

"I had two different sets of rules, and I had wants, yes."

"Now when Alan Goldstein arrived, it was you who drew your pistol first, wasn't it?" Marc stood with his feet slightly apart, tapping a pen on the palm of his left hand.

"Yes, it was."

"And you trained that pistol on Alan Goldstein, didn't you? You pointed it at him?"

"Yes."

The facts that the defendant knew how to shoot, knew the dangers of a loaded gun, knew he had a hair trigger on his pistol and still pointed it at Alan, were presented to the drowsy jury.

The events leading up to the shooting of Kari and Alan were answered in the same bored voice he had used earlier. He denied his father told him to "shut her up" and that he didn't walk over to her or point the gun at her.

"How then can you account for the angle of the bullet that Dr. Newsome mentioned yesterday if you did not raise your weapon? You'd have shot yourself in the the *foot* if you didn't raise your weapon."

He explained it by saying Kari was leaning forward. The angle would still have been wrong. Marc murmured, "So Kari was mistaken?"

Steve Ungar asked for a recess. We walked out to the balcony hoping for some fresh air, but it was as still as it had been at noon. The twitterers stood close by expounding to a woman reporter.

"Why, it's a crime the way he's picking on that boy!" exclaimed one. The other added, "Poor little thing. Just think how awful it would be if he were your son."

Karen Frauson took Mom's elbow and led her down the steps, away from the nonsense.

When court resumed, the defendant said the law and wrong didn't mean the same thing to him. Marc said, "Let's take a for instance. You knew that it was wrong and against the law, at least wrong in society's eyes, to shoot and hunt and kill people's cattle up there, didn't you?"

"Never hunted cows up there."

"You shot them up there, strays that wandered up there, didn't you?"

"I might have."

"Well, shooting a cow is a pretty hard thing to forget. Did you or didn't you?"

"It don't have nothing to do with this case!"

"I'll decide that, Mr. Nichols," admonished Judge Davis, leaning forward to study the defendant's angry face.

"Did you or didn't you?" demanded Marc.

"Yes!" He indicated with his next remark that if they were hungry they didn't think about the laws.

"Now, you remember when Alan Goldstein was shot?"

"Yes."

"Did you go to check on him?"

"No, I never."

"And you testified this morning that you knew that Kari Swenson was not shot fatally, that's why you left?"

"Dad told me that, yeah, I guess I believed it."

"And so you left?"

"Yes."

"Yet when you ran into the outfitter four months later in the mountains, you told him you thought you'd killed her?"

"No, I didn't tell him that."

"You didn't tell him that?"

"No. I said I was worried about her." Once again everyone else was mistaken. Dan said he couldn't have stayed to help Kari because his father was leaving, and he had to go, too, because he loved him.

"You mentioned this morning that you couldn't shoot anything when you were on the run?"

"For quite some time after that I missed everything I shot."

"Oh, you still shot at them, you just couldn't hit them?"

"It took me two or three times to get them."

"And, of course, you knew we had your diary from that period of time, didn't you?"

"Yes."

"And in your diary you document, don't you, how many things you've killed during that subsequent time?"

"Yes. I didn't write down how many times I shot at it, though."

"So you were still shooting, but you weren't quite as accurate as you were when you shot Kari Swenson; is that what you're saying?"

"I didn't aim at Kari Swenson."

"So your statement this morning about you couldn't shoot anymore—"

"What I meant was I wasn't very accurate."

"I think you said this morning that you couldn't shoot anything after that, trying to imply, weren't you, that you just simply didn't have the will and the desire to do that?"

"Yes." In his diary he had written of hunting grouse, and penned, "Got 'em all, momma, poppa, and baby."

"And you still wished that you had Kari up in the mountains with you, didn't you?"

"I wished I had somebody up there, yes."

Marc questioned until Nichols's involvement with a woman named Sue was revealed, then he quickly left the subject.

Later, the defendant implied that he never won any major arguments with his father, but Marc brought out some major decisions he had made against his father's wishes. He had gone to the Fundamentalist Christian church, was involved in the church youth group, and had had an affair with Sue for three years from the age of fifteen to eighteen. The father had opposed those decisions, but Dan ignored him even when his father became angry and wouldn't speak to him. His conduct in school, sports, music, and the community were disclosed, demonstrating that Dan followed the rules of society when he wanted to.

"And, in fact, isn't it that the real reason that you left school was because of Sue—had absolutely nothing to do with your father?"

"No."

"That's not right?"

"No."

They talked about the marijuana found in Dan's pack at the time of the arrest. He said a friend had given it to him and he carried it around for sentimental value. Marc had been tracing the extension cord with the toe of his boot, arms folded across his chest. He straightened up, stood still, and paused until you could hear a pin drop in the room. The defendant squirmed in the witness chair.

"Now, this wasn't the first incident, was it, where you'd had a confrontation with females. Do you remember Three Forks, 1979?"

Ungar was on his feet. "Your Honor, may I approach the bench?"

There was a discussion, and the judge and attorneys disappeared into chambers. During the lengthy arguments, Marc, Judy, and John cited points of law that would allow them to question Nichols about the assault on the Johnson girls. They insisted that Steve could not lead the defendant to testify that he would never do anything that serious and not expect the prosecutors to insist on the right to rebut the defendant's "sanitized life-style."

Steve argued that it wasn't permissible to use prior act evidence, and John pointed out it was character rebuttal, not prior act evidence. The judge mentioned the Youth Court Prohibition and asked if that law applied here.

"It says you can't refer to the proceeding," Judy answered. "It also says evidence in the proceeding, but there's no plan here to refer to any Youth Court proceeding, anyway. Once you open the door, certainly the truth outweighs any kind of prejudice. You can't just pick an incident and not let anything else in the door and claim prejudice, because you've got to show the whole picture."

"The primary purpose," Marc concluded, "is to rebut, to properly rebut, an impression that has been left with the jury that's to make a decision. I don't see how we can expect them to make a right decision if they don't know what we know as long as it's within the Rules of Evidence."

"Well, I've thought about it," Judge Davis answered, "ever since I got the brief, and knew it was coming. I'm inclined to agree with the state, Mr. Ungar, in view of what this witness has said on direct examination. I think this proposed evidence is relevant, and I'm going to admit it."

The cross-examination continued with the incident in Three Forks in 1979. Nichols admitted he was looking for Carrie Johnson, whom he had seen swimming at the gravel pit pond in Three Forks. She was a pretty girl with long, blond hair. He denied chasing her sister into the house, but, yes, he did go into the house, uninvited, with his knife drawn. He said he had not held the knife to the throat of the little girl while he questioned her about Carrie.

"And you scared the living hell out of all of them, didn't you?"

"Yes, I did."

"And you wanted Carrie Johnson."

"Yes."

"So when you testified either this morning or this afternoon about your concern for Kari Swenson and how you could never do something violent like that toward her, in fact, you had done it when you were fourteen years old?"

"No, I didn't! I didn't do anything to that girl!"

"Went in that house with a knife to get that girl, didn't you?"

"Yes."

"I have nothing further, Your Honor." Marc slapped his pen into his palm with a final snap.

On July 9, 1986, a year after the trial, the Nicholses asked for an interview with the news media. *The Bozeman Daily Chronicle* quoted Dan Nichols concerning the incident in Three Forks:

"It was basically the same thing," he recalled. "I wanted to get this girl and take her down the river. I had run away. I figured I'll just take this girl," he said. "Of course, she ain't going to like it for a while, but maybe she will later. That's what I thought."

Don Nichols

In the courtroom Mother gasped and looked over my shoulder. I glanced around and felt the blood drain from my face. I hadn't expected to see the older Nichols, and his abrupt appearance took me by surprise. He was tall, thin, and stooped, just as Kari had described him, but with short hair and no beard. His high-cheekboned, cadaverous face had an element of malevolence that was electrifying.

"My God, I'd have died of fright if I had been Kari," Mother whispered, gripping my hand. Sweat beaded her face. I asked her if she wanted to leave. "No, no, I'll be all right," she said, mopping her forehead with a handkerchief. A deputy appeared with a glass of water for Mom. Her hand shook and fluid sloshed onto her skirt. Bob sat on my left, leaning forward, elbows on his knees, hands clenched so tightly the knuckles were transparent.

The judge called for the court to be in session. Joking about the five-minute breaks that were at least twenty minutes long, he said, "You now know that five minutes court time is not like five minutes Naval Observatory Time."

Don Nichols took the stand. He was nervous and fidgeted, unsure of what to do with his hands. He stretched his neck and swallowed as if he were wearing a tight collar.

He went through the same childhood information that Mr. Ungar and the defendant had covered. He had trouble remembering dates, ages, and time spans that he had spent with his son in the mountains. Nichols frequently contradicted his son's testimony, but Mr. Ungar continued to try to establish that "Danny" had spent months and months at a time in the hills with his father. He couldn't do that, and when Marc finally objected, the judge asked Steve to move along.

Mr. Nichols was giving his opinions on education, which became so confusing and rambling that Marc interrupted. "Your Honor, we're going to object again. It's irrelevant to this inquiry. What in God's name does this have to do with the crimes for which he's charged?"

"It's hard for me to see that, too, Mr. Ungar, but I'm going to let you proceed. Go ahead."

The witness expounded on why he didn't like formal education, and said he taught Dan certain "things" that he refused to share with the court. He said he bought the chain in 1979 and told the court how he intended to use it. He denied using the word kidnapping when he talked to his son about taking a girl into the mountains against her will.

"Okay, what did you tell him in that regard?"

"Well, I said that if we met some girl that didn't have—wasn't tied up into society or obviously wasn't tied up, to the best of our knowledge, we would see if we could get her to go with us as easy way as possible for a couple days, and see what she thought of us." Nichols said he wasn't worried about getting caught by pursuers.

He was asked why the defendant ran away from him in the mountains when he was fourteen years old, and the witness became confused and so upset he had to stop to compose himself. He said Dan had captured a coyote, and it died. That, on top of a scolding from his father during a lightning storm, had made him angry, and a couple of days later he ran away and went to Three Forks.

"Did you ever teach Danny anything about the idea of a camp being like a castle?"

"Your Honor, can we object again? I hate to keep doing this, but I would like to hear the witness testify as opposed to Mr. Ungar," Marc said.

"Try not to lead him, Mr. Ungar," agreed the judge.

As Nichols began his version of "the incident," Judge Davis stopped him and reminded him of their conversation in chambers concerning his rights and asked if he still wanted to testify. The witness said, yes, he'd waive the right to avoid self-incrimination. His version of the kidnapping was so bizarre that it was hard to believe he was describing the same situation that his son, Jim, and Kari had testified to.

"It seemed on the surface she was the kind of girl that I thought, I have always thought of, you know, that would not have strong roots in society. And so I just took her by the wrist and just something like you'd flirt—but not—she could see I wasn't flirting. And I said—I said I'd like to ask you some questions and it's important."

"After the conversation what did you do next?"

"It just kind of worked into something; nothing really was definitely done. I just—she just started getting unhappy after awhile and saying she didn't believe me, and pulling her hands out of—trying to—starting to pull her hands away from me, you know. I just kept holding her wrists real tight." He put his hands in front of him, clenching his fists to show how he had held Kari. "And then she started pulling, you know, harder. You know trying to get her hands loose."

"Did you finally do something to restrain her?"

"No. I just—she just tried to get loose and couldn't. And I just kept saying I'm not—well, I'd also told her I wasn't going to rape her and all this stuff. And so finally she said okay. Okay. And so I took a nylon cord, like a shoelace-type—it wasn't a shoelace—but that size. And tied it to her wrist and so it wouldn't slip. And I tied a bunch of knots so it wouldn't slip tight and made it so it was just right. And then I handed one end to Danny and told him to wrap it around his hand." Nichols said the cord had been in his pocket. He was talking rapidly, gesturing nervously, crossing and uncrossing his legs.

He remembered telling her, "You would have a good—hell of a good story to tell your grandkids."

"She kept threatening me with her friends, and I finally said that—well, just hope they don't try anything because I'll shoot them."

After Kari was shot Nichols said Dan was hysterical. He remembered that his son asked Schwalbe to come into the camp to help Kari, and, yes, he had pointed his rifle at Jim until he was sure he didn't have any weapons. He said the three of them, Dan, Schwalbe, and himself, were all kneeling in front of Kari, and he didn't know where Al had gone. When Schwalbe realized Kari was chained up, his attitude changed, "and he wasn't so cool anymore." Now the witness changed his story and said his rifle was in its case.

"And so I picked them [guns] up and started back. I just was going to put them back a few feet, you know, more behind me, you know. And he stood up and he was looking real funny, and he started following me, you know. And I just kept backing up, and he just took a few more extra steps. Then when he could see that I was wondering what he was up to, and he stopped and he went back." Nichols swallowed and pulled at the skin on his neck. He said he heard Alan say, "You're covered."

"Okay. After you heard this other rescuer say that, what did you do?"

"My mind just went into—out into no-man's-land, I mean, you know? That just isn't something you expect, you know, and so—"

"Did it appear from your observations that Schwalbe expected it?"

"Your Honor, we'll object to the speculative—"

"Yes. I'm going to sustain that."

"I took the gun out of the case," the defendant continued. "I put it behind the tree and took it out of the case and put a shell in the firing chamber. I was used to doing that for game. And then I just kind of leveled it, I mean, I just kind of made it horizontal there." (Indicating low hip level.)

"And I thought if he saw that big gun he'd cool down, you know, so—so I said—I just stood there calmly, and I said put the gun down."

Ungar asked what Jim and Dan were doing, and he said he had no idea.

"Well, I said put the gun down, and he just said again, you're covered. And so I just—the gun was 'bout ten degrees away from me; I just pulled it over to what I thought would be the middle of the top part of his chest, right here," Nichols tapped the upper part of his chest with his fingers, "which was sticking out from behind the tree, you know. And I just pulled the trigger, and he just went down like a light and just real fast. I thought I hit him in the—through the lungs and through the spine because that's the way he went down." He looked at the jury and stretched his neck. Sweat ran down my back and I swallowed again and again to control the urge to vomit.

"Then Schwalbe said, 'Oh, my God.' He started running out of camp the same way he came in. He got down there, and he turned around and he looked back. And he said you can't get away; there's two hundred men here, or something like that. And then as soon as he said that, he ran up toward me just as fast as he could, and I put a shell in the chamber as fast as I could. And then he saw me do that, and he swerved away and went out there about five yards and turned around and looked at me. And he just looked at me like he wanted to say something, he didn't know what to say. And he took off running again and ran outside up there and went up there a ways and started screaming for help every few minutes. And he was still there when we left."

The witness stared at his hands, twisting them in his lap. He said it was obvious they had to leave, so they collected the chain, got Kari out of the sleeping bag, packed up, and left. He said Dan wasn't hysterical when they left the camp but became "guilty" after they hid from the helicopter because they weren't sure if Kari had been found alive or dead.

Ungar ended his questions after asking about the meeting with the outfitter, and court was adjourned until Thursday.

In Loren Tucker's office we talked with the prosecutors. Don Nichols's testimony had left all of us shaken, and at last we realized why Kari's nightmares were so terrifying.

John stood with his hands thrust deep in his pockets, head cocked to one side, looking out from under his eyebrows. "You know, I think he believes what he's saying, twisted as it is. He's convinced himself that it really happened that way."

"One thing about him that's rather pathetic. He loves his son, there's no doubt about it, and the kid has used that love to manipulate him into getting whatever he wanted," Marc said, lighting his pipe. "When Dan wanted to go with his dad, he did. When he got tired of the mountains, he asked to go home to Mom, and when she disciplined him too much, he asked to go back to Dad. He got pretty much everything he wanted by playing those two against each other."

Paul and Kari had prepared dinner for us. We discussed plans for Kari's trip to San Francisco and ignored what had gone on at the trial. The officials of the Women's Sports Foundation knew she was too frightened to travel alone and had made arrangements for her friend Becky Lohmiller to accompany her. While I hemmed her evening dress she read the program of events to us. They would be busy from the moment they got off the plane until they returned home.

After Kari went to bed, Mom said, "It's wonderful that she has something positive to do between the trials. When's the second one?"

"Marc thought it would be early July," Bob answered with a sigh. "Kari had hoped to train hard in July, but the emotional stress saps her energy, and she'll be lucky to train in August and September."

She had received a letter from the two vet schools telling her that she hadn't been accepted this year, but she was on the alternate list. I thought she'd be crushed, but she was relieved. Kari said she needed time to come to terms with "this mess," and felt she could not give school her complete attention. She also wanted to ski for one more year to see what she could do.

"Between Dr. Seitz and Dr. Morasky, I should be a pretty tough cookie someday." She draped her arm over my shoulders and said with a teasing look, "I'll keep applying to vet school, and if I don't make it you'll have to put up with a professional ski bum in the family."

Her schedule was full—too full. She was seeing Dr. Seitz, Dr. Morasky, the physical therapist, working for Dr. Gustafson, taking a class in genetics, training her dog every day, making an effort to see her friends, and dealing with the trials. This schedule would take its toll.

Cross-Examination of Don Nichols

Don Nichols sat in the witness chair, twisting his hands. His eyes darted nervously about the room. Marc began by asking about the early years in which he took his son into the mountains. He established the correct number of weeks Dan spent in the company of his father, and the fact that the son stayed with whichever parent he chose whenever he wanted to. Nichols said that in 1972 he kept his son in the mountains against the order of the court and spent one month in jail for contempt of court.

Dan had said two months. Nichols said he disciplined his son by spanking him with his hand and sometimes he hit him on the forehead with his fist.

"I thought that was the safest place to hit a kid without breaking my hand. I mean, you'd break your hand before you do your head, so I thought that was safe." He later learned that Dan didn't like that form of punishment. Marc asked if he encouraged his son to be unlawful, and he said no.

"You mentioned yesterday that you felt most of the laws that were passed were made to shove people around," Marc said.

"That isn't what I said, no. I said it's made for special interest groups of various kinds."

"And that they were used to somehow hamstring future generations, I think you mentioned?"

"Future generations of poor people, for sure."

"And you don't recall mentioning that they were made to shove people around?"

"Yes, I said that. That was part of it." Nichols was constantly moving his position in the chair, clearing his throat, crossing and uncrossing his legs, and covering his mouth with his hand.

"Now, would you agree with me that laws are also made to prevent you from shoving people around, and dragging people off into the woods against their will?"

"What lawyers do with laws, I don't know. I know what—what laws do to decent people. That's all I know."

"Isn't the bottom line that you pick and choose which laws you want to abuse and which ones you want to conform with?"

"I don't carry a law book around! I don't pick and choose with any natural law, no."

"Is it a natural law to grab somebody by force and tie them up and drag them off against their will? Is that a natural law to you?"

"It's a—what you're calling this is not the same as I would call it. I knew you wouldn't like it if you was there."

"And that didn't make a hill of beans to you, did it?"

The old man was sitting forward on the edge of the chair glaring at Marc. "Not what you would like, no. What the normal people—is a hell of a lot different."

"And you think that there are a large number of people out there, do you, that would think what you did was just fine?"

"Not just fine, no. But not as wrong as you're trying to make it."

"So the bottom line in this regard is that if it serves your needs and is what you want, you will take what you want regardless of what the law says?"

"No. That's not right."

"Isn't that true in this instance? Isn't that what you've confessed to?"

"I don't know what your laws are. I said I won't do anything that I know is unnaturally wrong, that is very wrong."

"You have different degrees of wrong then?"

"According to me and you, you damn right!" He squirmed in the chair, his eyes flashing with dislike.

"And taking Kari Swenson you knew was wrong; right?"

"A certain amount of wrong, yes."

"And you knew it was illegal?"

"I didn't think it was kidnapping, if that's what you mean!"

"Do you want to answer my question? Was it—or did you not know that was against the law?"

"I knew it was against the law, yes."

"And you knew you'd be followed?"

"No, I didn't. I said if we had turned her loose—I didn't think she would even be missed. I thought she was just a runaway girl or something."

"Just kind of a leftover, huh?"

"Yes, basically."

"So anyway, when you grabbed her, you did it knowingly; you knew what you were doing?"

"I didn't—I knew what I knew. I don't know. Like I said, I—you would have had a different idea about it."

"You find that distasteful, do you? That I would have a different idea about that?"

"I couldn't care less what you think!"

"You couldn't care less what anybody here thinks?"

"You damn right I care less!" He made a movement as if to rise from the chair, and a deputy standing by the television camera stepped forward. "What normal, decent people care, I give—I care a lot about, yes." He sank back into the chair, and the deputy relaxed.

Marc asked when the chain was purchased, what its function was to be, and what type of girl they had decided to take into the mountains. Nichols expounded on the "mixed-up" type of girl that no one would miss. The tempo changed suddenly when Marc asked about the illegal shooting of game and cattle.

"Well, did you do them?"

"I'm saying I have done illegal things. I'm not saying what, and I—I think you ought to bring charges, or—if you're going to make any accusations like that."

"So you refuse to answer my question?"

"I'm—no. I just said that my secret way of life up there is none of your business unless you want to bring charges about it."

"Don't you consider yourself a part of a community of people, Mr. Nichols, that you can't get along without?"

"I wished they were surrounding me up there, I wish I had a community. These people down here—I'm not sure who are my community and who isn't."

"You don't deny the fact that you need other people, do you?"

"No, I don't deny it. I'd like to have a tribe."

There were audible gasps in the courtroom, reporters scribbled, and the twitterers became vocal. My palms were slippery.

Nichols said his son went willingly to the mountains with him, that he did not restrain, threaten, or beat him to insure his presence. He said they had discussed the use of the chain, the cord, and the approximate age of the woman they wanted—not too young, not too old. He said Dan "tried to help me out" after he grabbed Kari.

"And so you were hopeful that they [women] would learn to appreciate the things that you appreciated up there, and would choose to stay?"

"That was part of it. If they started liking us right away, they would try harder, and that's something you could tell quite quick about."

"And you said that you had discussed this with your son for at least some time—before Kari Swenson came up?"

"Yes."

"Right. So you also knew, did you not, that there were frequently people down by Big Sky and Ulreys Lake?"

"That's why we went there, yes." He said that he and his son agreed to take a girl if they saw one who turned out to be what they wanted.

"And that's when he saw Kari Swenson coming around the lake. He told you that there's a girl coming around the lake?" Marc asked. I held my breath.

"He just told me there was—he was mostly excited because there was a—he thought she was a pretty girl. He just come up and said there's a hell of a pretty girl over there."

Dan Nichols banged his fist on the table and glared at his father.

"So knowing when you first met Kari Swenson that it was illegal to take her, and that in the eyes of some people it was wrong, and knowing that you would probably be pursued if you let her go, you took her?"

"Yes."

"And you weren't worried about being pursued at this point, I think you said yesterday? You have found it fairly easy to elude people looking for you?" Nichols answered that they stayed hidden from outsiders because they did "a lot of things" they didn't want people to know about. Especially game wardens. The witness's intense dislike of Marc was becoming more and more obvious.

"Now, were you against drug abuse?"

"Am I against drug abuse, like marijuana, or something like that?"

"Yes."

"It's—it depends on what you call abuse. I think every generation ought to be able to have their own vices. I think drugs is a reaction to the society." He fixed Marc with his glassy stare. "If they didn't do that, they would end up killing guys like you, probably!"

"Jesus!" whispered a reporter. The judge pushed his glasses up on the bridge of his nose and peered more closely at the witness. The venomous words echoed in the small room.

"Or maybe that's why they do, huh?" Marc said quietly. "Your son had an association with a person he mentioned yesterday, by the name of Sue. And you're aware of that?"

"Yes." He was also aware that Sue was considerably older than Dan, and he knew she was married. Nichols said his son maintained his association with Sue for three years despite his disapproval.

Marc returned to the scene where Kari first encountered the Nicholses. The witness said he knew she was lying about being married because later in the day she "completely forgot about him. She started worrying more about her mother."

My heart skipped a beat.

He said he decided to keep her even though she didn't fit the mixed-up personality they wanted. Nichols said he had the cord that was used to tie Kari's wrists in his pocket even though Dan and Kari said otherwise. He didn't remember his son pulling her arm out from under her, because he didn't recall that she was on the ground.

"And it was your son who led the way, set the course, he knew which direction he wanted to go?"

"Well, he had the girl, and I had to walk behind because I had the guns and I had to—so I wanted to look for footprints and things like that."

"Did he always set the course? Did he always lead the way?"

"That summer I let him lead a lot just to boost his confidence, yes. But I don't know what you mean by lead. He was in front."

He said Kari was mistaken when she said he had told her the reason he needed a woman in the mountains was to keep his son there, "or else I forgot."

"Well, he wanted one, didn't he? He told us yesterday he did."

"The girl is—was for both of us. Originally, it was my idea. I—when he was too young to even care much about girls, I thought of that idea."

"He sure did now, though, didn't he? At nineteen, he cared about them, he wanted one up there?" Marc paced back and forth, slapping the palm of his hand with his pen.

"Well, he wouldn't be normal if he didn't," snapped the witness.

"That's right. And he wanted one up there?"

"Yeah."

Marc established that Dan Nichols was the first one to pull a gun and aim it at Alan Goldstein, and that neither the defendant nor the witness pulled a gun on the outfitter when he approached their camp. The cross-examination completed, Judge Davis called a short recess—one of his "five-minute" ones.

Sweat stained the back of Bob's shirt and he was limping as we walked into the corridor.

"What's wrong with your leg?" I asked.

"I was sitting with every muscle in my body tensed, and I have a cramp in the arch of my foot," he laughed.

"I thought I'd have to have Karen pry my fingers off the seat, I was gripping it so hard," Mom said with a frown.

Mr. Ungar called the foster parents to testify after the break. They said that the defendant had been a quiet, sulky boy, but with time he improved, went to church, joined a church youth group, worked on the ranch, got good grades, and enjoyed staying at their home. He had lived with them for a year and kept in touch with them for two more years until he was eighteen. They said Dan made his own decisions in coming to stay with them when he had gotten into trouble with the law, and he decided when to leave them. He was dependable, law abiding, and acted independently and responsibly. He talked of his father frequently, to anyone who would listen. "He idolized him." Dan's affair with Sue wasn't mentioned.

Psychologist For The Defense

In chambers John Connor argued to prohibit the defense from using its psychologist as a witness. After long arguments by both sides, Judge Davis said he would allow the testimony.

Earlier, at the noon break, we had been joined by Dr. Herman Walters, a clinical psychologist at the University of Montana. He is a mild-mannered, reserved man with a delightful personality.

"We know what he's going to claim, and I imagine the therapist will repeat the same thing if he's allowed to testify," Dr. Walters said.

"What do they have in mind?" I asked.

"We're sure the psychologist will claim Dan is suffering from post-traumatic stress syndrome, depression, immaturity, and will conclude that he is dominated by his father even when they're apart," Judy explained.

"How do you know? Were you allowed to see the report?" Mom asked.

Someone explained that the psychologist who evaluated Nichols had suffered during the Vietnam War, and because of his personal experiences, often used the post-traumatic stress syndrome as a diagnosis for others who had suffered any type of trauma.

"But how does that apply to Nichols?" Bob said.

"They'll claim coming from a broken home, his father's weird ideas on laws and education, and the occasional smack on the forehead were trauma enough," John answered.

"I still don't understand how that affects his participation in the kidnapping, murder, and leaving Kari to die," Bob argued.

"They'll say he was in a state of mental shock, unable to act or think for himself; therefore, he went along with his dad's plans," John said. "After Kari was shot they'll insist he was in a survivalist mode, that his state of shock and hysteria made him blindly follow his father away from the scene, that he didn't have the mental capacity to stay and help Kari."

Dr. Walters nodded. "It will be along those lines, you can bet on it."

"What if the jury buys it?" I asked Marc.

"We have two excellent rebuttal witnesses. Dr. Walters and Dr. Stratford have evaluated Nichols, too, and know what Dan's problems are."

The psychologist for the defense took the stand and established his expertise in clinical psychology. Using the DSM-3, *The Diagnostic and Statistical Manual of Mental Disorders, Third Edition,* he developed the following diagnosis for Dan Nichols: post-traumatic stress disorder; mixed personality disorder; mixed conduct disorder.

After extensive testimony, the psychologist said that in his professional opinion, Nichols could not have "knowingly" kidnapped or shot Kari, that Dan saw the abduction as "something of a fantasy life." As John suspected, the witness said that after Schwalbe came into camp, Nichols was in such a state of shock that he could no longer function. He then took on survival attitudes and fled the scene.

Marc's cross-examination was long, and the questions asked indicated a thorough knowledge of the tests and diagnoses used by psychologists. He pointed out that evaluations are mainly subjective, depending on the clinician's ability, and that a number of studies say the tests used in evaluations are fine, "others say they are all wet."

Methodically, Marc destroyed the testimony, piece by piece, starting with the DSM-3 manual. The manual was critiqued, and it was explained that the diseases, disorders, or behaviors were included in it by a vote of the membership of the Psychological and Psychiatric Association. The current DSM is the third revision, and each revision has defined disorders differently from the previous one. Referring to the manual, Marc said, "And it changes with the mores of society, does it not?"

"I don't see it that way at all, no."

"Well, in 1952 homosexuality was included in the manual as a mental disease or defect. In 1967 it was eliminated; correct?"

"Yes."

"So it changes with the mores of society a little bit?"

"Some specific diagnoses, yes."

The Rorschach test and the thematic apperception test were taken to task for the possibility of wide and varied interpretation.

"So in that sense, you had to depend on the defendant in those tests to write down the answer that you—he believed was honest?"

"Yes."

"Now the things that the defendant told you, did you check with his family?"

"No, I did not."

"You didn't call his mother and talk to her? Or his sister, or his father?"

"No, I did not."

Marc paused and the jury shifted in their seats.

"I believe the first diagnosis that you reached, and, again, you would not have reached this had you not, I assume—you can correct me if I'm wrong—you would not have reached this one had you not had an order by the court, was post-traumatic stress disorder?" asked Marc.

The witness said that was not his first diagnosis, it was actually his *third*, thereby changing the emphasis placed on the post-traumatic stress disorder by defense counsel. Marc hefted a large book from hand to hand.

"Now," Marc said, "my understanding of the post-traumatic stress disorder is that the stress of producing that, or the event that produces that, according to the manual here, is that it's generally something outside the range of such common experiences as marital conflict and domestic problems—" Marc opened the DSM manual and read aloud. "Things like rape or assault, military combat, floods and earthquakes, large fires and airplane crashes, bombing and torture, death camps—" he snapped the book shut, "that those are the kinds of things that are the events that trigger this disease.

"My question is: Normal domestic problems are not a triggering mechanism for post-traumatic stress disorder, are they?"

The witness said they were not. There ensued a long question and answer session concerning whether or not Dan Nichols voluntarily told his father Kari was coming and participated knowingly, purposely, in the apprehension and kidnapping of Kari.

"If the facts are this: That he saw her coming; he was involved in the planning; he knew about the plan; and he notified his father, then he was acting purposely," Marc said.

"He was acting for his father's wishes."

Judge Davis addressed the witness. "I thought you said a minute ago that you would change your opinion if that were the fact."

"I thought I said that it would not change my diagnosis."

Marc interrupted. "That's what you said: It wouldn't change your diagnosis, but it would change your opinion about whether or not he was acting purposely or knowingly."

There was no response.

"God, what else can we use to determine people's conduct or their intent, but their own conduct?" Marc smacked his pen into the palm of his hand. "How can you look at a person a year later, ten months later, and tell us what he was thinking back then, other than by looking at his conduct?"

"I can look at his conduct. I can give you professional and clinical judgements right now on the way he is and make suppositions as to what went on back then."

"Suppositions," Marc repeated. The word echoed in the courtroom.

"And that survivalist mentality that you're talking about, he somehow regresses into himself and tries to survive the best way he can?" Marc asked.

No response. Marc repeated the question. No response.

"The law says that if a person acts voluntarily when he or she is capable, physically capable of performing an act, then the defendant was acting voluntarily, that's what the law says. Would you *disagree* with that?" asked Marc.

"No."

"If the law says that a person acts knowingly when he is aware of his conduct, then the defendant was acting knowingly— if that's what the law says? . . . Do you agree with that?"

"Yes."

"And if the law says that a person acts purposely when it is his purpose to engage in certain conduct—not talking about his motivation, now. We're saying if the law says that a person acts purposely when it is his purpose to engage in certain conduct, then the defendant was acting purposely."

No response.

Marc quoted some of Kari's testimony to demonstrate his point. He asked if those examples indicated to the witness that Dan acted knowingly.

"My contention has been that he cannot act independently."

"We're not talking independently. You just told me that if the definition of 'knowingly' means aware of your conduct, that he was acting knowingly up there in the mountains in July; correct?"

"Yes."

"Now, isn't it possible, Doctor, that he acted out of wanting that girl, wanting Kari Swenson, just as well as any other explanation?"

"That's a possibility, yes."

When questioned about the knife incident in Three Forks, the witness said he "hypothesized" that Dan was subconsciously carrying out his father's wishes.

"Even when he was apart from him?"

"Even when he was apart from him, the influence was still there."

"Isn't that what a criminal is—is when they simply ignore the rights and obligations of being a member of a moral community, and they essentially have no values and no feelings about anybody else?" Marc asked.

"Your Honor, I object. Argumentative."

"Overruled."

"I see Dan Nichols as having a value system that is very different than society's and very different than the ordinary criminal's," the witness answered.

"But that still doesn't excuse criminal responsibility, does it?"

No response.

"If we excused the responsibility for everybody that had different values, then we would be subject to siege by a wave of criminal activity virtually every day of our life."

"I object. Argumentative and irrelevant," Ungar insisted.

"Overruled!"

"I think Mr. Nichols has to learn the norms of this society and obey the norms and rules and regulations of this society, if he is going to stay in it," stated the weary psychologist.

"And he has to do that by assuming responsibility for his actions, doesn't he?"

"I agree."

"Nothing further, Your Honor."

The Therapist

We were subdued during the brief recess and talked about what we had just heard. I was beginning to understand how criminals who commit heinous crimes could get away with them.

While we waited, the attorneys were meeting in chambers to discuss the next witness—the therapist.

"Your Honor," Marc said, "the state would move in limine in the following regard: It is our understanding that the defense intends to call this man as an expert witness. We would move to exclude his testimony because it's not competent, expert testimony along the lines that a therapist or a counselor's testimony has not received such recognition within the scientific community as to be allowable evidence in a court of law under our Rules of Evidence. Therefore, he should not be allowed to testify as to his opinions and conclusions in that regard."

"Well, Mr. Ungar," said the judge, "What do you have to say? I had appointed the man several months ago to do some things."

Steve insisted that the therapist had the qualifications necessary to make him an expert witness, so his testimony was allowed.

The witness explained how he dealt with his clients and said he based his work on a method he had developed himself ten years ago. The judge's expression grew grim as he listened, and I wondered why he didn't stop the witness. When his testimony was completed I was so angry I could hardly breathe.

"Why was he allowed to testify? All that nonsense! And the jury didn't sleep through any of it!" I said to Larry Moran as we prepared to leave for the day.

"It will either be stricken from the record or Marc will rip him to shreds!" he stormed.

"But even if it's stricken, the jury's heard it, and it's the kind of drivel they'd probably remember. Damn!"

"Ah-ah," warned Larry. "If I can't smoke in here, you can't swear in here." He grinned.

The attorneys and the judge were in chambers preparing for the next day's session. Marc told the judge that in the morning he would make a motion to strike all of the therapist's testimony, "it being based on conjecture and unproven methods and a number of other things."

Judge Davis warned, "Show up early. Mr. Ungar, be prepared to resist that, because I wasn't too impressed with his testimony here." After some off-the-record comments, it was decided that the state's motion would be heard immediately.

"I guess our motion would be to strike the testimony of the man in its entirety because it simply does not comply with the provisions of Rule 702, as was suggested by Mr. Ungar when we were arguing this previously." John read the rule and continued, "He testified essentially that the methods he employed in ascertaining his diagnoses, I guess if you want to call them that—

he doesn't even go that far—were developed by himself. And upon those self-developed methods of evaluation, he comes to these conclusions.

"That is not within the purview of what is intended by Rule 702," John said. "As far as this particular rule is concerned, Your Honor, . . . he should not be allowed to come in here and do nothing more than confuse the jury by presenting a lot of ambiguous, so-called professional methodology that doesn't have anything to do with the legal principles of knowingly and purposely."

"Well, what's the effect, Mr. Connor? I've let him testify now. The jury has heard it."

"And the jury can be asked to disregard it," John answered.

"Or are we better off cross-examining?" Marc asked, knowing that was the last thing the defense wanted. Steve decided to accept having the testimony stricken from the record.

Marc brought up the subject of allowing the girls from Three Forks to testify. Mr. Ungar had submitted a brief arguing against the girls' testimony, saying that allowing them to speak would violate fair trial and due process rights.

"Could I be heard just briefly?" Marc said. He read the rule pertaining to cases such as this one, and presented his argument.

"Well, I may be wrong," the judge said, "but I'm going to be consistently wrong. So I'll allow you to call these witnesses if you want to, although, as I said before, in my judgement you've made your point on cross-examination, anyway. But if you feel that you need them, you can call them."

Rebuttal Witnesses

Friday morning dawned sunny and hot. In chambers Mr. Ungar sought to prevent Dr. Stratford's testimony because Dan Nichols and the woman named Sue complained about the doctor's interview methods. Steve said confidential and privileged information was gained from the Sue referred to in the case. He argued that Stratford had phoned her and asked questions about statements Dan made to her in her role as a youth counselor, and about their personal relationship.

Steve was angry when he told the judge that he had thought Sue would be at the trial because he had subpoenaed her, but when he phoned her he was informed she had hired an attorney from Helena to represent her, and he had advised her to refuse to cooperate with the defense attorneys.

Marc pointed out that Dr. Stratford's interview of Dan Nichols was conducted in the same manner as that of the psychologist and therapist.

"I advised him up front," Dr. Stratford told the judge, "that if there was any situation he did not want to talk about, that he should feel free not to talk about that." He said he advised him further to call his attorney if he wished and that on at least two occasions he did phone his lawyer.

"There was absolutely no harassment; there was absolutely no pressure for him to talk about anything he did not want to," said the doctor. He kept notes about the calls he made to Sue and Dan Nichols's sister.

"I said to her (Sue), 'You do not have to talk to me whatsoever. I do not want to talk to you about personal relationships, as it might be embarrassing to you. I would like to, however, ask you some questions about Dan Nichols and his relationship with his father.' She mumbled about three sentences of material that have no relevance at all, and I could not even understand. She said, 'My mother is right here and questioning as to whether or not you are who you say you are.' "

Stratford cut the call short by advising her to check with Nichols's attorney for advice and to call him collect. He phoned Dan's sister, identified himself, suggested she phone Ungar to verify his identity, and hung up after telling her to phone him collect, too. Neither returned his call.

The judge said he needed time to consider Mr. Ungar's motion. Meanwhile, the trial continued.

In the courtoom the judge admonished the jury to obey his instructions, said the therapist's testimony had been stricken from the record, and they were not to consider it in their deliberations.

Marc called Laurie Johnson, but before she testified, the jury was instructed that her testimony could be considered only to explain or rebut evidence previously offered by the defendant.

Laurie and Debbie Johnson told the court their version of the defendant's conduct the night he invaded their home. It was the same story Marc had told us weeks ago, and it didn't correspond with Nichols's testimony. There was no cross-examination, and the sisters were excused. In Ungar's closing statement he told the jury he hadn't cross-examined the girls because he hadn't known they would be called as witnesses.

Judge Davis allowed Dr. William D. Stratford to testify. He identified himself as a medical doctor who specialized in the practice of adult and forensic psychiatry. He was the only consulting psychiatrist for the Montana State Prison.

The witness said documents pertaining to the case, depositions from Kari and Jim, as well as police reports, had been made available to him, but he did not read them before the evaluation because he didn't want his reaction to the defendant prejudiced. He said he asked a clinical psychologist, Dr. Herman Walters, to do whatever testing and interviews he thought would be required. Correlating his interviews, the test results, and interviews with the psychologist, he came to the conclusion that Dan Nichols suffered from moderate depression, some from being held in jail. He diagnosed the defendant as having a dependent personality disorder.

In his professional opinion, he felt that Nichols had the capacity, at the time of the kidnapping, to act purposely and knowingly, and he was not under the domination of his father. He cited information from Kari's and Dan's testimonies and from his interviews and tests as his basis for his decision.

"He left school on his own, according to Dan," the witness said.

"He told you that, Dr. Stratford, that he left school on his own?" Marc said.

"Yes. . . . and that he went to the mountains on his own without his father's coercion for a variety of reasons."

"Now, were you able to discover whether or not the defendant was torn between his mother and father as has been presented here?" Marc asked.

"Well, sir, there are a variety of professional opinions which different people can have on that subject. In my opinion he was not torn. I was not able to elicit from him any positive feelings that he had toward his mother. He felt that she had been extremely critical of him and that other times had been permissive when she shouldn't have been." Dr. Stratford hesitated. "He described her in harsh terms."

"In harsh terms. How did he describe her?"

"On one occasion he described her as a bitch." Nichols's expression didn't change as every eye in the room slid toward him.

"Did you determine or can you give us a view, Dr. Stratford, of whether or not the defendant suffered from something known as post-traumatic stress disorder?"

"My professional opinion is that he did not. First of all, the diagnosis requires a specific stressor that is unduly traumatic and is usually outside the range of normal human experience. I'm unaware as to what specific stressor is being alluded to here. It usually refers to catastrophic circumstances: airplane accidents, war situations, significant traumas that would cause distress in almost all people."

"Thank you, Dr. Stratford, we have nothing further," Marc said.

Mr. Ungar was on his feet flipping through pages of a yellow legal pad. He cross-examined the doctor using the same tactics that Marc had used the day before, but the witness responded with calm, unflappable professionalism.

"Now, yesterday the state attacked our witness's finding of post-traumatic stress disorder, and apparently you agree that there was no basis for that kind of finding; right?"

"That's my opinion."

Mr. Ungar asked if many of the facts about Nichols's domestic life could be considered normal, and the witness said no, but they weren't of sufficient trauma to be categorized as catastrophic. Steve reviewed a long string of events in Nichols's life and asked, "Don't you think that if hypothesizing all these things as I just did, that a post-traumatic stress disorder would be a possible diagnosis?"

"No, sir, I think that's nuts." Reporters chortled and scribbled on their note pads.

Next, Dr. Herman Walters took the stand, gave his qualifications, and described his testing of the defendant. He had heard Dan's direct testimony and cross-examination as well as Don Nichols's direct testimony. Marc asked him if he had formed a professional opinion about whether or not the defendant had the capacity to act purposely or knowingly on July fifteen and sixteen, 1984.

"In particular, at the time of the first incident, the kidnapping, I believe he did have the capacity to act purposely and knowingly," the witness answered. "At the time of the second incident the following day, I believe that capacity may have been somewhat compromised, but that he was still capable of acting purposely and knowingly at that time."

"Dr. Walters, did you find that the defendant's testimony, when he testified on Tuesday, was the same as what he told you when you interviewed him concerning this incident?"

"On some points, yes, on other points, no."

"Did he specifically mention to you whether or not he was involved in notifying his father and planning this event?"

"Yes, sir."

"And that was different from what you noticed in his testimony?"

"Yes."

"We have nothing further for Dr. Walters," concluded Marc. It had been short, sweet, and to the point.

Antagonism showed in Steve's body language as he began his cross-examination. Dr. Walters was composed, as if he had expected this reaction. The attorney said he was going to give the doctor some hypothetical questions and would ask for conclusions from the doctor. He began a review of Nichols's family history, and Dr. Walters corrected him when he made mistakes in his story.

Finally, the psychologist held up his hand, stopped Ungar, picked up a pad of paper and a pencil, wrote down what had been hypothesized so far, and nodded for Steve to continue. Ungar's litany had been hypnotic, but the break of waiting and having to slow the delivery of his information released me and gave me time to find humor in the incident.

Steve concluded by asking if, given the preceding facts, Nichols could have acted independently of his father.

"Let me look at this please," Dr. Walters said as he scanned the pages of his handwriting. "Since this is hypothetical, may I ask just a couple clarification questions? . . . You note that the child or adolescent sustained being struck, beaten continuously during a prolonged period of time. By that are you meaning this is a daily event or that this is a weekly event, monthly event?"

"Let's say monthly," Steve answered. "Let's say he's hit once in the forehead with the fist and knocked down."

Dr. Walters made a note on his pad and said, "The second one: constant indoctrination to obey this philosophy. Now, that means there's no morality, there's no loyalty to each other. No loyalty to family. There's no morality of any kind is literally what you've said. Is that the assumption?"

Mr. Ungar sighed and said, "No, that would not be the assumption. The assumption would probably have as an exception the morality of loyalty toward one another."

"Okay. Thank you. And then I have one more question, and that is are there any other influences in the form of other family members or positive socializing sources that would be bearing on this, or are these the sole influences on this person?"

"Okay. The other influences that I would have you hypothesize are those influences that Dan actually had in his life that you know of from your interview with him."

The doctor turned the pages of his note pad, reading carefully what he had written. A reporter yawned. The sound of traffic and a barking dog drifted up to us from the street below.

Dr. Walters concluded that Nichols would find it difficult, but not impossible, to act independently. He said it was possible but "not likely" that Nichols suffered post-traumatic stress disorder because the specific element of a highly traumatic or catastrophic event was missing.

Marc conducted a redirect and gave a hypothetical of his own. The doctor turned to new pages in the notebook. Judge Davis's mouth twitched as he looked at the young prosecutor standing before him, arms folded, feet apart, rocking back and forth on the balls of his feet. Marc gave his information slowly so Dr.

Walters could jot it down. His information dealt with Nichols's ability to move freely between the worlds of his parents, his ability to conform to society when he wished, and his disregard for everyone but himself in his relationship with an older woman.

"Excuse me. I'll apologize. You've got the hopper just about full here," grinned Dr. Walters. Everyone laughed with Marc. "We should probably get to a question before I lose the whole thing."

"And then consider the kidnapping and abduction of a young woman takes place in the mountains, as you are aware they have taken place through the facts of this case," Marc continued.

"Yes."

"Do you have an opinion as to whether or not that person had the capacity to act voluntarily and freely and make choices, the consequences of which he was fully aware of?"

"Yes."

"What is your opinion?"

"That he would have the capacity to act voluntarily."

"Do you have an opinion concerning his capacity to act purposely and knowingly during that abduction? And could you give us that opinion?"

"That he did have that capacity." Dr. Walters's opinion was spoken firmly, with resolution. The defendant whispered and gestured to his attorney.

The state and the defense rested their cases, and the jury was sent home for the weekend. In the prosecutor's office, Marc said, "The testimonies of our witnesses went well. I don't think we could have asked for more from them."

John, hands stuffed in his pockets, looked out from under his brows and grinned at Marc. "You gave Herman a severe case of writer's cramp!"

Smiling, Marc tamped tobacco into his pipe and pulled out a chair for my mother. "Did you see Steve's face when Herman took out that pad of paper and made him lose the tempo of his questioning?" He clenched his pipe between his teeth and his grin broadened. "I knew he would do the same thing to me if I wasn't careful."

The attorneys and the judge spent the afternoon in chambers deciding on the instructions to be given to the jury. The three prosecutors went home for the weekend, and we drove to the cabin.

Kari was ill Sunday night but insisted on going to Virginia City to hear Marc's closing statement. "I'd like to get there just before the session starts so I don't have to worry about the cameras. I'm fair game when I'm not on the witness stand."

In the courtroom Kari sat between Bob and my mother and kept her face turned from the cameras. Paul glowered at the photographers.

Marc's closing statement was as eloquent and moving as his opening one had been. He recapped the important issues of the trial, stressing at one point, "This is not an epic story of two mountain men. It is an insult to the image of mountain men."

Nichols listened impassively while his attorney argued against the felony murder rule that could send him to prison for life.

We drove to the house on the hill to await the verdict. Each person was lost in his own thoughts. Three hours passed. Kari, exhausted and ill, went home with Paul, and the rest of us returned to the courthouse. We paced the corridors, sat in the prosecutor's room discussing everything but the trial, walked the rickety boardwalk along the main street, and talked to some reporters who asked why the Swenson family refused to be interviewed. I explained our anger at the romanticized, "mountain-man image" presented by the media. "You'll have to admit, Mrs. Swenson, the incident does have a romantic, old West twist to it," said a reporter from London. I saw Mother's expression and knew if

I didn't say something she would. She was exhausted and was running short of patience.

"You bet," I answered, "and I see that romantic aspect every time Kari wakes up screaming or crying; every time she goes through the pain of physical therapy; every time she goes to a biofeedback or counseling session; every time I think of Alan Goldstein and his family; every time I see the pain in our son's eyes, and when I see how this has aged my husband." The embarrassed reporter wandered off.

The jury returned at 11:40 p.m. Dan Nichols was found guilty of kidnapping and misdemeanor assault, but not guilty on the felony rule. Judge Davis accepted the jury's decision, but he didn't look pleased that they had disregarded his instructions, which said that if they found Nichols guilty of kidnapping, they were bound, by law, to find him guilty of murder.

Comments made by jurors to the newspapers confirmed my mother's impressions of them. "The law made it impossible to separate the two," said a juror, referring to the kidnapping and the felony murder rule. "We read the pages over and over to try and see a way out," said one of the women. "We finally decided to try and bluff them." She went on to say that the jury did not discuss the evidence given during the trial, only the problem they had with the felony murder rule. She said the testimonies of the four witnesses were essentially the same. "There wasn't any lying. All the stories were just alike."

"Just alike?" Bob stormed. "She must have slept through the trial!"

Kari hugged him and sighed. "It's over. You can't change the verdict, so let's forget it." She concentrated on her classes, treatments, and the coming trip to San Francisco.

Dan Nichols was freed on a $35,000 bond and released to a family who found him a job on a farm. His location was supposed to be a secret, but a reporter who called for my opinion of the bond told me he was located on a farm outside the town of Miles City.

I asked Marc about the terms of the bond, and he said, "He has to stay where he is until he's sentenced. If he leaves without the order of the court he'll be returned to jail. I don't think Judge Davis wants to sentence him before his father's trial."

"What? That's a month and a half away!"

"I don't have any say in it," Marc soothed. "It's up to Judge Davis, and he wants to avoid any more publicity. Besides, Steve says his schedule is too busy to free him for an earlier sentencing."

28

DON NICHOLS'S TRIAL

On May eighteenth, Kari and Becky Lohmiller flew to San Francisco, where Kari and nine other women received the Up And Coming Award. Then Kari continued with classes and her therapy sessions. Bob Morasky called us to his office in mid-June. Kari had been depressed, but we didn't understand how deeply until that meeting. With her permission, he conveyed her feelings about the stress placed on her by talking to attorneys, the class she was trying to finish, and by the discussions at home of the trials. I substituted at the veterinarian's office for her when she needed extra time to work on her class, and we decided not to discuss the trials with her unless she initiated the conversation.

Kari's friend Holly Flies returned from California and helped Becky shore up Kari's spirits. Tall, blonde, and soft spoken with a quick sense of humor, Holly was invaluable. They hiked, ran, laughed, floated the rivers, and rode the horses in the mountains around the cabin with Bob Naert.

June and July 1985

Don Nichols's attorney asked that all charges be dropped, stating that past publicity would make a fair trial impossible. Marc told me a hearing was scheduled for July second, and I reminded him I had just won our bet. Don White subpoenaed the newspapers and the television stations for copies of all the articles and film footage on the case.

"I'm sure the judge will deny the motion," Marc said, "because Nichols and his attorney didn't ask to have the cameras shut off during Don's testimony at the son's trial. Had they done that they'd have a more creditable argument. Also, it's on the record that the old man waived his rights in order to testify at his son's trial. This is just a formality."

July 2, 1985

It was hot, dusty, and unpleasant in Virginia City. The courthouse had gone back to business as usual, and no deputies waited to check the contents of my handbag. The doors to the courtroom were open, and I saw a group of reporters and photographers standing together on the far side of the room. They stared at me when I entered, and I felt uneasy. One woman glanced to my right and then back at me. I turned my head to see what had distracted her and saw Dan Nichols sitting with his sister. He looked away. The breath went out of me, but I kept walking until I joined the group of reporters. We watched his nonchalant behavior and wondered if he had been released from his bond agreement.

When Marc and Judy saw Nichols, Marc raised his eyebrows and shrugged at me.

Judge Davis entered, looked at the people in the room, and scowled when he saw Dan Nichols. He shuffled some papers, cleared his throat, and proceeded with the hearing. The judge eventually denied Mr. White's motion to drop charges against Don Nichols, as well as the request to ban cameras. Marc promised to find out why Nichols was not in Miles City. He phoned two days later.

"I talked with Frank Davis, and he was as surprised as we were to see Dan in Virginia City. He hadn't released him from the terms of the bond and suggested that I ask Steve Ungar what was going on. Steve said he forgot what the terms were, and he had told Nichols he could go live with his sister. Frank is unhappy but doesn't want to make a fuss that would cause more publicity, so he's given Dan permission to stay with his sister until his sentencing. Besides, White needs access to Dan if he's to testify at his father's trial."

"Don't the terms of a bond mean anything?"

"We can't do anything, Janet, but Frank promised me he'd sentence Dan within a week of the conclusion of the old man's trial."

I told him I didn't think it would be healthy for any of us if the son were to attend his father's trial.

"He's free to go where he pleases."

"Do you realize how dangerous it would be to have him there?"

"What do you mean?"

"Douglas and David Goldstein will be there listening to Nichols's unemotional tale of the murder of their brother, and I'll have to listen to the kidnapping and shooting story again. Do you think he's safe?"

The shock in Marc's voice embarrassed me. "Why . . . I hadn't thought of it in those terms!"

"Someone better."

Jonathan accompanied Kari to the second trial. Paul, with a double major in geology and physics, was obligated to spend the summer at a geology field camp.

The jury selection was long and tedious. Diane and Doug Goldstein were there, and Doug was quoted in the paper as saying Alan had been forgotten in the publicity surrounding the Nicholses and Kari. The article said Alan, a graduate of the University of Michigan, had been a member of the Flint Environmental Action Team. This group had had April 20, Arbor Day, declared as Alan Goldstein Day, and an oak tree was planted in his honor. Doug said Al was a wonderful, caring man, and people were drawn to him because of his kindness and concern for others.

"Mom, don't they know how we feel about Al?" Kari frowned.

"Yes. I wrote to the family several months ago asking permission to submit Al's name for the Carnegie Hero Award. I haven't heard from them, but I'll discuss it with Al's brothers this week."

"Did you nominate Jim Schwalbe for the hero award, too?"

"Of course!"

Kari made arrangements for Holly and Jonathan to ride to Virginia City with us. She and Bob slipped in the back door of the courthouse and went to Marc's temporary office before anyone realized we were there.

The twitterers were absent, but the courtroom quickly filled with curious tourists. Men in plaid Bermuda shorts balanced cameras on their ample paunches and stretched their pale, hairy legs into the aisles. Women in bright polyester slacks suits fanned themselves with brochures. The heat was oppressive. A tour group clustered around the deputy at the door and asked when the first act started. Vivian's jaw dropped in surprise.

A handsome elderly gentleman was seated across the aisle. He was stooped with age and used a dark wooden cane with an ornate silver knob on the top. He kept fiddling with a hearing aid that fitted his right ear beneath his snow-white hair, and his delicate, gray-haired wife fussed around him. He watched the tourists, frowned, and shook his head.

Douglas and David Goldstein arrived with Diane. Their suffering showed clearly in their eyes and the tightness around their mouths. Diane looked tired and nervous, which gave her beauty a haunting quality.

Sally Hollier slid into the bench behind me, sat with our friends from Lone Mountain Ranch, and squeezed my shoulder. She had come to the trials to be with me since my mother wouldn't be here. The last trial had been exhausting for Mom, and I had encouraged her to stay home.

Marc, Judy, and John were in chambers arguing to keep potential witnesses from being in the courtroom during the presentation of the case. The judge asked that they go off record, and there is no transcript of what was said. They agreed that Dan Nichols would not be allowed in the courtroom during the trial, but he was free to roam the building and the town. Kari stayed in the office with Bob while Marc made his opening statement to the jury.

Don Nichols remained expressionless as Marc recounted the kidnapping, chaining, shooting of Kari, and the murder of Alan. The Goldsteins were pale, their hands knotted in fists in their laps.

"Alan Goldstein had brought a pistol in his backpack in the event that while searching they ran into a bear. Who could have imagined that they would run into kidnappers? He had a limited number of choices. He could try to leave and get help, but one of his friends had already been shot, and a rifle was now trained on the other.

"And he had been accosted himself with two weapons, and there was no guarantee that he wouldn't be shot down if he ran. Or he could try to help his friends in the only way he thought he could, which would put his own life on the line. He chose to risk his own life for his friends; to lay it down for his friends because he wasn't sure he would have any friends to lay it down for if he did nothing at all.

"At the close of this case, we will ask you without hesitation that the lawlessness of this atrocity be declared by your verdicts and that justice not be disappointed."

The defense exercised its right to reserve a statement until later.

Marc called Joel Beardsley as a witness, and the defense immediately asked to be heard in chambers, where Mr. White argued against hearing her testimony, saying it would only be prejudicial. The motion was denied and Joel told her story. Marc showed the log with the Nicholses' names on it to the court, dismissed Joel, and called Kari to the stand.

Judge Davis told the press and tourists that the next witness had elected not to be on camera and to respect her request. Kari walked into the room, glanced at us, and joined Marc. She wore a white, blue, and mauve striped blouse with white slacks. She seemed to be in a trance as she took the stand. Drs. Seitz and Morasky's efforts had culminated in a type of self-hypnosis. Again she told of her kidnapping.

She began to cry when she testified that the defendant had threatened to kill anyone who tried to rescue her. Judge Davis called a recess, and Bob dashed off to be with her.

Sally and I walked into the corridor and came face to face with Dan Nichols. He was wearing a new black cowboy hat, and his western-cut shirt was unbuttoned at the throat to display a gold chain. The western trousers were cinched at the waist with a leather belt that had a large, shiny buckle. He wore new cowboy boots. Nichols laughed at something his therapist said and turned with a smile to stare at the Goldsteins edging past him.

I felt dizzy. Colors faded, and through the black-and-white haze of rage I started toward him. Sally and Vivian tugged at my arm, returned me to the courtroom, and held my hands until I stopped shaking.

"At least Nichols has the right hat. Don't the bad guys always wear black?" Sally said. The remark broke the tension and we laughed.

—

Kari and Marc went through her testimony. She used a set of photographs to show the jury where she had been chained and her relationship in distance to the firepit. Marc entered the color photographs taken by the forensics photographer as evidence, and Kari pointed out to the jury where she, Jim, Al, and Don Nichols were positioned in each of them. The last picture was one of Alan. It surprised her, and her voice broke when she identified it.

Mike Lilly, who had recently joined Don White for the defense, began the cross-examination. He made the mistake of being condescending, and I watched Kari's eyes flash. She clenched her jaw.

He asked if the conversations with the Nicholses, as they dragged her along, were friendly. She said that they discussed their philosophy of life and where they were going to take her. She didn't find their words friendly.

"Did you get the feeling during that walk that it was—I'm sure it wasn't friendly—but that there wasn't a lot of tension during that period of time?"

"Maybe not for them. It was for me."

"I'm sure. But they weren't exhibiting anything hostile to you from the way they were behaving other than the fact you were tied to Dan?" I couldn't believe what I was hearing!

"The defendant had his rifle the whole time, carried it with him, had it out of its cover, and walked behind me and his son with it pointed at our backs," Kari answered stiffly.

"Once you got to this point where you were camping, Kari, about how much time passed from when you first arrived there until you decided to go to sleep?"

"Two, three hours."

She said she asked questions about the Nicholses' life in the mountains, but they "got very hostile about that. But for my sake, I was trying to act as normal as possible because I didn't know, if I acted hysterical, what they would do."

"And Dan Nichols actually showed you some drawings that he had made; is that correct?"

"Yes."

He showed Kari the picture she had drawn and entered it as an exhibit for the defense after pointing out that the Nicholses had been good enough to give her a piece of paper to draw on.

"I originally asked for that paper to leave some kind of message behind."

Lilly ignored her. "Now, is there any drawing on the piece of paper that Dan made?"

"I don't know."

"The unicorn was not on that piece of paper?"

"No."

Lilly attempted to make the Nicholses sound like good ol' boys who "gave" her clothes and a sleeping bag. She corrected him by pointing out she had "*asked*" for the clothes, and the sleeping bag was almost useless because she couldn't pull it above the chain around her waist.

"But they were trying to make sure you were as comfortable as they could make you under those circumstances, weren't they?"

"I don't know how comfortable that is."

"They did what they could; would you agree?"

"No."

"As long as you brought it up, Kari, they told you on a number of occasions what their plan was, didn't they?" He repeated the idea of keeping her for several days, then releasing her if she didn't like them.

"Yes. And when I asked them that, I asked them if they would help me back to civilization. And they said, 'No. We'd let you find your own way back no matter how you wanted to do it.'"

"Okay. Did you get the feeling in their own way—and I emphasize 'own way'—were they trying to be friendly to you while you were in camp that first night?"

"I can't say. I would not call them friendly."

"In your eyes?"

"I don't think anyone would."

Jonathan's fists were clenched, and the muscles were working in Bob's jaw.

Lilly said that since Kari was familiar with firearms she probably understood that the most important safety rule is "you don't point your rifle in the direction of some person."

"Now would you agree with me that on the first day when Don Nichols had his rifle out, that he obeyed that basic rule?"

"No. He pointed it at me."

"Did he point it at you purposely or negligently?"

"I don't know. He was walking behind me with his rifle pointed at me."

He asked if she thought Dan Nichols meant to shoot her.

"Well, his dad told him to shut me up. I can only say purposely." She admitted there was no way she could know for sure if he had shot her purposely or accidentally.

Lilly said Nichols was hysterical right after he shot her, and Kari answered, "I wouldn't say hysterical, more scared. Oh, you know, he shot me. I mean, I would be scared, too."

"He was quite upset?"

"I would not say upset. Scared." She had not heard Jim give the same description, nor had she been told he used the word scared.

Mr. Lilly's next questions made it sound as if Kari didn't know where Alan had been when he was shot or what the distances were. Kari corrected him by saying she knew the distances, knew he had a radio but didn't hear his words as he called for help, knew he had moved behind the tree where he was slain, but didn't know if Alan had moved in any other direction before being shot.

Marc did a redirect.

"Why did you try to make conversation with these people?" he asked.

"To try to keep myself somewhat under control, try to stay as normal as I could under the circumstances."

"Did the fact that you were given a shirt and socks and sleeping bag really set your mind at ease?"

"No, not at all."

"Did it lead you to feel a sense of comfort and warmth that you were safe and secure in their presence?"

"No. I was scared. I didn't know what they wanted. And being chained up and dragged off, I just—I didn't feel safe at all."

"Why did you try so hard to maintain your composure?"

"I didn't know how they would react. He had told me earlier that if I started screaming, he'd beat me up. I didn't know what they would do if I became hysterical."

"And he had demonstrated his willingness to do that very early on, hadn't he?"

"Yes."

"We have nothing further, Your Honor."

Kari left the stand and sat between Holly and Jonathan to listen to Jim's testimony.

"What did Lilly think that was, a picnic?" Her voice shook with anger. Holly took her hand and calmed her. The elderly gentleman smiled and gave us a thumbs-up gesture. Jim took the stand to relate the same set of facts that he had testified to in the last trial. Marc displayed the photographs, and Jim pointed out where people had been. There was a recess before the cross-examination, and we retreated to the prosecutors' office to avoid running into the younger Nichols and the press.

"I was so upset with Mr. Lilly I'm not sure what I said!" Kari sputtered.

"You did just fine, Kari." John said.

"They wouldn't have turned me loose—not ever! Lilly implied that just because they said they'd let me go it was all right to kidnap me! To *borrow* me! I should have talked to Jim before the trials. His testimony has reminded me of some things I had forgotten."

"I think it was better this way. I don't believe in witnesses getting together to coordinate their stories. You and Jim are two of the most reliable witnesses I've ever interviewed. What makes your testimonies so creditable are the small details you don't agree on, such as the type of clothing they were wearing—but the major issues are the same," Marc explained.

Don White decided to cross-examine Jim. He asked time after time if Alan liked to hunt, and each time he was told no, but he and Jim had discussed the possibility of hunting in the fall. When he asked Jim if the other searchers were armed, Jim answered "one or two." It was never pointed out that those two men were law enforcement officers.

White handed Alan's pistol to Jim and asked him if he had ever seen it before. Jim said it resembled the pistol he saw when he returned to the crime scene with law enforcement officers. White let Jim sit there, the gun dangling from his fingers, while he asked a few unimportant questions. Jim stared at the gun, trembling so violently I thought he'd drop it.

"Thank you, Jim, for taking your time to come here today," White said and turned his back. In a split second Jim grasped the pistol in both hands, extended his arms, drew a bead on Don Nichols for one breathless second, then dropped the pistol back into his lap. It happened so quickly I thought I had imagined it until I saw the stunned look on my husband's face, Vivian's pallor, and the wide eyes of the reporters. The judge and the attorneys had not seen Jim point the gun.

Marc began the redirect, and it became clear that no one would have thought it unusual to take along a firearm, because most people thought Kari had been harmed or treed by a grizzly.

"Mr. White asked you on cross-examination or mentioned that in one of your early statements close to the time of the offense that you had hoped you could talk things out. Is that an accurate reflection of what you were thinking at the scene, that you could talk things out with these people?"

"When I first came up and saw Kari, I was hoping that I could talk them into just leaving and letting me take care of Kari."

"And in the ninety seconds that transpired, did that appear to be a reasonable probablility to you?"

"No."

"So how much time elapsed from the time that the defendant first trained his weapon on Alan Goldstein and asked him if he had a weapon, until he came back on you when you tried to grab it, and until he was swinging it back to Alan? Was there enough time for Alan Goldstein to have gotten off a shot? . . . Plenty of time?"

"Yes."

"But instead he made the comment, 'You're surrounded'?"

"Yes."

A recess was called. A reporter leaned toward a photographer and asked, "Did you see what I thought I saw?"

"The gun? It was so fast I thought I'd imagined it. Cripes, just the look in Schwalbe's eyes could've killed the old coot!"

Don Nichols Testifies

The air in the courtroom was hot, heavy, and stale. Tourists shed their jackets and complained about the lack of air conditioning. Last evening Kari had told us she, Holly, and Becky planned to spend the next few days together and would not attend the trial. We had dreaded a confrontation between Kari and Dan Nichols, so her decision gave us a measure of relief.

Dr. Rivers's testimony was similar to that of the first trial. Diane left when he began to describe Alan's wounds and had the misfortune of accosting Dan Nichols in the corridor. There was an unpleasant exchange of words.

Mr. Lilly gave the delayed opening statement.

"As they spent time in the mountains, Don will tell you they came to realize, despite their love for those mountains, for the wildlife and solitude, that they felt a need for female companionship. It just wasn't complete without women to share that experience, to share that love with them. . . . And it was their plan, Don will tell you, they they would hold her against her will in the mountains with them and show her their way of life and show her why they loved the mountains as they did. . . . And that's when they spotted Kari Swenson. And Don will tell you that they initially tried to talk Kari into going with them, but, of course, she resisted. So he did use force to take her with them, but after that initial force, Don will tell you that he and

Dan, in their own way, tried to befriend her, and tried to show her their way of life.

"It will be Don's position and it is our position that Don Nichols's conduct does not and did not constitute the offense of kidnapping as Montana law defines it. Rather that conduct constitutes the crime of unlawful restraint."

"Baloney!" the elderly gentleman hissed.

"And at the end of the trial we will ask you to find Don Nichols not guilty of deliberate homicide by reason of his right to exercise self-defense."

Don Nichols was nervous, constantly rubbing his forehead and his mouth with his hand, and clearing his throat. His childhood, marriage, discharge from the military, difficulties keeping his family together, the failure of establishing a homestead in the Cabinet Mountains, and the divorce were covered in great detail. He talked about his trips into the mountains with his son. He described himself as a social person who liked people. He had hoped to have a "tribe. Something like an Indian tribe."

His testimony was rambling, confusing, and difficult to follow. He described his dizziness and nausea after kidnapping Kari, the faulty firing pin in his son's gun, and insisted that he kept his rifle in its case.

He said his son pulled his pistol and trained it on Alan Goldstein, and he wondered at the time what Alan was going to do about it.

"When was Kari shot, then?" Don White asked. The defendant said he did not see the shooting, but his son had told him what had happened.

"You didn't actually see the shooting, though?"

"No, because I had turned over kind of toward—but I got this in my mind—I don't know where it came from, whether it came from what other people told me or whatever, and I might even saw it. I—I—my mind my eyes were on the scene, I know, because—and but I don't know what time they left, so—" Nichols shrugged and stopped speaking. Douglas was shaking his head in disbelief.

The defendant's uncertainties extended to whether or not he had his rifle in his hands and pointed it at Jim, and whether or not he asked Jim if he was armed. He said he picked up the rifles, in their cases, and moved them behind a tree when Jim looked worried. After Alan had said "you're covered," the old man said he took his gun out of its case, loaded it, and pointed it (from hip level) at Alan.

"And I shot him. I just pulled my gun around and shot him. My gun was just about like this. I just pulled it and shot him."

Diane buried her face in her hands and sobbed.

Nichols said he pumped another shell into the rifle, preparing to shoot Jim, who was running at him, but Schwalbe swerved away into the trees before he could shoot. He insisted that Jim stood out of sight in the timber and continued to yell for help, "and Kari yelled for help once in a while." He said he and his son quickly packed their gear, including the chain, and left the camp. He said they checked her wound and it "looked to me like the bullet went in right about here [he pointed to his chest] and then came out higher up on her neck. But there was blood kind of around, so we really couldn't tell too good." I felt sick. They hadn't tried to stop the bleeding.

"Why did you leave her there at that time?"

"Well, we couldn't take her with us, I mean, obviously." There was no mention of taking the sleeping bag away from Kari.

Judge Davis heaved a sigh when the direct exam was finished, pushed his glasses up on his nose, and said, "All right. You may cross-examine, Mr. Racicot."

Marc rose slowly, organized his notes on the podium, and looked at the defendant for a few seconds before speaking.

"Now there's no question, is there, that on July 15, 1984, that you restrained Kari Swenson?" he asked Don Nichols.

"No."

"And there's no question that you did that by secreting her or holding her in an isolated place?" This was the legal term for kidnapping.

"It's not what you're trying to make it, like kidnapping—if that's what you're talking about. Not on purpose just to be isolated in that sinister term, no."

"A sinister term, is that what you perceive my question to be?"

"Yes, it is!" spat Nichols, who slid to the edge of the chair and glared at the prosecutor.

"And there's no question, is there, that you restrained her and held her or secreted her in a place of isolation by using physical force? And there's no question, is there, in your mind, that you did those things knowingly?"

"This physical force thing was more intimidation than anything else, but we did use some force, yes."

"In other words, you could have gotten a lot rougher with her?"

"I had the potential to kill her if I wanted to."

Bob looked sick. He was clearly having more difficulty with this trial than he had had with the first one.

"How about when you grabbed her by the wrists, would you call that physical force?" Nichols answered no and said chaining her was simply "physical restraint."

"Now, there's no question in your mind, is there, that you caused the death of Alan Goldstein?"

"There is a question, yes. That's part of the equation. My part was the illegal part. It was the part of the equation. This world isn't that simple."

"It's not apparently as simple as you'd like to make it."

"I no more caused his death than he caused it or the sun had risen that morning that caused it. It was just part of the equation, the illegal part, that I admit was illegal." The illegal part was the kidnapping, he said.

Marc returned to the capture scene and asked, "But in your own mind, you could sleep with it, couldn't you? It didn't turn your gut inside out to think about dragging a girl off into the mountains, did it?"

"I didn't drag her off."

"It didn't turn your gut inside out to restrain her, did it? You could sleep with that at night?"

"Yes, I could. Yes."

"And you felt you had the right to kill Alan Goldstein because you were acting in self-defense—is what you believe?"

"Right." The defendant nodded his head again and again. He said he was sorry it happened.

"At the point in time when you made the decision to shoot that gun, that was a deliberate act?" Marc asked.

"Yes. Yes."

"And you knew precisely what you were doing?"

"I hoped I knew what I was doing. I didn't know if he was going to shoot me or I was going to shoot him. If I had missed, he would have shot me."

"Right. But it wasn't an accident you hit him, was it?"

"No, I tried to hit him." His eyes darted from Marc to the jury to his attorney. Nichols pushed himself back into the witness chair and crossed his legs. He said he hadn't discussed "taking" a woman with many people, because he knew most of them would be shocked at the idea.

"Did you really hold out some small amount of hope or even a great deal of hope that this could possibly work?"

"I almost knew it would work, yes, if I had been right. . . . I had to be right about the girl, and I had to be right about not having somebody that's a biathlete or something like that, which is not a very logical thing to assume, and a few things like that."

Nichols said he and his son had discussed the plans to kidnap a woman while they planted their garden in early June and decided that Ulreys Lake might yield the type of woman they were looking for. They had looked around the lake area for a girl on July fourteenth but didn't find one, and headed for the higher mountains. Since they had to head back toward the lake to exit the area without climbing over the Spanish Peaks, they decided to have one more look for a girl—they found her.

"I get the impression, Mr. Nichols—and you can correct me if I'm wrong—that this was kind of casual, that—" Marc was tapping his pen in the palm of his hand.

"Well, I thought about it for many years. It was pretty casual, yes. . . . I didn't think it was sinister, as you're thinking of it, so, therefore, it would be more casual than it would be for you."

"And that it was of no more significance to you than shooting a moose or getting a bear or burying your rutabagas?"

"Certainly it was, had a big impact on our lives."

"So it was significantly serious to you?"

"Yes, it was. But it wasn't that—I mean, life goes on up there."

"Some lives go on up there," Marc said pointedly.

The witness described the type of girl they were looking for, how he grabbed Kari's wrists and asked her questions. When he clenched his fists demonstrating how he held her, I felt faint and concentrated on the sweat trickling down Doug's neck.

"All the time she was talking, she was just—she was a social person, it looked like."

"You could tell, though, right then and there she was mixed-up and didn't have roots in society, huh?" Marc's voice was sharp.

"It was my impression she didn't, that she just acted like a bunch of other girls I'd seen."

"Well, isn't it really true that you just thought that because you wanted to think that?"

"I didn't want to think that. I hoped it was true, but it was obvious she was acting like a bunch of other girls I'd seen."

"Are you insinuating that was kind of flirtatious and loose and—" there was a quiet threat to Marc's voice as he riveted Nichols with his eyes.

"No, I wouldn't call her that at all, not at all. Just that—just mixed-up girls. They don't know—"

"Mixed-up girls smile a lot, or what?"

"Certainly. . . . I think she just thought I was a rude type of guy that flirted in strange ways at girls. That's what I thought. She didn't get real uneasy for a while because I—till some of these questions kind of got a little offbeat as far as she was concerned."

Nichols said he didn't hit Kari, only tapped her on the lips with three fingers because "I wanted her to stop screaming. . . . I said, shut up! Shut up! Shut up!" In the next breath he said he hit her.

"She pulled you down on the ground?"

"No, she didn't pull me down. She got down there. I just went down to follow her down." According to him they were just squatting on the ground having a conversation and he suddenly remembered he should tie her up.

Judge Davis called a recess. Sally went to find a pop machine, and I wandered into the hall. Someone touched my elbow, and I found myself facing Dr. Richard Cole, a physician I had worked with at the student health service.

"Jan, I haven't had a chance to tell you how badly we feel about all this. How's Kari?"

"Not great, but she's hanging in there."

"My God, it must have been horrible for her."

I looked up and saw Dan Nichols staring at me. He stood with one thumb hooked in his pants pocket, shoulders slouched, his face slightly shaded by his cowboy hat. A smile parted his lips and his teeth gleamed white. Dr. Cole's fingers dug into my arm as he held me back.

"No! He's not worth the trouble you'd get into, Jan. Don't look at him!"

Deputy Jerry Mason nailed me to the spot with his eyes. My anger evaporated. "It's nice to know there are people around to protect me from myself—and he's lucky, too." I nodded at Nichols, who turned away to talk to his therapist.

Deputy Mason stepped up to us. "Sorry, Mrs. Swenson, but it's my job to protect both defendants. I can't do a thing about his behavior."

"I know. I'll try to stop complicating your job, but someone should tell Steve Ungar to get him out of Virginia City before something dreadful happens. It didn't take him long to shed the little boy image, did it?" Several reporters had drifted up and overheard the conversation.

"Word has it that Ungar is certain Dan will get off with a suspended sentence, so he probably doesn't care what Dan's doing," said one of the newcomers.

"Suspended sentence? Why would he think that?" I gasped.

"Well, Judge Davis took the kid to the bus, gave him his ticket, and sent him off to Miles City. Guess Ungar reads that as sympathy for Dan." The reporter raised his eyebrows. "Any comments, Mrs. Swenson?"

"None you could print!"

Jerry laughed and returned to his station by the defendant's door while the rest of us drifted down the winding staircase—away from Dan Nichols.

"At some point in time," Marc continued after the recess, "did you tell Kari Swenson that she'd better not scream or you'd give her a couple black eyes, and it didn't make any difference whether or not she was a woman?"

"No. The only—in my original—when I was talking to her, all these questions, I told her were important, I said that, 'Try—we'll all try to make everything smooth, and if you don't cooperate I'm going to give you two black eyes.' That's all I said."

"Why did you tell her that?"

"It was part of the intimidation. I just thought it would make things go smoother. I just didn't want her to start screaming right away or anything like that."

"So it wouldn't make any difference if she was a woman?"

"No, I don't remember telling her. I don't think I did. Why would I say that?"

"It's beyond me why you said a lot of these things. . . . You told her that she'd also have a good adventure story to tell her kids, didn't you?"

"Her grandkids." He said he had made the comment to lighten the situation.

"Trying to be a good kidnapper, so to speak?"

"That was the truth. That's what I thought, she would have a hell of a good adventure story."

"So you told her you would live the way you want without interference from the system?"

"I don't know if I told her that. That's the way I believe."

"And you don't have to respect the values of the system?"

"I don't—I don't respect the values of the system. I think they stink." Nichols glared at Marc and crossed his arms across his chest.

"That's because it takes hard work to fit into the system?"

"Hard work? What do you mean 'hard work'?"

"It takes some compromise to fit into a system?"

"It takes your nose up some rich man's butt!" He glared at Marc.

"And you told Dan, your son, to shut her up?"

"No. I told Danny one time, I said, 'I'm getting tired of that girl screaming,' but that was when the—when Schwalbe and her was both screaming back and forth. And I think I said, 'I'm getting tired of all the goddamn screaming,' or something like that. And Danny—and that was after they was both—Schwalbe and her—were yelling there before while we was packing up."

"You don't remember saying shut her up—that's the bottom line?"

"I could have, yes. I doubt it." The elderly man thumped his cane on the floor and said, "I told you!"

"So the only time you told her you would shoot her friends or her relatives was when you said, 'She was threatening me with her friends'?"

"She just kept saying that, and I just told her that. I said, 'Well, just hope they don't try nothing, because I'll shoot them if they do!' "

"And you did." The room was hushed. A meadowlark's song drifted in from the foothills.

"I didn't know who I shot. And I didn't shoot him for that reason. I shot in self-defense, like I said." He cleared his throat and looked at White, who was whispering to Lilly.

"You thought his [Schwalbe's] efforts to save Kari Swenson and put this thing under control was a weird idea?"

"To save—she didn't need to be saved."

"You were going to do that, were you?"

"She was—I mean, the—only a madman would have thought anything else, but that she would have—that the whole thing was over. It was over. It was just too obvious it was over."

"Well, if it happened the way Jim Schwalbe and Kari Swenson remember it, it obviously wasn't over, was it, if you take that to be true?"

"If I took it—theirs to be true, yes."

Nichols said he got his gun out of its case in a manner that wouldn't alert Alan to what he was doing and loaded it behind a tree where Alan couldn't see him.

"So you'd have the element of surprise on your side so he didn't know exactly what was going to take place?"

"Yes. I didn't want him to think I was getting ready to shoot him. I didn't want him to think I'd shoot him."

"Otherwise he might shoot you?"

"Yes, he would have." Nichols was excited. He slid from the edge to the back of the chair and back to the edge again.

"Then you brought the gun over to where Alan was? And you knew it was pointing at him?"

"Yes, I thought I'd hit him. I thought it would hit him right about here. [Nichols pointed to the middle of his chest.] I remember—I knew I had to miss the tree, and so I—the tree was about like this, and I said I've got to miss that damn tree! So I raised it a little bit. I guess I raised it too much, but I thought I hit him—well, like in the upper part of his chest here [pointing again], and that's where I thought I hit him." He snapped his mouth shut and looked defiantly at Marc.

Nichols said Alan was holding the gun with two hands and pointing it at him. Marc said that was impossible because Alan had the radio in one hand and the gun in the other. This was verified by the positions of the radio and gun next to Alan's hands when he was found by the rescue team.

"Nobody had threatened to shoot any of you, had they?"

"That was part of the problem. He was locked in a trance."

"Do you ever think maybe he was afraid?"

"I don't stop to think and write a thesis and stuff like this. It's just you react. My impression was the fact that something is dreadfully wrong here that is not going to resolve itself. And *he* had started this incident!" Nichols was breathing hard. "He had his gun pointed at everybody, and that was completely unreasonable. And it just—the whole scene seemed like it was going to stay unreasonable. It was just impossible! That's all!"

Nichols said that after Jim fled the scene, he and his son unchained Kari and packed their gear.

"But you wouldn't leave her that sleeping bag, would you?"

"She didn't—no, I wouldn't have left her the sleeping bag. . . . She was going into shock when we left."

"Going into shock and you still took the sleeping bag?"

"You know, there's a thing here about shock, a medical thing, that I'm sure you believe about shock. I got my own opinions about it, and I suppose other doctors do. But shock—you don't cover them up to keep them warm."

"You felt you were helping her by taking the sleeping bag?"

"No. I took it. But I told Danny—I remember telling him later—I said Kari was going into shock, but she'll be all right. It's a cold morning and you go into shock because that's your body's way of making the blood leave the skin and go into internal organs where it's needed. And that's exactly what happens in shock. Some doctors are going to disagree with that, and some are going to agree."

"You took the bag?"

"I believe that. She was going in shock. She was in a cold sweat. She did not want to be warm. You do not want to be warm in shock. And later on when you're coming out of it, you want to be warm."

"My question was you took the bag because you wanted it not because—"

"I didn't even think about it."

"You left her there laying in the dirt, shot?" The elderly man thumped his cane in anger.

"No, not laying in the dirt. We just left her. What else could we have done? Taken her with us or just stayed around to direct operations? We thought there was going to be guys in there."

"If you thought you were justified in shooting Alan Goldstein, why did you think you had to run?"

"I didn't run. We left."

"Now, I believe this morning in your direct testimony that you said about two or three different times that you didn't remember all of the details. Do you recall saying that?"

"I probably did, because I don't recall all the details."

"You also told her [Kari] that you had hoped for an older woman for your son? Did you want an older woman?"

"I might have. I think I did tell her that. I said, 'As far as my son is concerned,' because I knew that's what I believed."

"Why did you want an older woman?"

"Because they got a lot to teach young men, that's why. That's just nature, that's all."

Nichols said they realized if Kari didn't "work out" they would have to try again, eventually.

Judge Davis called a recess. To avoid another encounter with Dan Nichols, I went to find Marc and found him in the prosecutor's office, staring out the window. Shadows of fatigue made him look ill.

"Are you all right, Marc?" I asked.

Startled, he turned and smiled. "I could use a little more sleep. Don's callousness in kidnapping Kari and murdering Alan give me insomnia. God, can you believe that man? How are you and Bob doing?"

"Okay, but this trial is harder on Bob than the last one was. He's not sleeping or eating well. Maybe it's the heat."

"Listening to Nichols's verbal garbage doesn't exactly whet my appetite, either," Marc grimaced.

"Our five minutes are up, Marc," said John Connor from the doorway.

Marc renewed his cross-examination with a curtness in his voice that hadn't been there before.

"Was Kari still chained to the tree when you shot Alan Goldstein?"

"Yes."

"Did you ever attempt to leave the scene before you shot Alan Goldstein?"

"No, that was—"

"That's fine. Did you ever indicate orally to Alan Goldstein or Jim Schwalbe that you were willing to give yourself up?"

"I thought—no, not give ourselves up."

"Okay. Did you ever suggest to Alan Goldstein and Jim Schwalbe that you were putting down your gun and that this could be worked out peacefully? Did you ever orally say that?"

"I thought it was obvious."

"Did you ever orally *say* it?"

"No, I didn't," snapped Nichols.

"Did you know why Alan Goldstein was there?"

"He was searching for Kari."

"Would you agree that Alan Goldstein would not have been shot if you hadn't taken Kari Swenson?" pressed Marc.

"Yes, I'd agree to that."

"Would you agree that it was you that started this whole chain of events?"

"The illegal part, yes."

"Now, you had choices that you could have made there at the crime scene, did you not, and you made some?"

"They were kind of made for me. They just came automatic."

"But you made choices as any individual human being . . . normally makes choices?"

"Yes."

"And you could have simply put down your weapons, surrendered, raised your hands, asked for help—those were choices you had, too, weren't they?"

"I could have shot myself in the head! I could have done anything. That wasn't a logical thing. There—it just didn't seem to have any reason for coming up."

"If the whole thing was over, why in God's name did you have to shoot and kill Alan Goldstein?"

White objected. Marc had made his point and had no further questions. Mr. White didn't do a redirect, and court was adjourned until the next day.

Marc stopped to talk with Bob before leaving the courthouse. I watched the two men standing side by side, heads bowed, speaking softly. Moving closer to them, I heard Bob say, "The posturing, arrogant behavior Dan's exhibited for the last couple of days is the personality Kari described to us when she was in intensive care. Do you think he'll get off with a suspended sentence?"

"I don't know. The presentencing reports didn't demonstrate that he was a poor misunderstood innocent, and the judge will seriously consider that report when he makes his decision."

"I like Judge Davis," Bob said. "I've been watching him carefully. Nothing about the defendants escapes his notice, and I think he likes the way you present an argument."

Marc laughed, "Let's hope the jury is half as attentive!"

Kari and Holly had a picnic dinner ready when we arrived home. The four of us briefly discussed the day's events at the trial, then talked about more pleasant things. The girls had taken Kari's puppy, Kicha, hiking with them, and the fuzzy black dog was exhausted. She was content to sleep with her head on Kari's foot during dinner and slept so soundly she missed a piece of French bread I dropped.

Bob spent most of the night wandering around the house. At 3 a.m. I joined him in the family room.

"You have to get some sleep, honey."

"It's too hot. Besides, every time I close my eyes I see that bastard hitting Kari, shooting Alan, or flopping Kari out of the sleeping bag. He's sick! My God, how could he walk away like that? When I look at him I almost choke!"

"I know, I know."

"He left her there to die. Alone! That wasn't some cow or deer, it was my daughter! My Kari!" He moaned and rubbed his hand over his fatigue-lined face. "I wish I could bang doors like you do. Sometimes I think I'll explode!"

Dan Nichols Returns

Dan Nichols strode to the witness chair with an air of importance that he hadn't exhibited at the first trial. He changed his testimony and said his father's rifle was in its case, that he hadn't pointed it at Jim Schwalbe when he entered the camp. Don White introduced as evidence a sketch drawn by Dan, and a series of photographs taken by White, in which the locations of Alan and Dan's father were different than anything we had heard so far. Listening carefully, I decided the defense was attempting to demonstrate that Kari was lying down after she was shot and could not have seen the defendant. Dan Nichols said Jim walked into the camp before Kari was shot, but Jim had testified at both trials it was the shot and Kari's scream that drew him to the campsite.

Marc began his cross-examination. The witness lounged back in the chair, legs crossed, and answered some preliminary questions with a distinct lack of interest. He started paying more attention when Marc asked, "Did you discuss with your father, the defendant, in June of 1984, that this was the summer or this was the time within the near future that you would take the woman that both of you wanted?"

Steve Ungar jumped up. "Your Honor, I would object to that question on behalf of my client and assert his Fifth Amendment privilege which might expose him to criminal liability beyond which he's already been tried for, and disposition has been reached in the prior case."

"I think the floodgate is open," Marc challenged.

"Yes. I think so. The objection, Mr. Ungar, is overruled."

Nichols answered, "We didn't discuss it like that. We said it could be."

"You didn't discuss it like that in June?"

"I said we didn't discuss it like that in June."

"Well, your father has told us that you discussed that it was going to be in the very near future—in June. So that isn't correct then?"

There was a long silence. "Yeah, that's correct. It would be."

They reviewed the capture scene again.

"But you saw him strike her, didn't you?"

"He didn't strike her to the ground, no."

"Excuse me?" Marc's eyebrows arched. "Well, you saw him strike her?"

"He didn't strike her in a sense. He tapped her on the lips and told her to shut up."

"He didn't strike her, huh?"

"Well, he—what do you mean by 'strike'?"

"What do *you* mean by 'strike'?"

"A strike to me is if you punch somebody and knock them down or something or slap them real hard."

"Do you recall at your own trial when you were asked, 'Did your father strike Kari Swenson?' and you answered, 'Yes'?"

"Yeah. Well, at that time—"

"Your definition has gotten more refined since your trial?"

"I guess it has." Nichols grinned at Marc. Judge Davis leaned forward, pushed his glasses up on his nose, and stared at the witness.

Marc crossed his arms and studied the toes of his polished boots. He switched to questions about statements the old man had made to Kari. Dan said his father had said things to make her realize "we weren't going to kill her or something."

"You were just going to kidnap her?"

"Yes. . . . Not kidnap, just restrain her. I don't know what you call kidnap."

"Your father used the word 'kidnap' all the time, didn't he? . . . Whenever he had these little talks with you, he would sit you down and tell you, 'Son, to get a woman up here, I'm going to have to kidnap her'?"

"Yes. I suppose that's his—the word he used."

"Not restrained? Restrained is a relatively new word in your vocabulary, isn't it?"

"Yes, it is. But it still meant the same thing." The corners of Nichols's mouth twitched upward. The judge frowned. The son said his father, not he, took Kari's remarks about her family and friends coming to look for her as a threat. He said he thought she made those remarks to encourage them to let her go by making them believe others were in the area with her.

"And you heard your father tell her that he would shoot any rescuers, didn't you?"

"Yes."

"And he did that, didn't he?"

"I wouldn't call him a rescuer, no."

Well, you knew why Alan Goldstein was there, you testified at the last trial. . . . You knew that he was with a Search and Rescue unit, . . . so he was a rescuer?"

"All right. Yes, he was."

"And you didn't make any advances toward Kari at any point in time, I believe you testified."

"Yes. I didn't want her to be more scared."

"So there was never any point in time where she just felt perfectly at home, was there?"

"I wouldn't say she felt perfectly at home."

The prosecutor asked questions about Schwalbe's approach to the camp.

"Now, there's no question in your mind, is there? You appeared to be a little bit doubtful when you testified on direct examination that when Jim Schwalbe came into that camp, your father had his rifle out. That's what you testified at the last trial."

"Yes." Nichols looked worried.

"There's no doubt about that, is there?"

"He had it out, yes, he did!" Nichols glanced apprehensively at the defendant's table.

"No question about that?"

"When he came into camp, yes, he did."

"And you didn't mean to suggest otherwise?"

He glanced at Ungar. "No, I don't."

"It wasn't sitting in a blue case laying off in the distance somewhere?"

"No."

The elderly man whispered loudly, "See! Didn't I tell you? That little gal knows!" He thumped his cane triumphantly. His tiny wife flushed and hushed him again.

Nichols was "vaguely" aware of his father's actions after Schwalbe entered the camp, admitting that everything happened pretty fast. He changed his testimony from his trial, and Marc refreshed his memory by referring him and his attorney to the transcript of Dan's trial.

"And you've previously indicated or said that in your view kidnapping is one of man's laws that's b.s.?" Nichols denied making that statement to Dr. Stratford.

"I said something to the—in the line that that's what the Indians have done all their lives or something. And I didn't—at the time we took Kari, I thought—I thought that there was different kinds of kidnapping."

"Now, did you move the body of Alan Goldstein?"

"Did I?" He looked surprised.

"Yes. Did anybody?"

"No."

Marc referred Nichols to the state's and defense's photographs. "And if you will look at State's Exhibit No. 19 . . . the body of Alan Goldstein was found perpendicular to the tree labeled 'G' on that particular photo. My question to you is how did his body end up behind that tree when you claimed he was up here in front of these logs when he had the weapon?"

"He had to fall someplace. I assume he fell backward, because if he would have fallen back to that tree, he would have landed out here in the—farther out from that tree, anyway."

"He landed a foot away from this tree, the testimony has indicated. Could you have been so shook up and could your position have been such, looking over your shoulder, that you obviously did not perceive the events as they took place?"

"I got a pretty clear picture of what—of where he was standing when he had the gun pointed . . . and I got a pretty clear picture of when he fell, too."

"And are you aware of the fact that virtually everyone else, including your father, the defendant, has placed the defendant or Alan Goldstein behind that tree?"

"I can't help where they seen—"

"And are you aware of the fact that he [Don] places himself on the right side of that tree?"

"I wouldn't have been able to see him if he was on the right side of the tree."

"You don't know if he took aim when he shot Alan Goldstein, do you?"

"I got my idea! I'm pretty sure he didn't."

"You didn't see that."

"No, I didn't see it."

The witness said Jim didn't run back toward his father, and Jim couldn't have run into the trees where his father said Jim disappeared.

"That's where your father says he went."

"Go up to—try running that way and see how far you get!"

"So he's wrong?"

"I don't know. I guess so."

"We have no further questions, Your Honor."

Don White called Don Nichols's daughter as a character witness. She and her two small children were attending Don's trial. She said her father didn't go hunting frequently when she was growing up, and that he taught all of his children the proper use of a gun. She said he had insisted that even toy guns be treated as if they were real. White didn't dare let her go into a narrative about what a wonderful father he was—true or untrue—because Marc, in chambers, told him if he tried it he would return Dan to the stand and ask about his methods of discipline.

Next, White called a man from Jackson, Wyoming, who had employed Mr. Nichols off and on before 1979. He said Nichols had been peaceful, "as far as I knew," and was perfectly honest, "as far as I know."

The third character witness was a woman from Jackson, Wyoming.

"Okay. And do you know Don Nichols?" Don asked her.

"Very well." She smiled at the defendant.

"How long have you known Don?"

"Since I moved to my present location, which was October 1973."

"Okay. During that period of time, Adele, have you heard around the community what his reputation is for peacefulness versus violence?"

"It's impeccable! He's a very peaceful person, always was. So much so he wouldn't even swat a mosquito or step on an ant!

I've been in his presence many times when he did that. He actually stepped over rather than step on them."

"Have you heard of his reputation for truthfulness—yeah, for truthfulness?" Don asked, consulting his notes.

"Uh-huh."

"And what is that reputation?"

"It's impeccable!"

Marc had no questions. Don White asked for a brief recess before concluding his case.

Vivian and Karen dashed to the basement to buy something cold to drink, and when they came back, Vivian's face was flushed with anger.

"Do you know what happened? Some tourist was asking if he could take Dan's picture and have his autograph! I was so mad I almost whopped the guy with the camera!"

White called Sheriff France to the stand, handed him Alan's pistol, and asked if he recognized it as the pistol found at the crime scene. France said it was, and that it wasn't used by law enforcement officers because of its recoil and because it made too much noise. The sheriff said he would not use the pistol to hunt bear.

Marc cross-examined Johnny France.

"Sheriff France, if you were called as a volunteer on a search and rescue effort where it had been indicated that it was possible the victim may be located in an area where there were bears, and you have one of these kind of weapons, and it was the only weapon you had, would you take it with you?"

"Yes, sir."

"Is this a good weapon to signal with because of the loud report?"

"Yes, sir."

"We have nothing further. Thank you."

Mr. White rested the case for the defense, and Marc had no rebuttal. Judge Davis grinned at the people in the courtroom and said, "I'm sorry. We're going to have to make a record on something. We'll be right back—don't go away." Laughter followed him from the room. In chambers Judge Davis addressed the defense's request to take the jury to the scene of the crime. The prosecution objected. Marc said a site visit wasn't necessary because there had been extensive testimony, photographs, and crime scene sketches placed into evidence. The age and health of some of the jurors was a worry, and the deerflies were outrageous, he argued.

Judge Davis denied the motion and dismissed the jury until nine o'clock in the morning. The elderly gentleman touched my arm as he left the room. "She's a sweet girl. Sorry this happened!" I was interrupted before I could ask his name.

The attorneys and the judge spent the afternoon arguing the instructions that would be given to the jury, and the rest of us headed home. It was hot. When we crested the hill above Virginia City, heat radiating from the highway distorted the view of the mountains into a shimmery fantasy world. We shrugged off the nightmare of Virginia City and reoriented ourselves to the real world.

Kari had decided to attend court in the morning for the closing arguments. She had a sleepless night, and when she tiptoed out to the deck at sunrise, I followed her. We didn't talk while we drank our tea and watched the mountain peaks turn to gold. The sun moved slowly down the purple-shadowed mountainsides like honey over ice cream.

"I remember watching the sun touch the treetops that morning before I was shot and Alan was killed," Kari said jerkily. "I thought I'd never be with you again, that I might never see another dawn." We were silent for a long time. The birds sang in the hayfield. "I never knew how much little things could mean to me, the sunrise, the meadowlarks, a cup of tea with you, Dad's puns, Paul's fish stories, Johanna's giggle . . ." She stopped and cleared her throat. "I'm not looking forward to seeing those two again today."

"I know, Punkin. You don't have to go."

"I want to hear Marc's closing remarks and say goodbye to the Goldsteins. Jonathan will drive me over, and we plan to return right away. I don't want to be there if the jury says it was self-defense. You don't mind if I leave before the verdict, do you?"

"No. Go take a shower and I'll get breakfast started."

July 12, 1985, The Verdict

Kari, Bob, Diane, Douglas, David, and I sat in the front row listening to the judge give instructions to the jury. Behind us sat our friends who had shared this ordeal with us and to whom we will be forever grateful.

Marc faced the jury. "As we discussed at the beginning of the week, the purpose of a trial is to ascertain and declare the truth by your verdict, to determine in a fair and impartial and orderly manner whether the defendant has committed the crimes with which he is charged, to convict him if he's guilty and if that guilt is proven, and to acquit him if his guilt is not proven . . . .

"Now a public trial is not solely to shield the defendant. It must protect the interests of society as well. In our concern for the defendant, it should be remembered that nice people have some rights, too. The rights of the victims are worthy of at least as much protection and consideration as those of the defendant. . . . The commission of a crime involves more than the infliction of an injury on an isolated individual. It's an offense against the public as well, which is why the public prosecutes it. A moral community, unlike a hive of bees or a hill of ants, is one whose members are expected freely to obey the law, and they're trusted to do so."

Marc pointed out that Don Nichols admitted he purposely and knowingly, without lawful authority, restrained Kari by holding her in a place of isolation and using physical force against her. "There's nothing redeeming about how they tried to treat her. We don't have *good* kidnapeprs and *bad* kidnappers. . . .

"So the question then becomes: Was the deliberate homicide of Alan Goldstein excused because the defendant was entitled to act in self-defense? The answer is an unqualified, unequivocal, and resounding no! The Court's Instruction number thirty-nine makes that unequivocally clear. The first paragraph of that instruction states, 'The defense of self-defense is not available to a person who attempts to commit, is committing, or escaping after committing the crime of kidnapping or aggravated assault.' . . . The last portion of that instruction states, 'A person who purposely or knowingly provokes the use of force against himself cannot rely on self-defense,' and again that makes sense.

"Unless he is in danger of death or serious bodily harm and he has exhausted every reasonable means of escape other than the use of force, there is no evidence here. This is the defendant's first option; this was his first choice. There's no effort to mitigate, no attempt at mediation, no try to somehow alleviate the consequences of his deadly acts. . . .

"How in God's name does a man who we've been told has such respect for insects and animals not remember that? [referring to Nichols's plan to chain Kari around the neck] Need I continue? I will suggest to you that in those instances where the defendant's testimony conflicts with that of Jim Schwalbe and Kari Swenson, it's more than obvious whose recollection is accurate . . . .

"Do you find a man believable who tells you with a grin that his definition of strike has gotten more refined in the last two months since his own trial, and that the word restrained is a new word in his vocabulary? No, I think not.

"What interest did Jim Schwalbe or Kari Swenson have in this matter? In what instances were they contradicted by the physical evidence of other witnesses? In what instances did they not appear candid and fair? I would suggest to you—none.

"And it is they who have had these facts indeliby etched into their memories now and forever. The entire truth is then revealed when we consider their testimony. There is no dream here. This is a nightmare of one crime after another! . . .

"This is not an epic story about the life and times of two mountain men. This is about common criminals who have ignored the dignity of other people to take what they wanted, shun society because they didn't like working, despise the law unless they could use it to their own advantage, and viewed those of us who tried to be contributing members of a community as people 'with noses up some rich man's butt.' "

Marc reviewed the shooting scene, pointing out that by law Alan was within his rights to try to rescue the victim.

"Well, any ordinary man, maybe me included, might have sat there and watched, but that wasn't the type of man Alan Goldstein was. That isn't why the city of Flint, Michigan, recognized him by proclaiming a day in his honor, not just for this event, but for a life of example and duty and honor. The very attributes people admired in him cost him his life." Kari cried softly.

"Even if convicted, he will retain more life than Alan Goldstein. We ask on behalf of the people of the state that the high-handed lawlessness of his actions be declared by your verdict, and that justice not be disappointed."

Don White began his final argument and shocked us by attacking Marc, Judy, and John for the manner in which they took notes during the trial and the way Marc conducted his direct of the state's witnesses. He attempted to place blame for Alan's death on Alan by saying that if he hadn't approached Don Nichols with a fully loaded weapon, he would be alive today. He said Nichols's failed attempt to establish a homestead in the Cabinet Mountains was the beginning of his withdrawal from society.

After more jabs at Marc for his thoroughness in preparing the case, Mr. White asked that the jury find Don Nichols guilty only of unlawful restraint for kidnapping Kari because he acted in self-defense in the shooting of Alan Goldstein.

Marc rose slowly and faced the jury.

"I don't feel an obligation to apologize to you for my preparation or the way I ask questions," he said. "If you find difficulty with that, that's something that you will have to deal with from your perspective, because I'm simply not going to accord those kinds of statements any dignity by even responding to them.

"And when Mr. White talks and suggests to you that perhaps we have misled you because we haven't discussed the lesser offenses of unlawful restraint and assault, that is simply because we find no evidence of it. There's no evidence of any lesser offense to the charge of kidnapping or to the charge of aggravated assault. . . .

"What kind of a man is Don Nichols? I think perhaps much simpler than what he was sometimes given credit for. Whether or not he's a social person, whether or not things are different in the mountains, whether or not we dispense with schedules and watches and certain feelings and emotions in the mountains does not remove us from our responsibilities as moral human beings. It does not give us a license to kill, to maim, to kidnap, to threaten . . . .

"So, ladies and gentlemen, the bottom lines, I believe, are still the same. But for the actions of the defendant, Alan Goldstein would be alive. But for, as the defense counsel states, the actions of the defendant, Kari Swenson would not have been scarred for life. But for the actions of the defendant, Jim Schwalbe would have not been placed in fear of his life. . . .

"We ask not that you rule on emotion or based on counsel's arguments or based on media coverage, we ask you to do your duty, to do simply what's right."

Kari wiped her eyes, Douglas had his arm around Diane, and David's face was contorted with grief. Marc, Judy, and John were grim faced as they scooped up their files and joined us.

The Goldsteins, Holliers, Schaaps, Karen Frauson, Bob, and I wandered the streets of Virginia City, moved in and out of the courthouse, and sat in the prosecutor's room with Marc, John, and Judy. Kari and Jonathan had gone back to Bozeman. I reminded Marc that Judge Davis had agreed to sentence Dan Nichols as soon as his father's trial was over, so the prosecutors sought out the judge to discuss the sentencing date. David and Douglas walked out into the corridor with me, and the three of us halted at the top of the winding staircase. Dan Nichols was posing for photographs out on the balcony. David's face blanched, and he strode toward the group.

"Doug, stop him! He wouldn't do anything would he?" I clutched his arm.

"Let him be. We can take just so much." Suddenly David stopped, whirled, and dashed down the stairs. Douglas followed him.

Judge Davis had stepped into the corridor from his chambers and witnessed the scene. He stretched, took his pipe out of his pocket, and glanced toward the photograph session on the balcony. He watched, listened, then turned back to his room and quietly closed the door.

I couldn't stand the tension in the corridor and went outside, where I walked aimlessly for an hour. Bob found me, and we joined our friends in a cafe for iced tea. Sally Hollier's foot was propped up on a chair, and a bag of ice covered her swollen, bruised toes. She had injured her foot earlier in the morning but insisted on coming to the trial. Reporters, attorneys, and finally Judge Davis drifted in for something cold to drink.

Sitting beside the window I watched the sun disappear behind ominous gray clouds. Dust devils sucked up litter and whipped down the deserted street. A black-and-white mongrel dog, tail between its legs, slinked across the boardwalk, peered into the cafe, and curled up beside the screen door. We remained in the cafe for a long time. There was little conversation as we wiped condensation off our tea glasses and glanced at our watches. It became darker and darker outside.

At approximately 4:30 p.m. a court reporter stepped over the dog and walked into the cafe to tell the judge that the jury had reached a verdict. The Goldsteins hurried toward the courthouse followed by Sally, who was limping, supported by her husband Dave. Karen walked with Vivian, silent and tense. Bob Schaap and my husband dropped behind the others. Schaap clasped Bob's shoulder with his hand and shook his head—it was a gesture I had seen him use one year ago tomorrow when our night search for Kari had failed.

I walked alone up the concrete steps we had traversed so many times since May. A raindrop splattered at my feet, then another. I looked at the sky. Black and purple clouds boiled, rolled, and tumbled over each other. Distant thunder followed flashes of lightning. The pungent smell of ozone hung in the air.

The foreman handed the verdict to the bailiff, who gave it to Judge Davis. He read it without expression and handed the paper to the clerk of court to read. The magnificent crimson drapes behind us billowed inward, and the wind moaned around the old courthouse. Nature was providing effects that were better than anything Hollywood could have dreamed up. Lightning startled us and was followed immediately by a clap of thunder so loud that the clerk of court had to raise her voice to be heard.

"We, the jury in the aforementioned cause, find the defendant, Donald Boone Nichols, of the crime of kidnapping, guilty." Thunder vibrated through the brick walls. "Of the crime of unlawful restraint, no answer; of the crime of deliberate homicide as alleged in Count I, not guilty; deliberate homicide as alleged in Count II, guilty; of aggravated assault, guilty; of assault, no answer."

The wind howled through the room, scattering papers and documents. Deputies rushed to control the wildly flapping velvet drapes and close the windows. Attorneys and clerks dropped to their knees to collect their papers. Thunder shook the building time after time, and rain pelted the windows. The wind wheezed and whistled through the old windows at our back and caressed our cheeks like a cold whisper. Then, strangely enough, my skin prickled and I had the strong impression someone unseen had joined us. I whispered softly, "Goodbye, Alan."

29

DAN NICHOLS'S SENTENCING

July 19, 1985

The courtroom was empty compared to the crush of the trial crowd. Kari had chosen not to testify, but would be present.

Mr. Ungar asked that his client not be sent to prison for his deeds, that incarceration would be "inappropriate" for his client, and the time he spent in jail, from December until May, was more than "sufficient time to serve." Besides, he said, the court couldn't "impose a long enough sentence by law to segregate him from society forever."

He said the defendant shouldn't be given the extra ten years for use of a weapon in the kidnapping of Kari. He insisted that the state enhancement law didn't apply because Nichols's mental capacity at the time of the crime was "significantly impaired."

The attorney asked for a suspended sentence, employment for his client, and a schedule for counseling. He said the defendant had talent in two areas: art and the "outdoors in general." Steve suggested that Dan's skills be directed, for instance, in working with the Boy Scouts and "other like groups."

Nichols took the stand. He said he frequently called his therapist and had even stayed with him for four days; he felt that he could change his social behavior; that he no longer admired his father or followed his advice; and that eventually, besides being an artist, he would like to be an outfitter.

The newsmen nudged each other.

Steve asked how Dan felt his special knowledge of the outdoors could help people.

"Just to get people over their fear of nature. Get them out there into nature and show them what it's like to—for one thing, nature's a good place for therapy. You know, a lot of people don't know how to get along out there. Just show them how to make it easier out there."

He boldly made those statements when sitting before him was a young woman who had understood and loved the mountains until he and his father changed that. They had stolen from her the inner peace and security we had so carefully nurtured for twenty-three years.

Steve excused Dan Nichols, but Judge Davis stopped him and asked if Marc had any questions.

Marc rose and slowly walked toward the defendant.

"Now," he said, "you talk about the tremendous amount of worry you had for the victims in the case between the time of the offense and the time that you were arrested, but your diary doesn't reflect anything of that kind, does it? Just talked about a leisurely life up in the mountains."

"I believe if you look at my diary, I've got teardrops written all over it."

"Teardrops?"

"Yeah. That's just an easy way to express sorrow without going into a big lot of writing."

"Well, your diary does nothing but mention the fact that you miss Sue and you'd shot a lot of game out of season and that you stole and robbed cabins and other people's food. That's about what it mentions. Do you agree with that—that those things are mentioned in there?"

"I just mentioned what we did from day to day."

"And that included all the things I've mentioned, didn't it?"

"It does. It mentions it."

"I have nothing further, Your Honor. Could I have just one moment?"

"Yes."

Marc left the area enclosed by the golden oak banister, leaned close to Kari, and whispered, "Well, do you have anything you want to say?"

"You bet I have!"

Marc turned to the judge. "We'd call Kari Swenson, Your Honor."

Kari strode to the witness chair, ignored the television camera, and looked directly at the defendant for the first time since he left her to die in the mountains. Up until now she had not been allowed to talk about the pain, physical or emotional, she had suffered because it had been irrelevant to the charges. The dam burst, and she told the court her feelings about Dan Nichols's behavior in the mountains. She said he had not acted under the duress or coercion of his father. He had appeared completely in control of himself and had made his choices freely.

"In fact, his father had asked him, 'Shall we keep her?' and he said, 'Yes.' If he would have said no, they may have released me."

"Was there ever any point in time, Kari," Marc asked, "that you can recall the defendant exhibiting any kind of an effort to assist you medically after you were shot?"

"No. He has stated that he felt bad about it, but I feel that if he really was sorry, he would have stayed and helped me somehow. He didn't help me at all. They flopped me out of the sleeping bag and left me to die. They didn't help me at all." Her eyes brimmed with tears.

"When you were lying there on the forest floor wounded and bleeding, did you believe you were going to die?"

"Yes. I—I thought I was going to die. I didn't think I had a chance." Kari talked about the strain the incident had put on her family and friends, and her difficulties with severe mood swings. "My brother and I were very close before this, and—and now it's hard—it's hard for us to even get together and talk."

"Did you ever think that you could feel the way you feel now toward another human being, like you do toward the defendant?"

"No. I have always trusted people and liked to meet and talk to them. Now I have a hard time going out or being alone—by myself."

"When you were lying there on the forest floor, did that four hours seem like forever?"

"Yes, it did."

"What's the one thing you can recall from that period of time as being the most difficult—one of the most difficult and insipid things to deal with?"

"Well, it was in the middle of the summer, and there were a lot of insects. I had flies, mosquitoes, and ants attracted to the blood, and I was took weak to keep them off of me. So they were swarming all over."

Judge Davis adjusted his glasses and scrutinized the defendant, who sat with his elbow on the table and his chin resting in his palm. He seemed bored. Marc looked upset and swallowed several times before he continued.

Kari returned to her chair and reached for our hands.

Marc discussed the testimonies of different witnesses, including the conflicting facts given by Dan and his father.

"In his diary he mentions the fact that he misses Sue. There's no remorse or exhibition of grief in that diary! He wanted her up there one way or the other, and I think he manipulated and encouraged and solicited his father in every way whatsoever to do the dirty work so he'd be able to take advantage of the fruits of the crime at some later time. . . .

"What kind of human being do we have here that finds amusement or some kind of sense of joy or thrill or excitement in the fact that he can list his occupation as a mountain man and pose for photographs under the circumstances? It's way beyond bad taste! It's to the point to where there's something substantially distorted with the way he views this particular incident, and with what he thinks he owes the rest of us, as people that have to live in this community and trust each other to obey the laws and not take advantage of one another. Even after he was arrested and even after we're getting close to trial, he told Dr. Stratford kidnapping as one of man's laws is bullshit. Now, what kind of an indication of intent is that? . . .

"He had an association, a relationship—an amorous relationship with an older woman twice his age—in spite of his father's condemnation of that. Now, let's talk about social skills. You know, how many social skills are you absent when you can carry on a successful relationship with a woman twice your age who's married?"

Marc listed Nichols's previous crimes for which he had not been charged: letting prisoners out of the jail his stepfather ran, assaulting the Johnson girls, drug and alcohol use, poaching, breaking into cabins, and shoplifting. "There's no respect for the law here. . . .

"He laughed! Damn near laughed at me when I asked him about the word 'restrained' being a relatively new word in his vocabulary where we were involved in a deadly serious matter about this. And he has the nerve and audacity to stand up there and answer a question in that regard! I think that's an indication of what moves inside the mind and soul of this man."

The next five minutes were devoted to advising the court of Kari's hospitalization, physical trauma, and rehabilitation.

"And the most peculiar kinds of difficulties confront her. She feels tremendous guilt. Of all things, *she* feels guilt over the death of Alan Goldstein! She's received mail from some perverted and tortured souls out there who accuse her of being the one responsible for all of this and being vindictive toward the defendants.

"The Goldsteins. I think very little more needs to be said about the grief and the extreme pain that's been inflicted on them. Alan left a wife; he left a daughter. He was thirty-six years old; he was bright. He graduated from the University of Michigan with a degree in business with a 3.9 gradepoint average. He was an active horseshoer and environmentalist. He was a peaceful man. And, obviously, as the city of Flint recognized, he was deeply loved by many people, and he—he's sorely missed. . . .

"If we allow the extravagance of his actions or his plan to seize our reason and to forget what he did or to forget his past record, I say that we have lost all moral sense. It's my belief, Your Honor, that substantial mercy and compassion were provided by the jury when they returned their verdict in the case.

"In my view the defendant is equally, under the law, responsible for all of the consequences that occurred as part of a common design which he willingly, voluntarily, freely, and knowingly associated himself with. This sentiment that has been utilized to depict him as poor, oppressed, cowering, frightened, bewildered, ignorant—who deserves nothing but sympathy and compassion and kindness, I think, is an outrage. That premise, in my view, that no one is responsible for their acts is essentially amoral. It ignores the ability of all of us to choose.

"I believe, Your Honor, that this is not the time that we should be measuring the delicate scruples of the defendant and to even care about whether he was a nice kidnapper or a bad kidnapper. He's a *damn* kidnapper who almost killed his victim, and knowingly, purposely, deliberately, and maliciously ignited this whole thing by his actions and association with it. . . .

"So the state's recommendation is that the defendant be sentenced to serve the maximum punishment possible in the case, twenty years and six months [ten years for kidnapping, ten years for use of a dangerous weapon in the commission of a felony, and six months for shooting Kari] at the Montana State Prison; and that he be designated a dangerous offender for purposes of parole eligibility."

"Well," Judge Davis sighed, "court is going to be in recess until one o'clock and also in a place of isolation."

Marc joined us at the cafe, but none of us were hungry. He looked exhausted, as if this last session had drained him of all vitality.

"Marc, you've done everything you could for me. He may not get more of a sentence than if we'd gone along with the plea-bargain, but at least we have a public record of what he is! It was worth the pain, as far as I'm concerned," Kari said.

Marc smiled. "I don't think Frank will let him off with a suspended sentence, but I really don't know what he'll hand down. It's very hard for a judge to sentence such a young person. If Dan had stayed away from the second trial and left us with the poor little boy image, he might have gotten his suspended sentence. But Davis didn't miss a thing, he saw the real person inside that body. The photograph of Dan on the front page of the *Chronicle* probably didn't help his cause."

1 p.m.

Judge Davis settled himself, pushed his glasses up on his nose, sighed, and began his statement.

"Sentencing of a defendant is often an awesome and agonizing responsibility, as everybody must know, and particularly so when we have a youthful defendant who has been involved in such a senseless and bizarre crime. And as I've often said, I wish this cup could pass from me. . . .

"What counsel this morning failed to articulate, but which must be apparent to everyone in this courtroom, is the dilemma facing the sentencing judge in these cases. To impose a sentence to achieve one purpose—for example, retribution—may frustrate the likelihood of achieving another purpose, namely, rehabilitation. To achieve one purpose may defeat the other, and this is why this responsibility is so awesome. And, absent the wisdom of Solomon, one has to do simply the best he can . . . .

"Mr. Ungar, you articulated well your appeal for probation for this defendant. And under the ordinary circumstances, considering his age, I would agree to it in principle. But in this case that punishment simply does not fit the crime.

"It would be in this court's opinion a gross miscarriage of justice of this court to give this defendant literally its blessing, and in effect tell him to go and sin no more, and go back into the wilderness. . . .

"The mental evaluators did use one term, which I think might describe my observations of this defendant, and that is self-dramatic. . . .

"The evidence in this case and in the other case in my observations demonstrate to me that this defendant has demonstrated sort of a subdued and benign arrogance and defiance almost from the moment he appeared as an actor in this tragedy. . . .

"The prosecutor has already mentioned his characterization of himself as an unemployed—self-employed mountain man. To me that was an act of arrogance and defiance. His father didn't do that. And conduct at his father's trial has been alluded to here, and that bothered me, and I'm sure Mr. Ungar was not responsible for it. But it appeared to me that he was literally basking in the limelight, his new-found glory. And what was so tragic about it, was it was in the presence of distraught victims of this crime. . . .

"I've seen no real indication of any remorse—not in his diary—just the opposite as was pointed out by the prosecutor this morning. There have been tears shed in this courtroom, but not by the defendant. We learned for the first time this morning the spots on his diary were teardrops, but there was no evidence that he was under agony and torment as a result of what he did.

"The defendant in my judgement is morally if not equally legally responsible for the death of Alan Goldstein, and I can't sentence him for that. He certainly is legally responsible for the ordeal that Kari Swenson underwent, and he didn't even have the compassion to leave her the warmth of the sleeping bag.

"So I can, and I must, and I do at this time impose sentence on the defendant in what I hope, Mr. Ungar, is a manner which is fair and which is just.

"So you'll stand up, Mr. Nichols." He waited for Nichols and Ungar to get to their feet. "It's the judgement and sentence of this court that you be sentenced to the Montana State Prison at Deer Lodge for the crime of kidnapping of which you were convicted for a term of ten years.

"For the crime of misdemeanor assault for which you were convicted, a term of six months.

"For the use of a gun for which I find no mitigating circumstances despite your pleas, Mr. Ungar, an additional ten years.

"These sentences will run consecutively, and you will be certified dangerous for the purposes of probation and parole. . .

"The formal judgement will contain a prohibition that you never receive any monetary profit or gain as a result of these crimes. The formal judgement will also take a recommendation by this court that the warden transfer you to the Swan River Forest Youth Camp when and if he deems it to be a proper case. I think he'll do that. I think there you'll be in our wilderness, not yours, and you'll be doing something constructive, and you'll have an opportunity to get counseling and maybe develop some occupational skills.

"Your bond is revoked. The sureties are exonerated, and you're remanded to the custody of the sheriff to carry out the terms of this sentence.

"Court will be in recess."

Marc joined us, said goodbye to Kari, and took Bob aside to talk to him. I answered a few questions for the press, and Kari, pale and shaken, left with Jonathan. Dan Nichols, solemn now, talked with his attorney.

A phoebe sang its plaintive song from the weedy vacant lot next door. A dog barked. Children laughed. The microphones were dismantled, and the electrical cords that had been taped to the floors and podium lay coiled like snakes on the polished floor. Cameras were packed away. The tour buses were leaving town. The circus was over.

30

THE LAST RACE

After the sentencing Kari could finally focus on training for the upcoming biathlon season. A friend from West Germany arrived in Bozeman to train with her, and the two of them put many miles on their roller skis, running shoes, and the roller board. She interrupted her training long enough to fly to Washington, D.C., to be honored as one of ten Healthy American Fitness Leaders by the President's Council on Fitness and the U.S. Jaycees, and to go to a reunion.

We had all looked forward to my family's reunion in Thermopolis, Wyoming. Johanna, cheerful, full of jokes, limping from recent orthopedic foot surgery, arrived by plane, and we drove to my mother's. The cousins, together for the first time in eleven years, told stories on each other and filled the houses with laughter. Mom and Milo were exhausted after the three-day celebration but invited everyone to return the next year.

Kari and Paul's friendship gradually returned to the loving, teasing pattern of the past. The trials purged the ghosts they had lived with for a year and broke down the barriers of guilt and uncertainty that had come between them.

Eventually, Paul returned to his studies at Montana State University, and Johanna went back to her job in Seattle. For the first time since the kidnapping she had a feeling of well-being—for herself as well as the rest of us.

Our Indian summer came to an abrupt halt with the onset of late October storms that dumped snow in Yellowstone Park and in the Gallatin Mountain Range. With the snow came the biathletes on their way to the winter training camp in West Yellowstone. Once again we shared Thanksgiving dinner with them at their condo and helped with the Alan Goldstein Memorial races held in early December at the Lone Mountain Ranch.

Johanna, Paul, and Kari were home for the Christmas holidays. The silence in the house was unnerving when Johanna returned to Seattle, Paul went back to school, and Kari went to Norway as a member of the U.S. Women's Biathlon Team.

March 1986, Holmenkollen, Norway

The sun reflected off the snow, and shadows of the seventy- and ninety-meter ski jumps stretched like giant tripods across the slope of a hill at the far side of the stadium. In the foreground the black circles of the biathlon targets stared like unblinking eyes. Kari squinted at the bleachers, surprised by the crowd of twenty thousand spectators who had come to watch the women's ten-kilometer biathlon race.

Kari's friends Lise Meloche of Canada and Kerryn Pethybridge of Australia joined her. The three young women wished each other well and separated. Kari closed her mind to the competitors and noise around her and began a session of imaging. In her mind's eye she skied effortlessly, and every target fell when she pulled the trigger.

"Kari, you're up!" her coach shouted, and she skied into the starting gate. Sixty seconds later she darted forward, sprinting, double-poling, lost in the thrill of competition.

She completed the first leg of skiing. Heart pounding, she skied into the stadium and unslung the rifle from its harness. In one smooth, graceful movement she dropped to her knees, opened the sight cover, shoved a clip of shells into the rifle, and lay on her stomach. She sighted down the barrel and squeezed the trigger five times in rapid succession—all five targets fell. She was so surprised she took a second look at the targets. Suddenly, her name blazed across the enormous electronic scoreboard. She was in first place. The crowd stamped their feet and yelled "Svenson! Svenson! Svenson!" The throbbing cadence of her name followed her out of the stadium, into the trees, and echoed in her ears as she crested the first hill.

The second leg of the course had long, hard uphills, and Kari's chest wounds ached as she came into the stadium again. She shut her eyes, took a deep breath, planted her skis firmly on the slippery snow, and began her off-hand shooting stage. When the fifth target fell, the crowd was on its feet. Their voices seemed to pick her up and carry her along on a rushing wave—"Heia, Svenson! Heia, Svenson! Heia, Svenson!" Her smile spread from ear to ear, and the volume of the crowd went up a few more decibels. Coaches and friends skied out on the course yelling, screaming, urging her on. Hot stabs of pain burned in her chest. She pushed away the pain and skied full out.

The crowd was on its feet when she entered the stadium for the last shooting round. Her pulse pounded in her wounds as she wiggled into the prone position, mentally shut out the noise, and squeezed the trigger. She missed.

"Oh-h-h-h-h!" the crowd moaned in unison. In that fraction of a second, Kari's pulse slowed, her arm steadied, and she hit the next four targets. The board flashed her name—she had dropped to third place, but the enthusiasm of the crowd was as high as ever.

She flew around the course and skied across the finish line in third place. The coaches crowded around, pounding her back, congratulating her. She reminded them that there were many good skiers who hadn't finished yet, but they were too excited to listen. Then it happened. Lise Meloche, almost the last skier, crossed the finish a fraction of a minute ahead of Kari and claimed third place for Canada.

The awards ceremony began with a procession across the snow-covered field of the stadium. The first ten finishers were to be recognized, so Kari walked between her Canadian friends Lise and fifth place winner Gail Niinimaa. Kerryn Pethybridge was sixth. Kari was called forward, shook hands with the three women standing on the winners' podiums, and turned to smile at the crowd who had cheered so enthusiastically for her. Someone tugged on her jacket, and the next thing she knew Lise had pulled her up onto the third-place podium with her. The spectators roared their approval as the two young women, arms around each other's shoulders, smiled, waved, and clutched their coveted silver Holmenkollen cups.

Epilogue

On September 27, 1985, Don Nichols was sentenced to a total of eighty-five years to be served in the state prison. He would be required to serve half his sentence before he'd be eligible for parole. His appeal for a retrial was denied by the state supreme court.

The Montana Sentence Review Board and the Montana Supreme Court turned down Dan Nichols's appeal for resentencing. The appeal to the supreme court concerning the ten years he was given for the use of a weapon was also denied.

Johnny France was defeated in the June 1986 primary for sheriff by Madison County Deputy Richard Noorlander. The week after the election Sheriff France fired Noorlander, then rehired him and ran a write-in campaign in the November election. He was defeated by another deputy, Lee Edmiston, who also ran on a write-in campaign.

Jim Schwalbe and Alan Goldstein were honored by the Carnegie Hero Fund Commission for the courage they displayed in attempting to rescue Kari.

On June 14, 1986, Paul graduated from Montana State University with degrees in physics and geology and entered graduate studies at Stanford University. He received a masters degree in geophysics in March of 1988 and returned to Montana to work for the summer as a fly-fishing guide at the Lone Mountain Guest Ranch.

In the spring of 1986 Johanna went back to college and majored in a paralegal program with the dream of someday going to law school. She is employed by a law firm in Washington and enjoys a renewed interest in the sport of tennis. Kari and Paul finally convinced her to try cross-country skiing, and our winter holidays are usually spent on the superb ski trails at Lone Mountain Ranch.

Marc Racicot was elected as Montana's attorney general November 8, 1988. John Connor had become an assistant attorney general in 1987, and Judy Browning continues to serve as an assistant attorney general.

In 1986 NBC Productions produced a made for TV movie, *The Abduction of Kari Swenson.*

Kari began her studies in veterinary medicine September 1, 1986. It was difficult for her to give up biathlon because she was afraid it meant leaving behind the friends she had made all over the world. She has kept in touch with many of them, and has continued to race when the opportunity arises.

Skiing remains an important part of Kari's life. She and Bill Koch traveled to the Snowy River Mountains of Australia in August of 1987 and made a ski instructional video called "Skating Away," a Westcom production in collaboration with ESPN.

ABC hired Kari as the biatholon "color commentator" for the 1988 Olympic Games in Calgary, Alberta, where she had the opportunity to renew friendships with fellow athletes from Europe, Australia, and Canada.

Kari still has nightmares, flashbacks, and emotional and physical pain associated with the kidnapping and shooting. Unlike television violence, real life trauma does not end with a fade-out and a commercial.

FORGET-ME-NOTS

"Go sit among the forget-me-nots, Punkin,
and I'll take your picture.

Aren't they beautiful this year?
They're so brilliant and large."

She sat grinning in the field of blue,
one arm thrown around her dog's neck.

"Hurry, Mom! It's cold in the shade. Another
minute and the goose bumps will show!"

"I'm trying to focus this thing, be patient.
Dad will love a picture of you sitting in the flowers."

We laughed and talked as we hurried,
eager to be off the windy ridge.

I admired my strong beautiful daughter as she strode along,
braid swinging,a long stride many teased her about.

I smiled to myself remembering I, too, had been teased.
"The Milek Walk" my friends called it.

After dinner at the cabin she kissed me and hurried to her car.
"Remember to press those forget-me-nots, Mom." She was gone.

Index